HEALTH AND HEALING
THE NATURAL WAY

———————

MANAGING
PAIN

———————

HEALTH AND HEALING
THE NATURAL WAY

MANAGING PAIN

Reader's
Digest

PUBLISHED BY

THE READER'S DIGEST ASSOCIATION, INC.

PLEASANTVILLE, NEW YORK / MONTREAL

A READER'S DIGEST BOOK
Produced by
Carroll & Brown Limited, London

CARROLL & BROWN

Publishing Director Denis Kennedy
Art Director Chrissie Lloyd

Managing Editor Sandra Rigby
Managing Art Editor Tracy Timson

Editors Richard Emerson, Hilary Sagar

Art Editor Simon Daley
Designer Jonathan Wainwright

Photographers Jules Selmes, David Murray

Production Christine Corton, Wendy Rogers

Computer Management John Clifford, Karen Kloot

First English Edition Copyright © 1997
The Reader's Digest Association Limited,
11 Westferry Circus, Canary Wharf,
London E14 4HE

Printed in the United States of America
ISBN 0-7621-0144-X

The information in this book is for reference only;
it is not intended as a substitute for a doctor's diagnosis
and care. The editors urge anyone with continuing medical
problems or symptoms to consult a doctor.

MEDICAL CONSULTANT

Dr. J.R. Wiles, MB, BS(Lond), FRCA
*Director of the Centre for Pain Relief, The Walton Centre for
Neurology & Neurosurgery, Liverpool, UK*

COMPLEMENTARY HEALTH CONSULTANT

Michael Endacott
*Research Director, The Institute for
Complementary Medicine, London, UK*

CONTRIBUTORS

Dr. E. Ghadiali, BSc, MPsychol, PhD, CPsychol, AFBPsS
Consultant Clinical Neuropsychologist

Dr. Andrew Baronowski, BSc Hons, MB BS, MD, FRCA
Consultant in Pain Management

Dr. Tim Nash MBBS, DObstRCOG, FRCA
Consultant in Pain Relief

Dr. Turo Nurmikko, MD, PHD
Consultant in Pain Management

Roger Newman-Turner BAc, ND, DO, MRO, MRN
Registered naturopath, osteopath and acupuncturist

Rosalie Everatt, RGN
Founder of Pain Concern UK and Pain Wise UK

Professor Philip-John Lamey,
BSc, BDS, MBChB, DDS, FDS, RCPS, FFD, RCSI
Professor of Oral Medicine

H.P.J. Walsh Mch.Orth, FRCS
Consultant Orthopaedic Surgeon

READER'S DIGEST

Project Editor Gayla Visalli
Cover Design Patrizia Bove

READER'S DIGEST GENERAL BOOKS

Editor in Chief, U.S. General Books David Palmer
Managing Editor Chris Cavanaugh
Editorial Director, health & medicine Wayne Kalyn
Design Director, health & medicine Barbara Rietschel

Address any comments about *Managing Pain* to
Editor in Chief, U.S. General Books, Pleasantville, NY 10570

MANAGING PAIN

More and more people today are choosing to take greater responsibility for their own health care, rather than relying on a doctor to step in with a cure whenever something goes wrong. We now recognize that we can influence our health by making improvements in lifestyle, for example, a better diet, more exercise, and reduced stress. People are also becoming increasingly aware that there are other healing methods—some new, others ancient—that can help to prevent illness or be used as a complement to orthodox medicine. The series *Health and Healing the Natural Way* will help you to make your own health choices, by giving you clear, comprehensive, straightforward, and encouraging information and advice about methods of improving your health. The series explains the many different natural therapies now available —aromatherapy, herbalism, acupressure, and many others— and the circumstances in which they may be of benefit when used in conjunction with conventional medicine.

A lack of information about the nature of pain and its causes can often lead to fear, which is the greatest barrier to the control of painful symptoms. MANAGING PAIN aims to fill this knowledge gap with clear and practical information to help banish that fear. It explains the positive role that the pain response plays in the functioning of the body and shows how pain can be relieved or controlled by self-help measures, changes in lifestyle, and, where necessary, by finding the most suitable treatment for your needs. While conventional painkillers have a major part to play in pain control, they can never provide a complete answer. In the case of persistent or recurrent pain, they can even lead to negative patterns of behavior in which pain and medication come to dominate your life. In MANAGING PAIN we show that appropriate measures, coupled with a positive approach, can enable you to regain control of your body and life and enhance your health and well-being.

CONTENTS

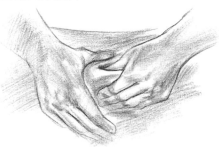

CHALLENGING YOUR PAIN

Pain, particularly chronic pain, is one of the most debilitating of conditions, yet there are steps you can take to avoid, minimize or relieve pain altogether.

THE PATH OF PAIN
The philosopher Descartes was one of the first people to describe the passage of pain messages to the brain. He envisaged a message travelling from the site of the injury up the body to trigger an alarm response in the brain.

NATURAL PAIN CONTROL
Many herbal remedies, such as chamomile tea, date back thousands of years and are still used effectively today for treating painful afflictions.

P ain often produces dependence on doctors and drugs. Many people expect their doctor to wave a magic wand and take pain away, or they prescribe for themselves over-the-counter pain relievers on a regular basis. But painkillers don't provide an answer to all pain, especially in the long term. In fact, there is no easy solution: increasingly we are learning that successful management of chronic pain requires the active involvement of individual sufferers, so that they gain an understanding of their pain—and ultimately take responsibility for controlling it. This book aims to describe the mechanics of pain, how it works, and what feeds it, and thus provide a key to effective pain management.

PAIN AND WESTERN MEDICINE

The traditional approach of Western medicine to pain management has tended to focus on blocking the experience of pain by chemical means. As recently as 1842 surgeons could use only alcohol as a painkiller. Morphine was employed during the American Civil War, but the problem of addiction made its widespread use undesirable. In 1847 chloroform was first administered to relieve labor pains and was soon in use during a range of surgical procedures. But high levels of the chemical proved to cause liver damage. It was only in the 1930s that anesthesia became a relatively safe practice.

Conventional medicine is still likely to be the first choice for the majority of pain sufferers. However, many people feel that modern medicine is still too focused on drug therapy and does not allow patients a sufficiently active part in the management of their conditions. In addition, Western medicine has had only limited success in managing complex pain problems. Chronic pain conditions such as arthritis or backache tend not to respond well to conventional treatment. Now many people are taking an interest in therapies that tackle pain in a different way. These methods offer patients a choice, but can also be used to complement conventional treatment.

PAIN RELIEF IN OTHER CULTURES

Although individual techniques differ, many Eastern systems of medicine share a focus in looking at patients' particular pain problems within the context of their overall general health and issues of diet, lifestyle, and emotional well-being. For example, traditional Chinese medicine incorporates a range of treatments such as acupuncture, herbalism, massage, diet control, and exercise—all based on the general philosophy that good health revolves round the correct flow of *chi*, the body's energy. Although Western science has been sceptical of the principles behind Chinese medicine, many practitioners are now becoming convinced of the efficacy of acupuncture and Chinese herbs in the treatment of a range of pain problems, including backache, muscular and joint pain, migraines, and menstrual pain.

Similarly Ayurveda, the traditional medicine of India, is another complete philosophy of health based on energy balance. In addition to placing great importance on diet and lifestyle, it emphasizes massage and meditation. Today many Western practitioners recognize that such techniques, which promote relaxation and reduce stress, can help people to cope better with pain. Many pain clinics offer a range of treatment methods, from counseling to aromatherapy, that can help the patient to learn to relax.

EARLY WESTERN MEDICINE
Until the early 19th century, Western medicine was based on limited scientific knowledge and a poor understanding of the body. Physicians were often lampooned in cartoons, such as this 1812 example by Thomas Rowlandson from his famous "Dr. Syntax" series.

THE HOLISTIC APPROACH TO PAIN

Increasingly modern science is recognizing what traditional medical systems have practiced for centuries: effective pain management must be holistic, addressing the lifestyle and emotional and spiritual health of the patient, as well as the physical problem. Recent research has proven that our perception of pain is controlled

MIND OVER PAIN
Eastern therapists take a holistic, or "whole body," approach to pain. Yoga, for example, enables some people to strengthen the link between mind and body and thus control pain impulses.

POSTURE AND PAIN
Recent research has shown the importance of good posture in preventing the onset of back pain. Carrying a backpack is better for posture than carrying a satchel or a suitcase, for example.

DIET AND PAIN
A balanced diet that includes plenty of fresh vegetables and fruit not only helps to ward off many painful disorders but also may help those with chronic conditions to control their pain.

by a whole range of factors: the experience of pain is highly individualistic and is affected not only by a person's state of health, but also by age, cultural background, and emotions.

Although most people find it easy to grasp the concept that general health can influence their pain, it is only relatively recently that doctors have begun to address diet and exercise as part of an overall pain management plan. Yet many kinds of pain can be avoided or relieved by simple lifestyle changes. For instance, reducing fat intake can have an impact on the pain of angina, lower the risk of some types of cancer, and reduce body weight, thereby decreasing the pain of disorders such as arthritis. Exercise is just as important in both preventing and relieving pain. It was once believed that people with chronic back pain should rest until they recovered, even if it took years. It is now known that both acute and chronic back pain benefit from regular moderate exercise. Moreover, exercise plays a vital role in preventing painful diseases such as osteoporosis and heart disease, as well as the painful stiffness that often comes with aging.

People are even less well-informed about the very real role played by stress and the emotions in pain. Science has now found evidence to show how prolonged stress reduces the body's own natural painkillers—endorphins—and makes the experience of pain more severe. A state of stress causes direct physical changes in the body; the muscles tense, which in turn aggravates the pain of such conditions as backache. Stress relief measures can play a large part in overcoming the anxiety and depression experienced by many sufferers of chronic pain. For this reason relaxation and meditation therapies are proving increasingly valuable in helping people cope with long-term pain.

UNDERSTANDING PAIN

While a great deal is being learned from traditional forms of medicine, modern science has also revealed much about the workings of the nervous system and the brain and how this affects the perception of pain. What is becoming increasingly clear is that there are steps that an individual can take to control his or her perception of pain messages. Understanding pain and how it works enables you to take these steps to avoid the pain or to minimize it. Pain is usually meaningful: it is your body's way of warning you that you have injured yourself, or that you are about to come to harm, or that you need to rest. All pain sensations are processed in the brain. Your brain will decide what a pain message means, how serious it is, and the most appropriate action to take. In the case of a cut finger, for example, the pain message effectively forces you to rest the injured part, in order to avoid further damage, and allow the body's natural healing processes to take place. However, in the case of chronic pain, the pain message is not a useful one. Arthritis can in fact be made worse by rest, yet the pain experienced by the sufferer when he or she tries to become more mobile discourages any kind of exercise at all.

Pain research is now focusing on how individuals can influence the way in which the brain deals with information received from the nervous system. Studies have shown that when an individual is experiencing moments of extreme stress, an athlete taking part in a major competition, for instance, serious injuries can be sustained without the person being aware of the injury until the event is over. The brain has decided that the event is more important than the pain. In the case of chronic pain it might be possible to refocus the brain so that instead of prioritizing, say, a persistent message of back pain, it decides that completing a 20 minute daily exercise program is more important and overrides the pain message.

THE STRENGTH TO ENDURE
Dancers provide an ideal example of how the mind can control pain. As they strive to achieve perfect form and movement, ballerinas endure great pain—and rise above it.

WHERE EAST MEETS WEST
Acupuncture was the first therapy with roots in Eastern philosophy to be accepted by orthodox medicine. Western doctors say it controls pain by releasing natural painkillers. But the philosophy behind it is based on a belief in more complex forces.

THE BEST TREATMENT FOR YOUR PAIN

No pain experience is straightforward, and each individual's experience of pain is unique. It follows that finding the best therapy is a highly individualistic process. In some cases, an orthodox approach such as surgery may be necessary, but in other cases you might seek help from a naturopath for advice on diet and herbal remedies, an osteopath for back and neck manipulation, or an acupuncturist for pain relief, or combine a range of treatments to best manage your pain. The key to success is understanding how pain messages are processed, so you feel in control of your pain, rather than ruled by it.

MEDICINE IN A MOMENT
Most households contain a range of items that can relieve the discomfort or pain of everyday ailments. For example, mild sunburn can be soothed by cucumber slices, cold tea bags, milk, or apple cider vinegar.

BEATING PAIN
If you let it, pain can ruin your life, forcing you to retreat into a world of isolation. With a positive mental attitude, however, you can dominate and control pain and continue to lead a full and active life.

MANAGING PAIN

The purpose of this book is to provide you with the ability to acknowledge and understand your pain and to enable you to make the right decisions on how to cope with it.

Chapter 1 explains the physiology of pain – how pain works, what causes it and why people experience the same pain differently. In Chapter 2 you will learn how to recognize pain as a warning system – what pain means, how serious it is, and when you should consult a doctor. In addition, there is a guide to combining conventional and natural treatments, along with a description of painkillers, both orthodox and natural.

Changing your lifestyle to prevent pain is covered in Chapter 3, with advice on balancing your diet, exercising, and adapting your habits to avoid pain. The array of traditional treatments now available to combat pain can cause some confusion; Chapter 4 describes how they can help to manage your pain more effectively.

Chapters 5 to 8 focus on various pains experienced in different parts of the body, giving the possible causes for each type of pain and the best approaches for them. In Chapter 5 you will find out how to deal with headaches, earache, sore throats, toothache, and some other less common ailments. Chapter 6 explains the causes of chest pain, ranging from a cough to angina, and abdominal pain. The pain from disorders of the reproductive and urinary systems is covered in Chapter 7. Advice is given for women's problems such as menstrual pain, breast pain, and pain related to uterine disorders; men will find information on problems that cause pain in the testes and penis. Chapter 8 describes ways to cope with back and neck pain, as well as painful joint problems such as frozen shoulder or tennis elbow.

Chapter 9 aims to help people who are living with chronic pain and those who care for them, discussing the problems experienced by both and presenting ideas on how to overcome them.

Finally, Chapter 10 offers first-aid advice for the pain caused by minor injuries, with alternative and conventional treatments for cuts, burns, bites and stings, sunburn, and other minor ailments.

Do you know how to manage your pain?

Many people who experience pain either use painkillers regularly or suffer in silence. Perhaps they are not aware what effect the painkillers are having or what the latest advances in pain management are. Do you know how to ease a headache or relieve back pain without using conventional painkillers? There are simple steps that you can take to avoid many types of pain.

Q WHEN WAS THE LAST TIME YOU TOOK A PAINKILLER?

If you are one of those people who pops a pill at the first sign of pain, then you could be damaging your health. While painkillers can be an effective remedy for short-term and nonrecurring pain, their prolonged and excessive use can have unpleasant side effects (see Chapter 2). Also, by simply treating the pain itself, you are not dealing with its underlying cause. And prevention of pain altogether is far better than the treatment of symptoms.

Q ARE YOU UNSURE WHETHER TO CONSULT YOUR DOCTOR?

Many minor pains, if recurrent, can become an irritant in your life, and you may be tempted to visit the doctor if you get no relief. However, pain can often arise from factors such as stress or diet that are within your power to control once you establish the trigger. For example, frequent migraines might be linked to something you eat, such as chocolate. Chapter 2 shows how keeping a pain diary allows you to build up a picture of when you feel the pain and what does or doesn't affect it. You may be able to take steps to correct the problem. If the pain seems to warrant medical attention, or if you experience any of the 'red flag' pain signals described in Chapter 2, then see your doctor. To prepare yourself for a consultation, complete the pain questionnaire and read the feature in Chapter 2 that explains the kind of questions your GP will ask you.

Q DO YOU FEEL THAT MODERN MEDICINE HAS NO ANSWER TO YOUR PAIN?

Perhaps you have already visited doctors and specialists and been through a battery of tests without finding effective relief for your pain. If so, turn to Chapter 4. It is possible that one of the natural treatment methods may provide a potential answer to your problem. Bear in mind, however, that there are no miracle cures out there—it is simply a matter of finding what works best for you.

Q DO YOU GET HEADACHES FREQUENTLY?

Headaches are the most common pain experience; millions of people suffer them every year. The most frequent cause of which usually results from stress or today's hectic pace of life. Regular exercise is one of the most effective ways to dispel tension before it causes a headache. Relaxation techniques can also be invaluable in helping you to slow down. Chapter 5 gives details of other ways to prevent or relieve headaches.

Q ARE YOU A BACKACHE SUFFERER?

At least 80 percent of North Americans suffer from back pain at some time in their lives, and for 15 percent the problem is chronic. Many people believe that backache is a fact of life and they despair of any real relief. But there are many measures one can take to alleviate this debilitating and often depressing condition. Chapter 8 describes how exercise can prevent and relieve backache and gives sound advice on the many complementary medical treatments, including massage, acupressure, and osteopathy, that can have an amazing impact on back pain.

Q ARE YOU LIVING WITH A PERSON WHO SUFFERS CHRONIC PAIN?

It has been estimated that 10 per cent or more of the population of North America suffers from chronic pain (medically defined as pain that occurs daily for more than three months). Caregivers of chronic pain sufferers know that it is hard to give the right amount of support without undermining the sufferer's independence. They also know that pain sufferers experience a range of emotions, including depression and fear, which can make the pain worse and further impair a person's quality of life. The key to dealing with the emotional side of chronic pain is effective communication that promotes understanding.

Chapter 9 offers pointers on how to achieve this. In addition, there is particular advice on caring for children and elderly people who are in pain.

CHAPTER 1

WHAT IS PAIN?

Pain is an unpleasant sensation that most of us do our best to avoid. It can vary in severity from mild discomfort to excruciating agony and can last for just a few seconds or as long as a lifetime. Although the primary function of most pain is to protect the body from injury, there are some kinds that are not so easy to define, for example, the pain caused by certain diseases.

THE PROCESS OF PAIN

The process by which you experience pain is a complex one involving the brain and nerves. Understanding the mechanism, however, may help you to avoid or minimize your pain.

Although pain is one of the most unpleasant of human experiences, it is, in fact, also one of the body's most important functions. You may not appreciate this when you experience a blinding headache, a throbbing toothache, or a cramping stomachache, but the pain is providing you with vital information about your current state of health or external risks to your health, and forcing you to take steps that will allow healing to take place. A headache, for example, might be a warning that you are fatigued and stressed and need to rest; a toothache is probably informing you of damage to the tooth that needs to be attended to before more serious damage occurs; and a stomachache might be drawing your attention to poor dietary habits. Learning to understand and also properly respond to your body's pain messages can help you to avoid many painful disorders.

WHY YOU EXPERIENCE PAIN

When the body is injured, two types of pain are triggered. For example, if you twist your ankle, you immediately feel a sharp intense pain that grows worse in a matter of seconds and then rapidly begins to fade. This is known as the first pain. Then another pain sensation, a deep, diffuse, throbbing pain emerges and starts to spread slowly outside the affected region. This is known as the second pain.

The first type of pain is a warning of possible injury, and the first response is to stop whatever is causing it. If this pain response didn't occur, then more serious injury could result. This type of pain also teaches you not to repeat certain actions, such as touching something hot. The dull, relentless pain that follows makes you attend to the injury that has occurred. Without this second type of pain, there would be no motivation to protect the injured part from further harm,

or to rest and allow the body's own repair functions to take over and start mending the damage. Apart from making you rest—the oldest known cure—this kind of pain may drive you to seek treatment.

However, there are other kinds of pain that do not seem to serve the purpose of warning the body. They may be triggered by causes that do not pose any threat at all to your well-being. For example, if you overexert yourself at the gym after a period of inactivity, you will almost certainly have aching muscles the following morning. This is not because your body has experienced serious injury but because your muscles were not prepared for such a degree of exertion. Muscles prefer regular use and so exercising regularly will reduce the likelihood of experiencing this kind of pain.

In some cases the pain experienced can seem to be completely out of proportion to its cause. For example, passing a kidney stone can be extremely painful, although the condition itself is not life-threatening.

The pain-warning system can also be triggered by such diseases as cancer and arthritis. This kind of pain appears to have no primary function, though it does encourage the sufferer to consult a doctor.

HOW YOU FEEL PAIN

Pain messages are relayed from the injured area to the brain via the nervous system. The skin and deeper tissues of the body contain highly sophisticated nerve endings that sense changes both outside and inside the body. These nerve endings can respond to external changes, such as heat, cold, or pressure, and to internal stimuli like stretching and the release of chemicals from damaged cells. When these nerve endings are activated by direct stimuli, pain messages are sent to the brain. First the messages are relayed to an area in the spinal cord called

PAIN AS PROTECTION
Although pain is an unpleasant sensation, it actually functions to warn and protect the body from injury.

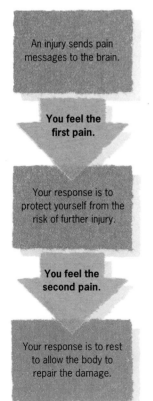

An injury sends pain messages to the brain.

You feel the first pain.

Your response is to protect yourself from the risk of further injury.

You feel the second pain.

Your response is to rest to allow the body to repair the damage.

NERVES AND THE BRAIN

The nervous system is a highly integrated mechanism that detects, analyzes and responds to changes in conditions both inside and outside the body. The system is divided into two main parts: the central nervous system, which comprises the spinal cord and the brain; and the peripheral nervous system, which is made up of all the nerves that connect the brain and spinal cord to the rest of the body.

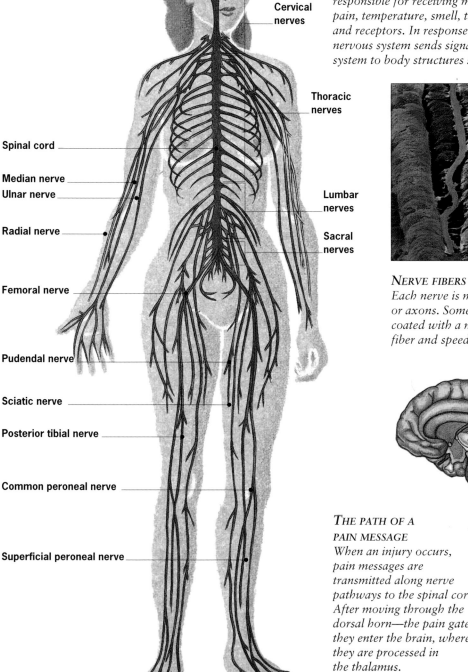

Brain

Brainstem

Cervical nerves

Thoracic nerves

Spinal cord

Median nerve

Ulnar nerve

Lumbar nerves

Radial nerve

Sacral nerves

Femoral nerve

Pudendal nerve

Sciatic nerve

Posterior tibial nerve

Common peroneal nerve

Superficial peroneal nerve

THE CENTRAL NERVOUS SYSTEM
The central nervous system consists of the brain and spinal cord and is the body's most important nerve system. It is responsible for receiving messages concerning stimuli such as pain, temperature, smell, taste, and sound from sense organs and receptors. In response to these messages, the central nervous system sends signals via the peripheral nervous system to body structures such as the muscles.

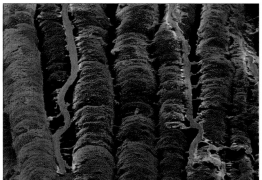

NERVE FIBERS
Each nerve is made up of bundles of nerve fibers, or axons. Some axons, called "A" fibers, are coated with a myelin sheath which insulates the fiber and speeds transmission of nerve signals.

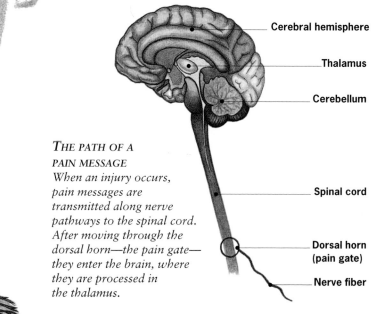

Cerebral hemisphere

Thalamus

Cerebellum

Spinal cord

Dorsal horn (pain gate)

Nerve fiber

THE PATH OF A PAIN MESSAGE
When an injury occurs, pain messages are transmitted along nerve pathways to the spinal cord. After moving through the dorsal horn—the pain gate—they enter the brain, where they are processed in the thalamus.

WHY AN INJURY FEELS TENDER

If you cut your finger the injured area will usually feel inflamed and tender. Even a gentle touch to the area can be extremely painful. The inflammation of the area around the cut is caused by the release of chemicals such as prostaglandins from the damaged cells. These substances enlarge the blood vessels so that more blood plasma and cells can enter the tissues to start the healing process. The increased blood supply makes the area hot, and as plasma collects in the tissue it starts to swell. The chemicals also cause exaggerated responses from the nerve endings in the injured area, so the cut feels tender even to the slightest touch. The pain serves to protect the area from further damage. Because the injured part becomes more sensitive to pain, the body is forced to rest the damaged area to allow healing to take place.

CROSS-SECTION OF A CUT
When you cut yourself, your body reacts immediately to repair the damage.

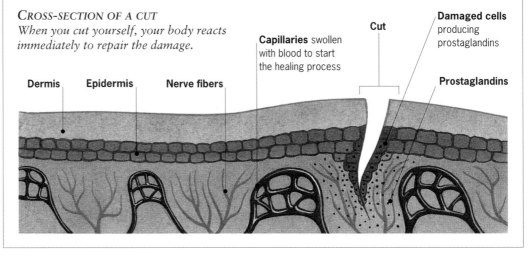

Capillaries swollen with blood to start the healing process

Cut

Damaged cells producing prostaglandins

Prostaglandins

Dermis   Epidermis   Nerve fibers

"A" AND "C" NERVE FIBERS
"A" fibers are surrounded by a thick, insulating sheath that helps them to transmit pain messages more quickly. Messages transmitted on the "C" fibers move more slowly. If insulating sheaths are destroyed, as occurs in multiple sclerosis, nerve fibers cannot transmit impulses, so numbness or weakness may result.

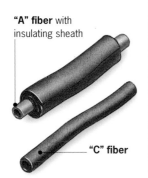

"A" fiber with insulating sheath

"C" fiber

the dorsal horn, where they are processed. From here the pain message travel up the spinal cord to the brain. Because all pain messages from the body pass through the dorsal horn before being transmitted to the brain, this part of the spinal cord is known as the pain gate.

Once the pain message reaches the brain it is processed in an area called the thalamus, and pain is then experienced. Nerve impulses are then passed back from the brain to the muscles and internal organs to produce the response to pain in order to safeguard the individual.

The response to pain will be influenced by the properties of the tissue that is stimulated or damaged—for example, some parts of the body are more sensitive to stretching while others are more sensitive to extreme temperature or pressure. However, no matter what part of the body is stimulated or what the nature of the stimulation is, no pain can be felt without the brain – this is the reason why general anesthesia is used during surgery. It works by neutralising the part of the brain that recognises pain.

PRIORITIZING PAIN MESSAGES

The brain is constantly bombarded with messages from different parts of the body giving information about changes occurring internally and externally. The thalamus deals directly with the most important sensory messages, such as those concerning pain, and acts as a kind of filter. Other messages are transmitted from the thalamus to the outer layer of the brain, where the sensations are analyzed. However, the body has its own system of making sure that important pain messages take priority, to ensure the individual's safety.

If the body faces injury from an external threat such as heat, priority will be given to the pain message so that the body can act immediately to deal with the potential threat. The body does this by transmitting urgent pain messages along nerve pathways that conduct messages especially quickly. This produces the first pain. These fast-conducting nerve pathways are known as "A" fibers. The pathways that conduct pain messages more slowly are known as "C" fibers. These produce the second pain.

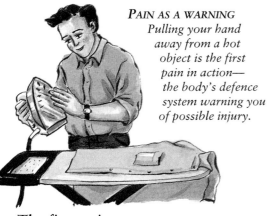

PAIN AS A WARNING
Pulling your hand away from a hot object is the first pain in action— the body's defence system warning you of possible injury.

The first pain

The skin contains mostly fast-conducting "A" fibers. This reflects the fact that the skin is the first line of defense against external threats to the body. For example, if a child places a hand too close to a candle flame the "A" fibers in the skin will quickly send a pain warning message to the brain, even before injury has actually occurred. The brain processes the message and quickly reacts, instructing the muscles to pull the hand away from the flame to avoid injury.

The second pain

After the initial sharp warning signal, a duller, relentless pain message is passed along the slower-conducting "C" fibers. These continue to transmit pain messages until the stimulus is removed and the tissue has recovered—and in some cases long after. The teeth and internal organs have mainly "C" fibers, which explains why we are usually aware of them only when they are already damaged.

PAIN AND THE BRAIN

Once the pain message has passed through the pain gate and on to the brain, it reaches the thalamus. This is where the various aspects of the pain message are analyzed in order to determine appropriate action. However, the brain not only analyzes the physical details of the pain message—such as where the pain is located, the form or type of pain, and any associated tenderness—but also it takes into account other factors such as the emotional aspects of the pain experience, the unpleasantness of the pain, and its degree of severity.

Memory, too, is important in the overall processing of the pain message. The brain draws on earlier experiences of a similar pain, and on any stored knowledge about

what such pain might mean, including pain experiences that have been reported by other people, in order to analyze the pain messages and arrive at an overall impression of the nature of the injury (see below).

THE BODY'S OWN PAIN CONTROL SYSTEMS

If a child falls and bruises his knee, his mother's instinctive reaction often is to rub it better. The mother may not realize it, but by simply rubbing the injured area she is causing the pain gate to close, thus preventing the transmission of any more pain messages to the brain. Rubbing the injured area stimulates other nerve fibers that feed into the dorsal horn with the pain messages. These impulses overload the pain gate so that eventually it closes and causes the pain to diminish.

The body's own pain control system explains why the degree of pain felt is often at odds with the type of injury suffered. If, for example, you fall off your bicycle and scrape your hands and also break your wrist, initially you may be aware only of the pain from the cuts and grazes. This is because sensory overload has closed the pain gate, blocking access to "C" fiber (or slow) pain impulses from damaged tissue around the bone, which would indicate that

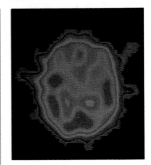

PET SCAN
Pain perception can be studied using a technique called positron emission tomography (PET). This produces images that show the precise location of areas of brain activity. In the image above, the red areas indicate high activity and the blue areas show low activity. PET is being used to investigate the brain's reaction to pain and is greatly expanding our knowledge of the subject.

WHAT SHAPES PAIN PERCEPTION

Pain is felt entirely in the brain. But there are various external factors that contribute to any pain that we feel. The brain considers the psychological aspects of the injury as well as the actual physical damage when shaping the type of pain.

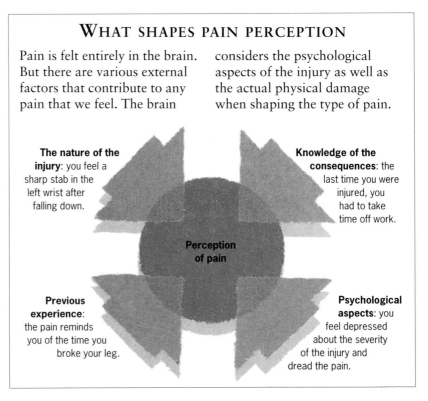

The nature of the injury: you feel a sharp stab in the left wrist after falling down.

Knowledge of the consequences: the last time you were injured, you had to take time off work.

Perception of pain

Previous experience: the pain reminds you of the time you broke your leg.

Psychological aspects: you feel depressed about the severity of the injury and dread the pain.

HOW TO INCREASE YOUR ENDORPHINS

Research has shown that stimulation and pressure can encourage the release of endorphins, the body's natural painkillers. This may explain the benefit of oriental massage methods, such as acupressure, that focus on applying pressure to acupuncture points. You can help to increase the release of endorphins by:

▶ *Gently rubbing and moving the painful part.*

▶ *Doing exercise.*

▶ *Trying energy therapies such as acupuncture, acupressure, and shiatsu.*

ENDORPHIN PRODUCTION

As recently as 1973 scientists discovered that the body produces its own pain-relieving substances. Known as endorphins, these natural painkillers act in the brain, spinal cord, and nerve endings at sites known as opiate receptors to relieve pain. In addition to their painkilling effect, endorphins are also believed to influence mood and regulate the body's response to stress.

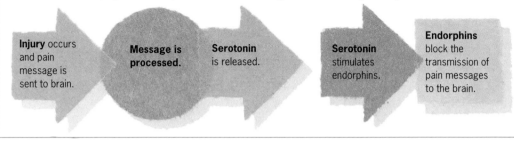

Injury occurs and pain message is sent to brain.

Message is processed.

Serotonin is released.

Serotonin stimulates endorphins.

Endorphins block the transmission of pain messages to the brain.

a more serious injury has taken place. By registering only that the skin has been cut, the brain is effectively prioritizing pain messages: if the skin is damaged, there may still be an external threat that the body should move away from.

In the same way that the brain classifies pain messages according to importance, it also prioritizes other messages unrelated to pain. For example, survival instincts are of paramount importance. If you are trapped in a burning building, your brain's first priority is to help you to escape from the fire, rather than assess messages that your hand has been burned.

Although the above is an extreme example, pain management specialists are interested in the fact that the brain's ability to override pain has been observed during non-life-threatening situations such as sports. If a player is injured in a soccer match, he may register the pain of a serious injury only when the game is over. This is because pain messages have been blocked, since the brain perceives them as less important than the need to win the game.

If we can persuade the brain that winning a game of soccer is more important than acknowledging a torn ligament, we can also learn ways to persuade the brain that a constant message of arthritic pain is less important than, say, the desire to attend and enjoy a much-anticipated social event. Ways of achieving this are explored in Chapter 4.

The body's own painkillers

The body produces its own painkillers in the form of chemicals known as endorphins. When pain messages reach the brain, the production of a chemical called serotonin is stimulated. Serotonin in turn helps to release endorphins, which block the transmission of pain messages at specific sites, known as opiate receptors, that are located in the brain, nerves, and spinal cord.

Recent research has established that a person's emotional state can influence the release of endorphins. Stress and anxiety are known to inhibit the production of endorphins because the more depressed a person is, the lower the level of serotonin produced. This situation, in turn, reduces the amount of endorphins released. The body's natural

DEFENSE SYSTEMS

The brain is informed of changes in the environment by messages sent from highly sensitive nerve endings in the skin. These nerve endings, or nociceptors, have different sensitivities. Some respond to extreme stimuli such as a cut, for example, while others respond to changes in pressure.

SENSORY OVERLOAD
The skin is particularly rich in nerve endings. Rubbing the injured skin after falling down may help to relieve pain by closing the pain gate.

pain-coping mechanism is therefore diminished, because pain messages can be transmitted freely to the brain.

TYPES OF PAIN

Although people can experience pain in many different ways, it is often helpful to consider the two major categories of pain: acute and chronic.

Acute pain

Everybody has had some experience of acute pain, which may have lasted a few days or, in some cases, a few weeks. This kind of pain is part of the body's response to injury or disease. Its primary purpose is to make us rest and allow healing to start. Physiological changes that take place include increased pulse rate, raised blood pressure, sweating, heightened awareness, and decreased response to other stimuli. Acute pain normally responds to painkillers, which are usually required for only a short time and thus pose no long-term problems.

Chronic pain

Although acute pain usually serves a purpose, chronic pain may continue for years with no benefit. It could be the lingering aftermath of an injury that has healed. It may also occur in response to a disease such as cancer or arthritis. Often the cause of chronic pain cannot be diagnosed.

Emotional and psychological factors can play significant roles in the experience of chronic pain. Emotions, in particular, affect the body's release of endorphins. As a result, the more depressed and anxious you are feeling, the more intense the pain experience is likely to be.

It is also possible that chronic pain can become more severe due to conditioning. The long-term experience of pain can lead to constant tensing of the muscles near the affected area. The nervous system may become conditioned to perceive pain whenever these muscle tension sensors are stimulated, so that any form of movement or exercise becomes painful.

The commonest occurrence of chronic pain is in the lower back, followed by the neck and joints that are affected by arthritis. These particular pain problems tend not to respond well to pain-relieving drugs.

Referred pain

Pain from injury to the skin is usually felt precisely at the point of injury—it is said to be localized—and often has a sharp, stinging quality. In contrast, pain from deep internal organs is hard to pinpoint, and it is often difficult for people to describe exactly where they feel the pain. The symptoms are also quite different: the latter pain is deep and aching and often the sufferer feels nauseous and generally unwell.

ACUTE PAIN AND CHRONIC PAIN

Acute pain is characterized by the rapid onset of symptoms, which can be extremely changeable, but last only a few days. In contrast, chronic pain persists for a long time. Listed below are the physical and physiological differences that have been established between acute pain and chronic pain.

TYPE OF PAIN	PAIN EXPERIENCED	BODY RESPONSE	PHYSICAL CHANGES	TREATMENT
Acute pain	It is often severe but normally of short duration (hours or days).	Pain signals the body to rest so that damaged tissues can be repaired.	The pulse rate becomes faster, the blood pressure rises, sweating increases, and there is a heightened sense of awareness and decreased response to other stimuli.	Conventional painkillers work well and are usually required for only a short time, enabling a resumption of activities.
Chronic pain	Degree of pain often outweighs original cause. Link between source of pain and actual pain decreases as chronic pain continues over a long period (weeks, months, or years).	Pain messages can still be generated long after initial stimuli have gone.	If the nerve transmitting the pain messages is paired with muscle tensing pathways for a long time, the nervous system may become conditioned to perceiving pain whenever muscle tension sensors are stimulated.	Herbal medicines used over a long period of time are often more effective than conventional painkillers; narcotics may demotivate. The sufferer's mental attitude and relationships can play a significant role in alleviating the pain.

Chronic Backache Sufferer

Chronic backache is one of the commonest pain conditions. If back pain doesn't respond to the usual treatments given by a GP, fear of the consequences may lead to overprotection, which in turn can cause more pain. Strategies such as relaxation and gradually increasing activity can help the sufferer to cope with backache and lead a happier and more productive life.

John is a successful 47-year-old businessman, with a wife, Ann, and three children. He developed backache following a football injury in his teens. His pain never troubled him until recently, when it started to interfere with his activities. Work has become more stressful and he has had to stop playing squash, as this makes his backache worse. He has become irritable and his relationship with Ann and his children has suffered. He is becoming increasingly worried about his inability to cope and his deteriorating relationship with his family. His doctor prescribed painkillers and rest, but these have had little effect. X-rays have revealed there is no surgically treatable cause for his backache.

WHAT SHOULD JOHN DO?

John needs to consult a specialist in pain management, to develop a strategy to help him cope with his pain. He should have his painkillers reviewed and think carefully about his lifestyle and emotional state. He also needs to pace his exercise, doing limited workouts frequently rather than a more strenuous routine just once a week. He should practice relaxation techniques and study ways of managing his stress, to help him handle his workload and manage his pain better. He needs to recognize that not getting along with his wife and children is adding to his stress and may be contributing to his condition. He should try to set aside more time to spend with them in recreational activities.

Action Plan

STRESS
Delegate work in the office and review responsibilities. Spend more time with the family, take up an interest and practice relaxation exercises on a regular basis.

FITNESS
Plan an exercise regimen and set goals to increase physical activity. Targets could include swimming once a week with the family and helping Ann in the garden.

FAMILY
Make more use of the babysitter so that there is more time to spend alone with Ann. Plan more family outings.

FITNESS
Lack of exercise and inactivity can diminish lack of confidence, which in turn reduces tolerance to pain.

FAMILY
Chronic pain often causes difficulties within the family, sometimes leaving the sufferer isolated and with the tendency to avoid activity for fear of increasing pain.

STRESS
Stress can cause increases in muscle tension that, when prolonged, can lead to more pain.

HOW THINGS TURNED OUT FOR JOHN

John reorganized work responsibilities and found he could leave the office earlier. He paced activities, didn't overexert himself, and spent more time with his family. As a result, his confidence increased and in three months he was able to go for long walks, had taken up gardening, and was becoming much more active. Although some of his pain persisted, his sleeping patterns improved and he was able to cope with it more effectively.

Pain from internal organs may be felt in other parts of the body, sometimes a great distance from the diseased or damaged area. This is known as referred pain. This occurs because a number of different parts of the body are supplied by the same nerve or group of nerves as the damaged tissues that are the source of pain. The brain can misinterpret or confuse the signals supplied from the same group of nerves. For example, pain caused by angina, where the heart muscle is starved of oxygen, is often referred to the arm: the heart and the arm are served by the same group of nerves.

Describing pain

Within the broad definitions of acute and chronic pain, doctors further categorize pain into three distinctive types. The first type, called somatic pain, occurs in the skin, muscles, and bones. Generally it is constant and localized, and is characterized as aching,

throbbing, or gnawing. Throbbing pain is often due to inflammation. Blood vessels dilate to increase the flow of blood to the area. With each pulse of blood a throb of pain occurs.

Pain from the inner organs of the body is called visceral pain. It is characteristically vague in distribution and quality, often described as deep, dull, aching, dragging, squeezing, or pressure-like. When acute, it may be colicky. It can be due to distension of the smooth muscle walls of the intestine, rapid stretching of the enveloping sheath of such organs as the liver, or lack of blood supply and oxygen to tissue.

Neuropathic pain involves the nerves and can be further sub-divided into paresthesia, dysesthesia, and allodynia. Pain may be due to the nerve being damaged as a result of injury or disease. It is often described as a burning sensation. Other symptoms commonly include tingling and numbness.

DIFFERENT KINDS OF PAIN

Various parts of the body detect pain in different ways. The skin has a large number of pain receptors so injuries to the skin are felt acutely. The intestines, however, mainly contain receptors that detect when the tissues are being stretched. This means that distension resulting from excess gas, for example, is felt acutely, but a cut is not registered. Recognizing the characteristics of pain can help to identify its cause.

CHARACTERISTICS	TYPE	AREA	NAME	TYPICAL CAUSE
Aching, throbbing	Constant and localized	Skin, muscle, and bone	**Somatic**	Injuries to skin, muscle, and bone such as cuts, bruises, burns, and fractures; inflammation; vascular headaches.
Deep, dull, dragging, squeezing, pressure-like; colicky	Vague in distribution and quality	Internal organs	**Visceral**	Distension of walls of intestine due to excess gas, a food that is not well tolerated, lack of exercise or bowel inactivity after an abdominal operation; lack of blood supply and oxygen and death of tissue. Colicky pain is caused by an overactive bowel, in which contractions are too fierce or rapid.
Tingling with numbness, occasionally a burning sensation	Abnormal sensation without a stimulus	Nerve tissue	**Neuropathic** Paraesthesia (pins and needles)	Occurs when conduction of nerve sensations from the body to the brain are partially blocked, for example, when the foot is in an awkward position for too long.
Unpleasant, even intolerable sensation	Abnormal sensation	Nervous system	**Neuropathic** Dysaesthesia	Occurs with disease or injury to nervous system.
Hypersensitivity to stimulus such as touch	Pain is out of all proportion to light and touch stimulus. In extreme cases even the touch of clothing can cause extreme pain.	Nervous system	**Neuropathic** Allodynia	Pain caused by prior damage to nerve endings, which has made the area oversensitive. Frequently accompanies damage to the nervous system, as in the case of shingles.

PERCEPTION OF PAIN

The way the brain perceives pain is not only based on the actual physical sensation, but also is influenced by the individual's cultural background, personality, and previous experience.

Fast pain, which travels along the "A" fibers, primarily has a warning function; it signals the body to take immediate action to protect itself from further injury. However, slow pain, which travels along the "C" fibers, is processed in a more complex way: the brain draws on other types of information, which influence its response to the pain message. These include memories of similar types of pain experienced before, how family members or friends may have coped with similar pains, and alarm about what the pain may lead to.

This means that the same kind of pain can be experienced in very different ways by different people, according to factors such as their age, gender, culture, and personality, as well as their previous experience of pain.

INDIVIDUAL PAIN TOLERANCE

The term "pain threshold" refers to the level at which we experience pain when some kind of stimulus, such as pressure, is applied. Laboratory tests have shown that most people have a similar pain threshold. However, the level at which a person labels a pain as unbearable—known as personal pain tolerance—varies significantly according to age, sex, and cultural background.

Our perception of pain depends to a large degree on past experience and knowledge about what is likely to be painful. The more anxious or solicitous our parents are about any pain we may experience as children, the more we learn to fear pain. For example, if a parent is nervous and tense about how a child will cope with an injection and communicates this anxiety to the child, the child stores this information about injections and comes to expect all injections to be painful. The brain's expectation of pain heightens the actual experience of pain.

In the same way, research has shown that an over-solicitous caregiver can reinforce the sufferer's perception of being in pain, which in turn heightens the brain's perception of actual pain.

Emotions play another important role in influencing our perception of pain. Being fussed over by a caregiver may cause an emotional response in the patient, who learns subconsciously that a heightened sick role gains extra attention and care.

Negative emotions about pain can also heighten the sufferer's pain experience. Feelings of anxiety, fear, and stress produce increased sensitivity to all external and internal stimuli, including pain. This aspect of pain perception is looked at in more detail on page 30.

PAIN TOLERANCE AND THE INDIVIDUAL

The intensity of pain can vary from person to person, and also within the same person. Perception of pain varies according to the way one feels or the circumstances at the time. In addition, there are a variety of other factors that make the tolerance of pain unique to each individual.

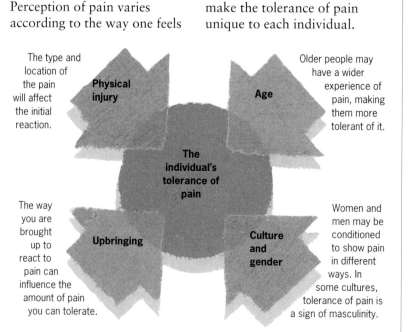

The type and location of the pain will affect the initial reaction.

Physical injury

Older people may have a wider experience of pain, making them more tolerant of it.

Age

The individual's tolerance of pain

The way you are brought up to react to pain can influence the amount of pain you can tolerate.

Upbringing

Women and men may be conditioned to show pain in different ways. In some cultures, tolerance of pain is a sign of masculinity.

Culture and gender

Cultural differences in feeling and dealing with pain

People from different cultural backgrounds have been shown to react differently to the experience of pain, even when the injury or illness causing the pain is the same. Although the pain threshold is similar, the outward expression of pain may differ enormously. In some cultures, people express their feelings openly and visible expressions of pain and discomfort are positively encouraged. In other cultures, people are conditioned to hide or mask their feelings and may not be encouraged to express pain openly. For example, by tradition Japanese women are not expected to vocalize their pain during childbirth.

Richard Sternbach, a California psychologist who specializes in pain, studied pain tolerance levels in a group of American women from various ethnic backgrounds, in order to determine the influence of their cultural background on experimental pain. His research revealed that women of Italian descent, who were conditioned to voice their suffering openly, tolerated less pain than women of British or Jewish origin.

An understanding of the ways in which your cultural background can affect your pain perception and pain tolerance may help you to gain control over your own reaction to pain and devise strategies to control the amount of pain you feel.

Gender differences in feeling and dealing with pain

Gender and age influence how people react to pain. In many cultures, males are encouraged to be more stoical and reserved. If they have a physical problem that is causing pain, they are not encouraged to complain about it. Any outward display of pain or suffering may be taken as a sign of weakness or insecurity. In contrast, women are more able to discuss their emotions openly and, as a result of this, may display pain and suffering to a greater degree.

Some cultures go so far as to regard the ability to withstand pain without showing any reaction as a sign of great manliness, and so adolescent boys are encouraged to demonstrate their high pain tolerance. The same ability in a young woman, however, is seen as unfeminine and is discouraged.

Pain clinics (see page 69) usually have a slightly higher proportion of women attendees than men. This may be due in part to the fact that women are more likely to seek

Munchausen's syndrome

In extreme cases, enjoyment of the sick role can lead to Munchausen's syndrome, a psychological disorder in which the sufferer complains of pain that is pretended or self-induced. In some cases sufferers may actually experience pain, so strong is the conditioning of their subconscious mind. Physical symptoms may include fever, skin rashes, dizziness, and pain in the abdomen. Patients are usually well versed in medical matters and often bear the scars of previous treatments or examinations. In Munchausen's syndrome by proxy, parents insist that their children are suffering from painful medical conditions.

CULTURAL DIFFERENCES IN PAIN PERCEPTION

Although different people may experience the same intensity of pain, the way they perceive and cope with it will vary according to their backgrounds. In some cultures internalizing emotions is encouraged, but in others an extravagant display of feelings may be standard. The film styles of northern and southern Europe show how culture can condition the expression of emotions and pain.

NORTHERN REPRESSION
The languid movements and solemn expressions typical of films made in northern Europe are symbolic of the internalized emotions of their characters.

SOUTHERN EXPRESSION
Dramatic or passionate gestures and displays of high emotion are common features in films of southern Europe or Latin America, reflecting the expressive nature of the culture.

Origins

The influence of environment, experience, and knowledge on our perception of pain has been the subject of many studies during this century. Dr. Henry K. Beecher, who later became the first Professor of Anesthetics at Harvard University, was involved with treating soldiers during the Second World War. He observed that soldiers wounded in battle were much less likely to ask for or need morphine than civilians who had received similar injuries. The difference lay in the emotional response: whereas the soldier felt relief at escaping from the battlefield alive, the civilian saw the injury as a depressing and calamitous event. As a result, Beecher came to the conclusion that "There is no simple direct relationship between the wound per se and the pain experienced." His theory explains why a person can feel the same pain differently according to his environment and current mental and emotional state. For example, a child will laugh if smacked in play but cry if the same slap is given as a punishment.

DR. HENRY K. BEECHER (1904–76)
Dr. Beecher was one of the foremost researchers into the perception of pain.

Does a fetus feel pain?

From the 20th week of pregnancy a fetus begins to show responses to painful stimuli. Initially, these responses are more like primitive reflexes, but as the nervous system matures, the responses become more specific to the area of stimulation. Thus it can be assumed that a fetus feels pain.

---

help for a pain problem than men. Studies have shown that women tend to report chronic pains that are more severe and last for a longer period. Also, according to experiments women generally report pains in a wider range of areas than men.

Recent research suggests that the gender difference in pain perception may actually have a specifically biological basis, as well as a cultural one. In experiments carried out on a group of men and women who had just had their wisdom teeth removed, medical researchers in California discovered that opiate painkillers had a longer-lasting effect on the women than on the men. This research could have major implications for the way that men and women are treated for pain in the future.

Age differences in feeling pain

Age, too, has a bearing on how pain may be perceived. The older a person is, the more likely he or she is to have experienced a wide range of acute and chronic pain conditions. As a result, the person is more likely to have developed a higher degree of tolerance and can also draw on past experience in order to recognize the pain and come to terms with it and manage it.

How children communicate pain

Children are not as articulate in describing their pain as adults. They have less knowledge and experience to draw on to determine what kind of pain they are feeling. Thus a pain anywhere may be described as a tummy-ache, or nausea may be described as a sore throat. Pain may also be communicated through other means such as temper tantrums, crying, sulking, and resorting to behaviors like bedwetting. It may not be clear if a child is feeling pain, is generally distressed, or simply wants attention. For example, a youngster who is experiencing problems at school may develop "pains" in order to stay at home.

Children may find it easier to communicate their pain and its location through drawings. These can help a doctor diagnose the problem more accurately.

Sometimes children mimic their parents' or older siblings' reaction to pain. Similarly, they may develop the same fear of pain shown by other family members. In a child this is accentuated by a lack of emotional maturity and inability to rationalize fears. Parents should always be aware of their reactions to both their own pain and that of their children.

THE CAUSES OF PAIN

We usually think of pain as emanataing from a specific injury or disease. However, pain can arise from other causes, and an individual can learn to control or avoid such conditions.

Physical pain is frequently caused by injury to the body. Chemicals such as prostaglandins are released after an injury to help the healing process get underway. Paradoxically, these chemicals intensify the pain, because they stimulate the nerve endings to transmit pain messages to the brain. These messages have a protective function, as they induce the body to rest the injured area to allow the damaged tissues to be repaired.

Localized physical pain may also be experienced as a direct result of tissue damage that is the result of disease. For example, a tumor pressing on or disturbing a nerve can cause pain. However, illness and disease can also be responsible for a more generalized pain response—even if there is no actual tissue damage. Generalized myalgia, or painful aching of the muscles, is commonly experienced during a bout of influenza and warns the body of the need to rest.

Pain is almost inevitable after surgery. It may be minimized, however, by the skill of the surgeon and the anesthetist, and by the knowledge that the pain is only temporary while healing occurs.

PAIN DURING EXERCISE

Although exercise is vital for keeping the muscles active and promoting general good health, pain can arise both during and after exercise. If you do brisk exercise after a long period of inactivity, your muscles will probably be tender and actually feel swollen several hours later. This type of pain is due to mechanical damage of the muscles. You can avoid it by warming up your muscles before exercise, and by building up your exercise regimen gradually.

If you find that chest pain comes on during exercise and rapidly increases until the activity has stopped, you may be suffering from narrowing of the arteries, and this condition is causing a limited blood supply to reach the heart. Narrowing of the arteries can be caused by elevated blood

WARMING UP

Warming up exercises are an essential part of any exercise routine. Gentle, rhythmic movements such as stretching prepare the heart, lungs, and muscles for more strenuous work to come. Warming up also helps to lubricate the joints, so they can work more efficiently when you start your exercise program. If you don't warm up sufficiently, you may suffer dizziness, muscle cramps, and chest pains. Cooling down is just as important—gentle movements after an exercise session help the blood flow to return to normal. As part of a warm-up and cooldown, try the illustrated exercise.

THE SWAN
Bend knees with feet wide apart. Put your left hand on the hip, right hand above the head, and lean to the right. Repeat in both directions several times.

27

CAPTAIN AHAB AND PHANTOM PAIN
One of the most famous literary figures to suffer phantom pain was Captain Ahab in Herman Melville's epic novel Moby Dick *(1851). The legendary whaler lost a leg in a terrifying accident but continued to have frequent bouts of agonizing pain in the limb that had been removed. The picture above shows Gregory Peck as Captain Ahab in the 1956 film version of the story.*

ICE-CREAM HEADACHE
Eating cold food like ice cream can bring on a headache. Though troublesome, this type of pain is not a cause for serious concern.

PHANTOM PAIN

People who have lost an arm or a leg often feel as if the limb is still there, because the nerve pathways serving that part of the body are still transmitting messages to the brain. They may also experience pain in the part of the body that has been removed, just as they did before amputation took place. The pain is no less real than if the limb were still in place. This condition is known as phantom pain and is usually described as crushing, cramping, or burning. The pain may persist as long as the nerve pathways continue to transmit pain messages. Phantom pain usually dissipates in time. In some cases, however, the pain is severe and does not decrease. Transcutaneous electrical nerve stimulation (TENS) has been shown to relieve phantom pain in many cases (see page 83).

pressure or high blood cholesterol levels, smoking, diabetes, and obesity. If you fit into any of these categories, consult your doctor before starting an exercise program.

DYSFUNCTION OF PAIN NETWORK
Damage to a nerve or nerve pathway can lead to a malfunctioning of the pain network and consequent pain symptoms. Even minor injuries can trigger extensive, persistent pain problems if the nerve pathway relevant to the affected area is damaged. In such cases the nerve pathway becomes hyperexcitable, sending erratic pain messages to the brain for no apparent reason. Similar sensations are frequently experienced by people who have lost a limb (see box on phantom pain, above).

THE EFFECTS OF COLD
In extremely cold weather, you may find that your fingers and toes begin to ache. This is because in subzero temperatures, the arteries supplying the fingers and toes can go into spasm, restricting blood flow and releasing chemicals that send warning pain messages to the brain. Even if you warm the affected area, the pain will persist until all the chemicals released in connection with the muscle spasm have been cleared. In some cases, cold can cause minor, but often painful complaints such as chilblains and chapped skin. Chilblains result from too rapid rewarming of the skin after it has been exposed to extremely cold conditions. Chapped skin occurs most frequently in cold weather when oil-secreting glands produce less oil to lubricate the skin. In severe cases persistent lack of blood flow due to cold leads to tissue damage, as in frostbite, or tissue death, as in gangrene.

PAIN IN MENTAL ILLNESS
Sometimes people suffer such severe psychological trauma that they actually experience it as physical pain. There are several possible reasons for this response. One is that physical pain, rather than a psychological problem, is often easier for a patient or his family to accept. Or sometimes the role of the invalid is seen as offering greater benefits, such as sympathy or a chance to avoid responsibilities. In extreme cases, the body copes with painful emotions by converting them into physical pain. For example, a man who has caused injury to another with his right arm might be so traumatized that he too will start to feel pain in his right arm. Although the pain originates in the mind, it feels completely genuine to the sufferer. Known as conversion disorder, this problem is usually resolved by coming to terms with the underlying psychological problem.

Some people develop delusions that their body has altered in some way, for example, that an arm is being eaten away or disfigured. Pain may accompany such delusions, which are common in schizophrenics.

SELF-MUTILATION
Self-mutilation, the act of deliberately cutting or otherwise injuring oneself, often involves pain. It is common among people suffering from depression, schizophrenia, bulimia, or feelings of hostility. The need to relieve tension, the influence of alcohol or other substances, aggressive impulses, and a desire for attention are some of the possible reasons for self-mutilation.

SELF-INFLICTED PAIN

Cultural factors are known to affect the way pain is perceived. This is evident in traditional customs and sacred rites where pain plays a part, such as tattooing, body-piercing, and mutilation for religious reasons. For example, the ceremony of hook-swinging, practiced in parts of India, involves suspending a male member of the community from hooks that have been embedded in his back. The man seems to suffer no pain during the ceremony but rather appears to be in a state of exaltation.

In Western culture, body-piercing and tattooing are often a way of promoting self-identity or affinity with a group. Some people who have undergone body piercing have reported a pleasant sensation at the time of piercing, described as a rush or high, that lasted as long as several hours. This may be due to release of endorphins, the body's own painkillers.

The states of pleasure and pain and the thin line dividing them have been much discussed by philosophers since the days of Plato. Ecstasy is commonly understood to be a state of intense delight, although, as in "the agony and the ecstasy" of Christ, it also refers to the overwhelming state of any emotion such as fear or pain. This overwhelming state is somewhat similar to a trance. The suffering may be endured as a means of obtaining the heightened state.

BODY PIERCING
Piercing the body with a variety of objects is a common phenomenon throughout the world. In some cultures this kind of piercing may be linked to initiation rites, indicating that a male or female has reached a certain phase in maturity. In the West, ear piercing became fashionable in the 1960s, and today piercing other parts of the body, such as the nose or the navel, is increasingly common.

FIREWALKING
Rituals involving fire, such as walking over hot coals, exist all over the world (this photo was taken in Sri Lanka). Many cultures believe that firewalking is a test of faith, and firewalkers claim that they are aided by strength of belief. Scientists surmise that a crucial factor in successful firewalking is the amount of time that the foot is in contact with the coals. However, there is no doubt that willpower also plays an important part in distracting the mind and blocking the pain.

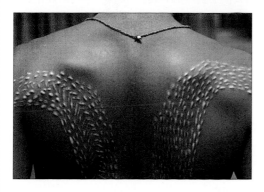

RITUAL SCARRING
The practice of producing raised scars in decorative patterns on the human body is particularly common in parts of Africa, New Guinea, and Melanesia, and among Australian aborigines. The scarring may indicate an individual's status or tribal allegiance, or it may be done purely for cosmetic reasons. The patterns are produced by cutting with a knife or sometimes by burning. In some cases, protective charms may be placed under the skin.

Sadomasochism
Sadomasochism is an abnormal condition in which sexual pleasure derives from the infliction (sadism) and receipt (masochism) of pain. The term can refer to the combination of both sadism and masochism in one person, or a couple may indulge in sadomasochistic practices whereby one partner has heightened sexual arousal from inflicting pain and the other derives pleasure from receiving it.

EMOTIONAL PAIN

Emotional pain is experienced completely within the brain, but painful physical symptoms often follow because of the close link between the brain and the physical functioning of the body.

Mind over body
Studies have shown that some patients suffering a terminal illness are able to delay death in order to be present at an important event such as a birthday or holiday celebration. This phenomenon illustrates the power of mind over body and forms the basis of visualization therapy. It appears that the mind can be trained to exercise more control over the body than was previously thought.

Emotional pain can have many causes, for example grief over the loss of a loved one, or feelings of rejection after divorce, or shock at being unwanted following a downsizing. Such emotional trauma can lead to depression and anxiety and, in extreme cases, to physical pain, because the areas of the brain that process emotional pain and suffering are the same as those that deal with physical pain.

For example, after being rejected by a partner, a person feels a complicated mixture of emotions—including anger, hurt, betrayal—which in turn produce threat and insecurity. Once a threat message has been perceived by the brain a typical stress "fight or flight" response is activated: heart rate increases, muscles tense, and soon the individual feels tense as well as hurt and unhappy. After the initial shock fades, many people pass through phases of profound sadness, anger, guilt, depression, helplessness, confusion, and erratic or impulsive behavior. Physical symptoms are often similar to those experienced under stress: appetite loss and insomnia are common.

HOW EMOTIONS AFFECT PAIN
Your emotional state can strongly influence the sensation of pain. According to your feelings and character, your response to an initial pain message can either intensify and prolong the pain experience or reduce the amount of pain perceived.

Anxiety and pain
Anxiety about the pain one is feeling or anticipates feeling has been shown to intensify the perception of it. When a group of medical students were told they were going

THE VICIOUS CYCLE OF PAIN

Your perception of pain is closely linked to your thoughts and behavior. Emotions such as anxiety can actually heighten the perception of pain and lead to further stress and negative emotions, which in turn cause yet more pain.

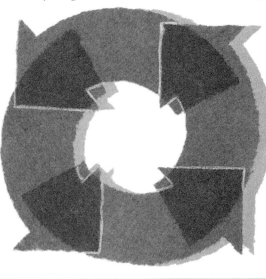

Feeling anxious about the consequences of your condition can actually make you more sensitive and increase your pain.

Fear and uncertainty about the nature of your condition can make pain receptors more sensitive, increasing the perception of pain.

Depression caused by a long-standing condition can heighten your pain by inhibiting the production of endorphins.

Stress brought on by a painful condition can increase muscle tension in the body, which in turn causes more pain and more stress.

THE LANGUAGE OF EMOTIONAL PAIN

The extent to which physical manifestations of emotional pain affect us is reflected in the language we use to describe painful emotional states. A statement such as "I felt as though my heart would break" indicates how emotional pain can be transferred to a physical experience. Many people describe their initial reaction to the death of a partner or friend as a feeling of numbness. This feeling, which has been called the heart's analgesic, may be the brain's way of playing for time before admitting the loss of a loved one and having to come to terms with the intense emotional pain that is associated with it.

to be subjected to high levels of pain when asked to hold hot metal rods, the students grimaced and dropped the rods even though they were not hot at all.

When you feel anxious, you tend to feel much more sensitive to external and internal stimuli – for example, noises may seem louder and lights brighter. This can heighten your perception of pain and make it feel worse. Relaxation and being well informed about any pain you may be about to feel can help to dispel anxiety and so reduce the amount of pain you experience.

Anxiety about something other than your own problems, however, can serve to distract you from pain. It is not uncommon for people with chronic backache to find their experience of pain diminishes if a close family member falls seriously ill.

Depression and pain

Depression can make pain feel worse, particularly if it is long-standing. This is partly because depression can reduce the body's ability to produce endorphins.

In severe cases of depression people may become completely preoccupied with their physical problems. They may come to believe that part of their body is damaged or altered in some way and causing severe pain. In such cases the pain is actually caused by the underlying depression.

Fear and pain

If you don't know the cause of a pain, the fear and uncertainty may increase its intensity. As with anxiety, fear heightens the body's receptiveness to stimulation making pain receptors more sensitive. Sometimes people avoid doing exercise for fear that strenuous activity might cause an injury, even though exercise would clearly be beneficial. People recovering from a heart attack, for example, are often advised to exercise. They might notice that their heart rate goes up following exercise and, although this is a normal response, they may interpret the raised heart rate as signaling the onset of another heart attack. The resulting panic causes their heart rate to rise even more, and they may even develop pain symptoms.

Stress and pain

Stress can increase the experience of pain and make it more difficult to cope. When you find yourself in a stressful situation, your body responds by increasing the production of certain hormones such as adrenaline. These hormones cause a variety of changes in the body, including raising the blood pressure and heart rate. When stress is experienced over a prolonged period, the body's reaction is to tense the muscles. Muscles in a state of sustained tension in the neck, shoulders, and head can cause pain, which then produces more stress and more tension, thus increasing the pain. Tightening of the muscles in the face, scalp, and neck can trigger a tension headache, which can last for hours or even weeks.

Making a conscious effort to relax and reduce your stress levels is often recommended as a way of decreasing the risk of pain from stress-related problems. There are various relaxation therapies (see pages 91 and 92) you can try that can help to prevent some of the first signs of stress, for example, shallow breathing, lack of concentration, and disturbed sleep. All of these manifestations can heighten your perception of pain.

DEALING WITH EMOTIONAL PAIN

Most counselors and therapists agree that profound emotional pain is best confronted head on:

▶ *Don't hide or repress your feelings, otherwise they may re-emerge in physical stress-related disorders such as eczema and tension headaches.*

▶ *Discuss your emotions openly with a friend or counselor.*

▶ *Consciously call a halt to negative feelings; these can generate chemical reactions in the brain that lead to a cycle of depression.*

▶ *Try to focus on the positive aspects of your life.*

▶ *Pinch yourself to direct your brain away from negative thoughts.*

▶ *Try visualizing yourself in a relaxing scene such as you might experience while on vacation.*

COPING WITH FEAR

Fear of the unknown, feelings of uncertainty, and lack of understanding can all intensify the feeling of pain. In some cases fear of pain can be worse than the actual pain itself.

The way you feel pain is greatly influenced by your upbringing, experiences, education, and culture. If you are frightened by the pain you are suffering or the treatments that you are about to undergo, the fear may prevent you from thinking and behaving rationally. Perhaps most significantly, fear and anxiety will actually heighten your pain experience (see page 30). Although changing deeply entrenched attitudes to pain is never easy, learning to cope with and minimize fear is one of the most important pain management strategies you can acquire.

WHY WE DEVELOP FEAR OF PAIN

Fear of pain most often develops in childhood when we are less able to analyze experiences in a rational manner. While an adult may understand the need for undergoing a certain amount of pain in order to benefit in the long term, a child may find it difficult to appreciate the value of pain when set against the fear it causes. One bad experience in childhood, such as a very painful injection at the dentist, can cause long-standing fears, which may continue into adulthood. Anxiety can exaggerate the initial fear and lead to avoidance, which in turn can exacerbate the fear and anxiety.

Having an operation or other medical treatments and tests may produce fear not only of the pain but also of what may be done to the individual and in what condition the individual will be left even after recovery. Fear of ongoing treatment, fear of recurrence of the problem, and fear of what will happen if treatment is unsuccessful, all contribute to general anxiety about pain.

The role that fear plays in increasing pain is perhaps most clearly seen with victims of torture. Many have reported that the anticipation of pain was worse than the actual experience of it. The work of Amnesty International has brought to light the disintegration of the personality that results from prevention of sleep, the expectation that pain will be worse each time it is inflicted, and the fear that the torture will become more severe as the process continues.

HOW TO AVOID FEAR

The experience of torture victims highlights one of the most important aspects of pain management: when people feel they have some control over the amount of pain they will suffer, they are able to tolerate higher levels of pain. When others are responsible for inflicting the pain, however, the level of pain tolerated drops dramatically, primarily due to anxiety. This phenomenon has also been demonstrated in scientifically controlled experiments. The first step in coping with fear of pain must therefore be to become as informed as possible about every aspect of your condition and treatment:

continued on page 36

PREPARING A CHILD FOR AN OPERATION

The key to preparing a child for a painful operation is communication. Open discussion and explanations of what is going to happen are likely to make young patients feel relaxed and more secure. If your child is young, you can explain medical procedures using familiar toys. Talking through a puppet and drawing pictures may also encourage a child to open up and express his feelings.

GIVING SUPPORT
Using a familiar toy to explain procedures can help to allay a child's fears.

Fear of the Dentist

A single unpleasant experience during dental treatment as a child can lead to a lifelong fear of dentists. People who fear dentists may avoid all dental work, but this will only make the fear worse and will likely have serious consequences for their teeth. By gradually facing up to the feared situation, and using relaxation and coping techniques, they can learn to overcome such fear.

Paula is 14 years old and living with her parents and younger brother. She is doing well at school, and enjoys sports. She developed a fear of dentists as a young child after having a painful tooth extraction. As she has grown older the fear has become worse. Paula's mother has been trying to get her to go to the dentist but she herself is frightened and this has prevented her from forcing her daughter to go. Paula developed a severe toothache recently and after much persuasion went to see her dentist. She managed to sit in the waiting room but when it was her turn to sit in the dentist's chair, she panicked and rushed out in tears. Although the toothache persisted she could not face having treatment.

WHAT SHOULD PAULA DO?

Paula needs to feel more in control of the situation. She should discuss a strategy with her parents for coping with a visit to the dentist. One thing Paula could do is visit the dentist's office before making an appointment, to familiarize herself with the waiting area and examination room without having the anxiety of treatment. She might also discuss with the dentist exactly what the treatment involves and how long it will take. To feel even more in control, Paula could agree on some kind of hand signal with the dentist, so that if she does feel pain she can make a sign for the dentist to stop. Paula would also be helped by learning visualization and breathing techniques to help her relax.

Action Plan

STRESS
Practice breathing and relaxation techniques on a regular basis. Visualize scenes that will help to distract the mind from pain.

FAMILY
Family members should not show anxiety, which might influence behavior. Watch other people successfully undergoing treatment to help to develop ways of coping.

HEALTH
Find out about the treatment, how long the procedure will last, and what the effects will be. Learn about the consequences of not undergoing the treatment.

STRESS
Stress causes heightened anxiety and tension, which can result in muscle spasm.

FAMILY
The reactions of family members can influence a person's response to pain and feared events.

HEALTH
A poor understanding of a feared event will increase anxiety levels, which in turn can increase the amount of pain that is felt.

HOW THINGS TURNED OUT FOR PAULA

Paula practiced relaxation exercises. Taking deep breaths while visualizing lying on a secluded beach helped her to relax. She discussed her treatment step-by-step with her dentist and arranged a hand signaling procedure. She successfully underwent a dental examination, and her anxiety slowly decreased over subsequent sessions. Although she never had to use the hand signal, she felt more in control knowing it was available.

A Painful Event

There are strategies you can adopt to help you cope as you approach a potentially painful event. They will lessen the fear and anxiety and help you to feel more in control. In turn, this preparation should diminish the pain and aid in recovery.

FEELING AT HOME
Familiarizing yourself with a place where you will go for treatment, and assuring yourself that there are others in the same situation, can help to reduce your fears.

Facing a potentially painful test or treatment at a clinic or hospital is stressful and sometimes scary. Described below are a few things you can do to prepare yourself

First, make sure you know exactly what is involved by discussing with your doctor what will happen. You may find it reassuring to visit the hospital or clinic before your appointment to become familiar with the environment. If possible, take a friend or relative with you the day of the event. This should be someone who is calm and not easily alarmed by medical situations.

THE NIGHT BEFORE

Start preparing for the event the night before and do all you can to put yourself in a relaxed frame of mind. First, write down a short description of your condition to date, making it as clear and accurate as possible. Think rationally about your case and write down any questions that you would like to ask, because they may easily slip your mind once you are there. If you've been noting pain symptoms in a diary (see page 44), it would be helpful to take that

with you. Don't forget to pack a notebook and pencil, too, for writing down any information about when and where to obtain test results, future treatment that may be necessary, or dosages of medications.

If you are feeling anxious, practice relaxation and breathing exercises. For example, visualizing yourself in the feared situation and then imagining a successful outcome can help you to gain confidence and overcome fears of the impending

treatment. To decrease your anxiety levels, relax in a hot bath with soothing music and perfumed candles, or read a good book or some favorite poetry. It's also a good idea to avoid caffeine, because this can increase anxiety and pain. Have instead a cup of hot milk or a soothing herbal tea such as chamomile

Finally, when your bag is packed, go to bed early. A good night's rest before a procedure can help you cope better with whatever ensues.

WAKING UP

When you wake up on the morning of your treatment, make sure your first thoughts are positive.

▶ *Breathe deeply, relax, and then flex your muscles.*

▶ *Make a mental list of the things that you enjoy about life and the attributes that others value in you.*

▶ *Think about the good things that happened to you the previous day and imagine that tomorrow you can add the treatment to the list.*

SLEEP EASY
A good night's sleep will ensure that you're refreshed and better able to deal with the coming event.

BE INFORMED

One way to reduce fear of pain is to be as informed as possible about the treatment options available to you. Talk to your caregivers and don't be afraid to discuss your health and ask probing questions about surgery and medication. The following questions cover the main points, but there may be other issues you want to raise:

▶ *Do I understand the procedure step-by-step?*

▶ *How long will the procedure last?*

▶ *How long will the short-term effects of treatment last?*

▶ *What are the usual effects and expected outcome of the treatment?*

▶ *Is there a chance that more pain might be caused?*

▶ *Are there any other treatment options available, such as pain clinics, osteopaths, physiotherapists, chiropractors, alternative healers?*

▶ *Are there any risks associated with the treatment?*

▶ *Will I be allowed to control the amount of painkilling medications that are prescribed?*

WHILE YOU'RE THERE

Enter the hospital or clinic believing that everything will go smoothly. Imagining positive scenarios can help to engender a positive outcome. Before undergoing the procedure, try practicing a visualization exercise (see page 141) to help you relax. Imagining a pleasant scene will enable you to think more positively about the treatment you are about to experience. Sit as comfortably as possible, keeping your head, neck, and body straight but relaxed. Keep your eyes closed or focus on some neutral site, then call up the scene. If you have difficulty in choosing a suitable image, it may help to bring along an illustrated book. Look at a picture for three or four minutes, then close the book and try to remember the image and what was going on. How many people were there? What were they doing? What were the colors? How would you yourself have painted or photographed the scene?

Later, during the procedure, you can apply the same visualization techniques. First, try to imagine the situation as being far away and not part of you. When you have achieved a feeling of detachment, call up your scene to distract you from any pain you might experience. You can choose any visual image that you find has a calming influence.

Breathing exercises can also be effective at calming you while you're waiting as well as during treatment. Breathe in and imagine the breath travelling through your body down to the tips of your toes and back up along your spine. Then imagine the breath has reached the painful area and that when you exhale, you are getting rid of the pain. Practiced correctly, a combination of visualization and breathing techniques can relax you, help conquer fears, and turn a potentially unpleasant event into a positive one.

Another calming technique being used more widely today by many physicians and hospitals is music therapy. Studies have shown that people who listen to soothing music during medical treatment exhibit positive effects on heartbeat, breathing, blood pressure, and tension. Talk to your physician about having music played during the procedure.

DISTANCING PAIN
Thinking of a pleasant experience such as a holiday in the countryside can help to distract your mind and distance you from the pain.

FEAR OF HEIGHTS
One of the most famous fictional depictions of the obsessive behavior of people suffering from phobias is in the film Vertigo (1958). The actor James Stewart plays a man who suffers from an irrational fear of heights after the woman he loves commits suicide by jumping off a tower.

PHOBIAS

Phobias are irrational fears, which can develop following sudden pain or shock. Some people may, for example, find they have a fear of hospitals after a painful operation or an associated frightening experience as a child. Subsequently the feared situation will be avoided, so the fear is never confronted and tends to get worse. Other more generalized fears may then develop. Whenever the feared situation is experienced anxiety levels rise. If the situation is then immediately avoided the anxiety level will fall and the relief becomes associated with avoidance of the feared situation. If this happens repeatedly for a long period, conditioning can turn the fear into a phobia.

Fear of pain may mask a fear of something else. People will rationalize a fear, such as agoraphobia (fear of open spaces or entering public places), as being a fear of pain, because fear of physical pain is considered more understandable and therefore a more acceptable reason for not doing things than the apparently irrational fear. So, for example, a person might exaggerate a back pain as being so disabling as to prevent him or her from leaving the house, when in fact the underlying problem is psychological.

what it entails, how long it will last, what the side effects will be, and what the long-term effects will be. Being informed will help you to feel in control and, in turn, will reduce your anxiety. A recent study in the United Kingdom compared levels of anxiety among terminally ill patients in two types of institutions: ones that had an open policy about discussing their patients' illnesses and those that had a policy of greater reticence. It found less anxiety and depression in the more open institutions.

The importance of relaxation

After becoming well informed about your treatment and the pain you are likely to experience, the next most effective coping strategy is to learn how to relax. Relaxation can change your perception of pain and reduce its severity. The power of the mind over the body has been recognized since ancient times, but an interesting modern application of the phenomenon is demonstrated by the placebo effect.

The word placebo comes from Latin, meaning "I please," and describes the use of a pill or other sham treatment in place of a genuine painkiller or other active treatment. Although placebos are generally believed to be effective in cases of "imaginary" pain, experiments now show that placebos can relieve actual physical symptoms related to diseases like angina. According to research, an individual responds differently to placebos under different circumstances, at times receiving a benefit and at others not. The exact way that placebos work is uncertain

but the therapist's interest in the well-being of the patient, the patient's own belief that positive steps are being taken to relieve pain, and a consequent decrease in anxiety all seem to help contribute to a sense of relief and relaxation.

Therapies for relaxation

A number of therapies are particularly effective at promoting relaxation. For example studies have shown that blood pressure, one of the indicators of stress and tension, drops during massage. Massage can also be very helpful in encouraging a good night's sleep, and sleep is perhaps the best form of natural healing and pain relief available.

Meditation is another extremely useful relaxation tool. Studies have shown that meditation can bring about a decreased heart rate, decreased respiration rate, decreased level of cortisol (a stress hormone) in the bloodstream, a lower pulse rate, and increased EEG (electro-encephalogram) alpha, a brain wave associated with relaxation. Defined simply, meditation refers to any activity that keeps your attention focused in the present rather than dwelling on thoughts of the past or the future. Techniques to achieve this include concentrating the mind's attention on deep breathing to the exclusion of all other external stimuli. Some therapies, yoga and reiki, for example, also include a meditative aspect.

Chapter 4 describes in more detail relaxation techniques, energy-rebalancing, and mind therapies, all of which can help to reduce anxiety and stress.

CHAPTER 2

PAIN AS A SYMPTOM

Pain is the alarm bell of the body's sophisticated signaling system, alerting us that something is wrong. It serves not only to warn and protect, but also to promote healing. Some types of pain can be safely ignored or treated at home, while others should be taken seriously and may warrant seeing a doctor. An ability to distinguish the different types of pain will help you to decide whether a visit to a doctor is advisable.

WARNING SIGNS

Deciding when to call a doctor is not always easy. Knowledge of the different kinds of pain symptoms can help you decipher any serious warning signs.

If you learn to recognize different pain symptoms, you can begin to distinguish between pains that you can manage yourself and those that need to be treated by a doctor. In addition to helping you decide whether or not to see a doctor, an understanding of your symptoms and an ability to describe them clearly and concisely will make it easier for your doctor to diagnose the cause of your pain and decide on the best possible course of treatment.

LEARNING TO DISTINGUISH DIFFERENT KINDS OF PAIN

Many common discomforts, such as headaches, muscle pain, indigestion, and cold hands and feet, usually do not signal any real threat to the body. The pain felt in these cases is caused by activation of the body's sensitive protective system by harmless stimuli. Although at times the pain may be strong, it does not indicate a serious problem and can usually be safely ignored. For example, women often feel pain during menstruation. This does not herald a major injury or disease, but is the body's reaction to hormones, which are released to stimulate the uterus to contract and shed its lining. These contractions can be very strong, causing severe cramps.

Sometimes the body's nervous system may break down and send faulty pain signals to the brain, resulting in chronic pain that has no meaningful purpose for its sufferer. An example of chronic pain is the prolonged discomfort that can follow a bout of shingles after the skin has healed and the virus causing the condition has been combated by medication or the body's own defences. Complementary medical techniques described in Chapter 4, such as massage and acupuncture, can help to alleviate chronic pain.

Sudden pain, for example, the kind that is felt in the chest preceding a heart attack, serves as a true warning signal that the body is under threat and needs immediate treatment. In such cases it is vital to consult a doctor as soon as possible.

RECOGNIZING THE WARNING SIGNS

Pain that signals a life-threatening condition is usually intense, starts abruptly, and is associated with other symptoms and signs. For example, a sudden severe headache accompanied by a feeling of weakness on one side of the body, or clouding of consciousness, may signal an acute brain hemorrhage. A chest pain that rapidly intensifies to unbearable levels, together with severe shortness of breath, dizziness, or physical weakness, may indicate serious heart or lung disease. Acute abdominal pain accompanied by other major symptoms, such as nausea, vomiting and signs of shock may indicate a perforated ulcer, inflammation of the pancreas, appendicitis, or a similar condition requiring emergency surgery. Usually in such instances the severity of the pain clearly tells a person that the symptoms are not trivial and that they need to seek help.

DEALING WITH GRADUAL PAIN

In many cases pain comes on gradually, slowly building to a point at which it interferes with daily life and it's necessary to take action. It may arise as a discomfort and then slowly turn into an actual pain that does not abate. Or it may result from an injury or another easily detectable cause such as indigestion, menstrual cramps, over-strenuous exercise, or bruising. In such circumstances you will probably decide to treat your own pain, and if you use common sense this should be quite sufficient. There are a variety of home remedies that can safely be used to treat common painful conditions like headaches and coughs (see table opposite).

SHINGLES CELLS
The most excruciating pain in shingles can occur after the blisters have healed, because the virus may remain in some nerves. Part of an infected cell is shown in yellow in the lower right corner of the picture.

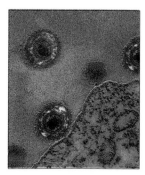

Two effective treatments for various types of common pain, such as muscle strains and rheumatic aches, are heating and cooling. However, it is important to distinguish between their uses. Cooling should be used to treat the inflammation caused by strains and sprains. It soothes the skin and helps to neutralize the release of chemicals in the damaged tissue, such as prostaglandins, that cause inflammation and pain. However, an icepack should be used only to soothe very painful and highly inflamed injuries, because it can inhibit the healing process.

Warming is effective for chronic pain such as aching joints caused by rheumatism. Warming the damaged area stimulates the pain receptors further, so that even more pain messages are transmitted to the brain. As a result the pain gate becomes overloaded and no further pain messages can be interpreted. Stimulating the skin also helps to relax the underlying muscles.

In some cases a judicious mix of warming and cooling techniques, for example, hot compresses followed by cold ones, or alternate hot and cold baths, can also be beneficial. Pain-relieving sprays, which are often used by physiotherapists for first-aid treatment of sports injuries have a longer-lasting effect than superficial cooling of the skin. For more information on how to make and apply a compress, see pages 87 and 155.

HOME REMEDIES

Some types of pain can be safely treated at home without the need for prescribed painkillers. In many cases, such as a sprain or menstrual pain, applying heat or a cold compress can be extremely effective. Simple measures like herbal remedies or gentle exercise may also provide relief in some situations. However, if pain persists after treatment with a home remedy, you should consult a doctor for further advice.

PAIN	TREATMENT	AIM	METHOD	WARNING
Rheumatic aches	Heat	Soothes soft tissue and causes counter-irritation.	Hot-water bottle; hot compress; rheumatic liniment and spray	Don't use in cases of flare-up of existing symptoms.
	Pressure	Relaxes tense muscles and causes counter-irritation.	Acupressure; gentle massage	
Strains and sprains	Cooling	Reduces inflammation by neutralizing prostaglandins in damaged tissue.	Ice bag or pack of frozen peas; apply for 10 mins, reapply 1 hour later.	Wrap ice bag in a towel to prevent ice burn.
	Rest	Reduces swelling.	Raise injured part.	
Headache	Over-the-counter painkillers; herbal remedies	Reduces inflammation; blocks pain; relaxes muscles.	Take recommended dose with water.	If headaches persist consult your doctor.
	Relaxation	Reduces nervous tension.	Rest in the dark; massage temples; relax in a hot bat.	
Menstrual pains	Heat	Reduces muscle spasm	Take a hot bath; apply a hot sponge or hot-water bottle.	If pain persists after menstruation see a doctor.
	Gentle exercise	Stimulates release of endorphins; relaxes muscles.	Go for a bicycle ride; go swimming; take a walk.	
Indigestion	Herbal remedies and antacids	Neutralizes stomach acid and soothes inflammation of stomach lining.	Take milk, yogurt after meals; drink chamomile or peppermint tea.	If indigestion is persistent or recurrent, see your doctor.

LOCATING THE LIKELY CAUSE OF PAIN

The human skin contains an intricate network of nerve endings that accurately locate the site and nature of any painful stimulus. For example, if you cut your finger, you will feel pain on your finger at the site of the injury. However, other organs are not as well supplied with nerve endings, and so the exact location and cause of pain, say in the abdomen, is more difficult to pinpoint.

Furthermore, many pain messages are bundled together and transmitted along a common nerve pathway. This may result in the brain misinterpreting a pain message as coming from a different part of the body. In such cases pain is felt at another site, sometimes in a completely different area from the original injury (see page 21). This is known as referred pain. For example, pain felt in the mid-back can actually be a warning signal of problems in the pancreas in the abdominal cavity. Determining the originating site of and reason for a pain can therefore require considerable skill and is best trusted to professionals.

THE LOCATION OF YOUR PAIN

To understand the nature of your pain, it's important to remember that discomfort felt in certain parts of the body might be referred from an injury in another part.

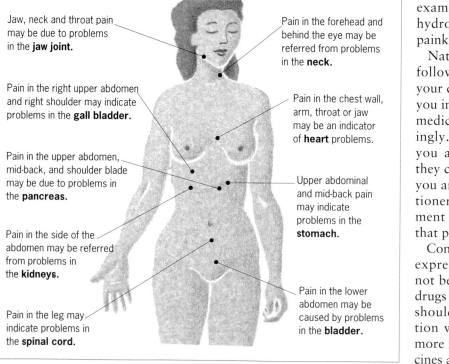

Jaw, neck and throat pain may be due to problems in the **jaw joint.**

Pain in the right upper abdomen and right shoulder may indicate problems in the **gall bladder.**

Pain in the upper abdomen, mid-back, and shoulder blade may be due to problems in the **pancreas.**

Pain in the side of the abdomen may be referred from problems in the **kidneys.**

Pain in the leg may indicate problems in the **spinal cord.**

Pain in the forehead and behind the eye may be referred from problems in the **neck.**

Pain in the chest wall, arm, throat or jaw may be an indicator of **heart** problems.

Upper abdominal and mid-back pain may indicate problems in the **stomach.**

Pain in the lower abdomen may be caused by problems in the **bladder.**

SEEKING HELP FROM NATURAL THERAPISTS

Pains can often be relieved by acupuncture, massage, chiropractic treatment, osteopathy, relaxation therapies, or other natural techniques. The approaches can have variable outcomes, and individuals may have different responses to them. But with proper precautions, these treatments are safe and becoming increasingly popular.

It's important to remember that complementary medicine does not always show immediate results, so don't expect a miracle cure. Although starting a new treatment can make you feel optimistic about a cure, the realization that a technique is not working for you can lead to depression, which in turn can heighten your perception of pain. Some treatments, such as chiropractic, acupuncture, and transcutaneous nerve stimulation (TENS) may even cause additional pain initially, but in the longer term they can help alleviate the pain associated with chronic diseases. Unless you suffer from frequent recurrences of an old condition, you should see your doctor first. This is especially important if your pain features any of the warning symptoms (see page 38).

Combining natural therapies with medical treatment

Complementary medical treatment is often combined with orthodox medicine. For example, you might try aromatherapy and hydrotherapy in conjunction with medical painkillers to help relieve a migraine.

Natural remedies are generally safe if you follow a few simple guidelines. Always let your doctor know what additional methods you intend to try, so that, if necessary, your medical treatment can be adjusted accordingly. You should also tell your doctor if you are using herbal medicines, because they could interfere with drug treatment. If you are receiving physiotherapy, the practitioner should be made aware of any treatment by an osteopath or chiropractor, so that practices do not overlap.

Conversely, some alternative practitioners express concern that their treatment may not be as effective if a patient is also using drugs prescribed by a doctor. However, you should not stop taking prescribed medication without consulting your doctor. For more information on complementary medicines and their uses see Chapter 4.

THE MCGILL PAIN QUESTIONNAIRE

The McGill pain questionnaire was originally developed as a research tool at McGill University in Montreal, Canada. Ronald Melzack, one of the world's top pain researchers, compiled a list of common words used by pain sufferers to describe their pain. Doctors then started to give the words to patients to help them describe their own symptoms.

To use the questionnaire, look carefully through the 20 groups of words. If a word in any group applies to your pain, circle that word. Do not circle more than one word in a group. If there are groups of words that do not apply to your pain, there is no need to circle a word. Then go over the circled words in groups 1 to 10 and choose the three that most closely represent your pain and write them down. Similarly, choose the two most representative circled words from groups 11 to 15. Write down the one circled word in group 16, and one word chosen from the remaining groups 17 to 20.

You should end up with up to seven words that describe the quality and intensity of your pain and give an indication of how it affects you. These words should help your therapist to assess the impact of your pain on your well-being and then to plan a possible course of treatment to try to alleviate it.

GROUP 1	GROUP 2	GROUP 3	GROUP 4
Flickering Quivering Pulsing Throbbing Beating Pounding	Jumping Flashing Shooting	Pricking Boring Drilling Stabbing	Sharp Gritting Lacerating

GROUP 5	GROUP 6	GROUP 7	GROUP 8
Pinching Pressing Gnawing Cramping Crushing	Tugging Pulling Wrenching	Hot Burning Scalding Searing	Tingling Itching Smarting Stinging

GROUP 9	GROUP 10	GROUP 11	GROUP 12
Dull Sore Hurting Aching Heavy	Tender Taut Rasping Splitting	Tiring Exhausting	Sickening Suffocating

GROUP 13	GROUP 14	GROUP 15	GROUP 16
Fearful Frightful Terrifying	Punishing Grueling Cruel Vicious Killing	Wretched Blinding	Annoying Troublesome Miserable Intense Unbearable

GROUP 17	GROUP 18	GROUP 19	GROUP 20
Spreading Radiating Penetrating Piercing	Tight Numb Drawing Squeezing Tearing	Cool Cold Freezing	Nagging Nauseating Agonising Dreadful Torturing

The GP

Building a good relationship with your GP (general practitioner) is an important step in successful management of pain. With careful preparation, you can help your GP to diagnose your problem and suggest appropriate treatment.

Origins

Health care is one of the oldest professions. In medieval times apothecaries, or pharmacists, used their knowledge of herbal medicine to cure sick members of the community. Their modern equivalent is the GP, or general practitioner. (A similar category is the family practitioner.) Before the Second World War, GPs operated mostly alone. After 1945 they began to ally themselves with other doctors, and today's partnerships are well equipped and staffed by teams of qualified nurses and clerical staff.

ANCIENT TRADITIONS
Medieval medicine was based on a knowledge of herbal lore that had been handed down for centuries.

When it is time to visit your doctor, it pays to be prepared. A body chart indicating the location of your pain, a pain diary (see page 44) describing your pain in detail, and a daily record of the intensity of your pain will help your doctor to diagnose the cause of your pain and suggest appropriate treatment. It is also a good idea to rehearse what you plan to say to the doctor to make sure your description is accurate and complete: although you need to be concise, it is important not to leave out details that may be relevant to the doctor's diagnosis.

Does my doctor need to know exactly where the pain is?

Yes. A body chart showing the precise location of your pain or pains is extremely helpful in giving your doctor a good idea at a glance. It's particularly important to keep a body chart if the site of your pain varies, as in the case of some migraines. Do not clutter the chart with detailed information, but try to concentrate only on the main issues. Your doctor can always form a more detailed picture to pinpoint your pain by asking you for more information.

I find it difficult to explain my pain. Any suggestions?

Many people find it helpful to follow the McGill pain questionnaire (see page 41), which can help to pin down the particular nature of their pain. The questionnaire was originally developed for use in

research and has been translated into many languages. It lists 77 words chosen from those most commonly used by patients to describe their pain. The first 10 groups of words describe the quality of the pain, groups 11 to 15 describe how the pain affects you, group 16 evaluates the intensity of the pain, and the rest are miscellaneous.

How can the doctor measure my pain?

You can help the doctor to get a picture of its intensity and its fluctuations by measuring your pain yourself. One system of measurement is the visual analogue scale (VAS), which you can easily make at home (see opposite page). By marking the intensity of your pain on a blank scale every day, you can detect changes in the degree of pain felt over a period of time. Prepare several VAS scales so that you can record the intensity of your pain once or even twice a day for a given period, say over a week or two. Every day try to make time to mark the point that you think represents the level of your pain, then write the date and time on the scale, so you can track any fluctuations. It's important that you don't look at previous recordings before making your mark on the line. Although a VAS report can help your doctor to understand your pain, remember that it is subjective and relates only to your own experience. It is not possible to compare pain reports from different people, as individuals have different perceptions and experiences of pain.

Does my doctor have time to go over all this information?

If you have your pain scales and pain diary on hand, your doctor will be able to grasp the essence of your pain quickly and will be able to devote more time to examining you and planning further tests and treatment. He will probably ask you to continue recording your pain in the same way, so that it is possible to monitor whether the treatment is working or not.

Why can't I just ask my doctor to investigate what is wrong with me?

Remember that pain is a personal and subjective experience—your doctor cannot actually feel your pain. She has to rely on your description of it in order to decide on appropriate treatment. It is best to do all that you can to convey information about your pain precisely and concisely. If you are unable to record notes and keep pain charts, one way to describe your pain is to imagine what you would have to do to someone to cause that

---

MAKE YOUR OWN VISUAL ANALOG SCALE

Draw a line on a piece of paper and divide it into 10 equal sections. At one end write "No pain at all" and at the other write "The worst pain I ever felt." Now put a cross on the scale to represent your current level of pain. Prepare enough scales to use a new one each time, so that you're not influenced by previous recordings (for more details, see opposite page). You can use a similar scale to record the effectiveness of different types of painkillers. At one end write the name of the drug and the time you took it. Mark on the scale the length of time that you are pain-free. This will help your doctor to adjust the dosage correctly.

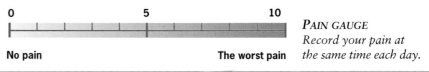

PAIN GAUGE
Record your pain at the same time each day.

---

kind of pain. Thrust a dagger between the shoulder blades and twist it? Tie a belt around the head and pull it tight? After you form as clear a picture as possible of what you are feeling, the doctor can then start planning your treatment.

Can the doctor advise me about long-term treatment?

To plan your treatment program and remain in control of it, you need to have as much information as possible about the options available. If your GP suggests new treatment,

always ask for a clear explanation of what is going to happen and about any possible risks. Your doctor can help you interpret any data you may have from journals or specialist groups. He can also advise you about the possibility of combining orthodox medical treatment with complementary approaches such as chiropractic, osteopathy, pain clinics, hands-on healing, and self-help groups. Many GPs themselves have been trained in alternative health care, and some group practices include alternative practitioners.

EXPLAINING YOUR SYMPTOMS
Keeping a diary of all your symptoms can help you to describe your pain more clearly and concisely.

WHAT YOU CAN DO AT HOME

Before a visit to the doctor go over in your mind how you are going to explain your pain symptoms. Use the checklist below to make sure you have everything you need to support your description:

▶ *Pain diary (see page 44).*

▶ *VAS scales measuring the intensity of pain (see above and opposite).*

▶ *List of words describing your pain (see page 41).*

▶ *Notebook and pen to write down advice and prescription details.*

▶ *Details of medication and its effects.*

Pain Diary

Pain, particularly chronic pain, is notoriously difficult to describe, but your doctor or alternative health practitioner needs a clear description in order to determine the possible causes for your condition and suggest appropriate treatment.

GETTING TO GRIPS WITH YOUR PAIN
A good way to form a clearer picture of the nature of your pain is to record your symptoms in a pain diary.

By making a careful daily record of what you are feeling, you will start to reach a clearer understanding of the type of pain you suffer – its nature, intensity and fluctuations. Note down your pain in a diary alongside events in your daily life; this should give you a good idea of any factors that make your pain worse, such as stress, as well as conditions that help to ease the pain, such as a good night's sleep. This knowledge will help your therapist to choose a suitable form of treatment and to suggest ways of avoiding such pain in future.

The amount of pain and whether the pain started abruptly or gradually may be important factors in assessing your condition.

Words from the McGill pain questionnaire can help your therapist to understand the particular quality of your pain.

The painkillers you take and their effects should be recorded so that your therapist can check your progress.

Changes in the nature of your pain and whether the pain is constant or intermittent can be highly significant in the correct diagnosis of your condition. Note how long each bout lasts.

Stressful events that may influence the onset of your pain should be carefully noted down.

14 MONDAY

10-30	Dull ache on left of head at top; gradually extends all way down left side; left eye feels heavy.
11-10	Headache subsides
22-30	Bed

15 TUESDAY

4-45	Woken by throbbing pain after restless night: 3 hrs sleep
5-00	Pain intensifies
5-30	Take 2 aspirin – takes effect in 30 mins: sleep for 3 hrs
12-00	Bed

16 WEDNESDAY

7-00	Another restless night
7-30	Faint aching develops into constant throbbing pain
9-30	Meeting to discuss Friday deadline
19-30	~~Barbecue at David's~~ -cancelled due to rain.
23-30	Bed

A clear description of your pain is particularly important in the diagnosis of conditions such as migraine and irritable bowel syndrome. These may not be characterized by any obvious physical abnormality, and so the doctor's or health practitioner's diagnosis depends heavily on an accurate pain description. Also, a pain diary will help you and your doctor to see the patterns of your pain. This is useful for such conditions as , cluster headaches, gallstones, kidney stones, gout, and angina, as these often feature recurrent pain attacks.

The diary will give a solid account of your pain for the doctor or health practitioner to review and provide further leads to follow as required. He or she may also ask about your mood, appetite, personal relations, and work, especially if the pain is chronic. All of this information has a bearing on the distress you feel, and will help to determine what type of tests and treatment you should undergo.

If you are taking any medication, you may find it useful to keep a record of the type, dosage, its results, and any side effects, so that your doctor can monitor your treatment.

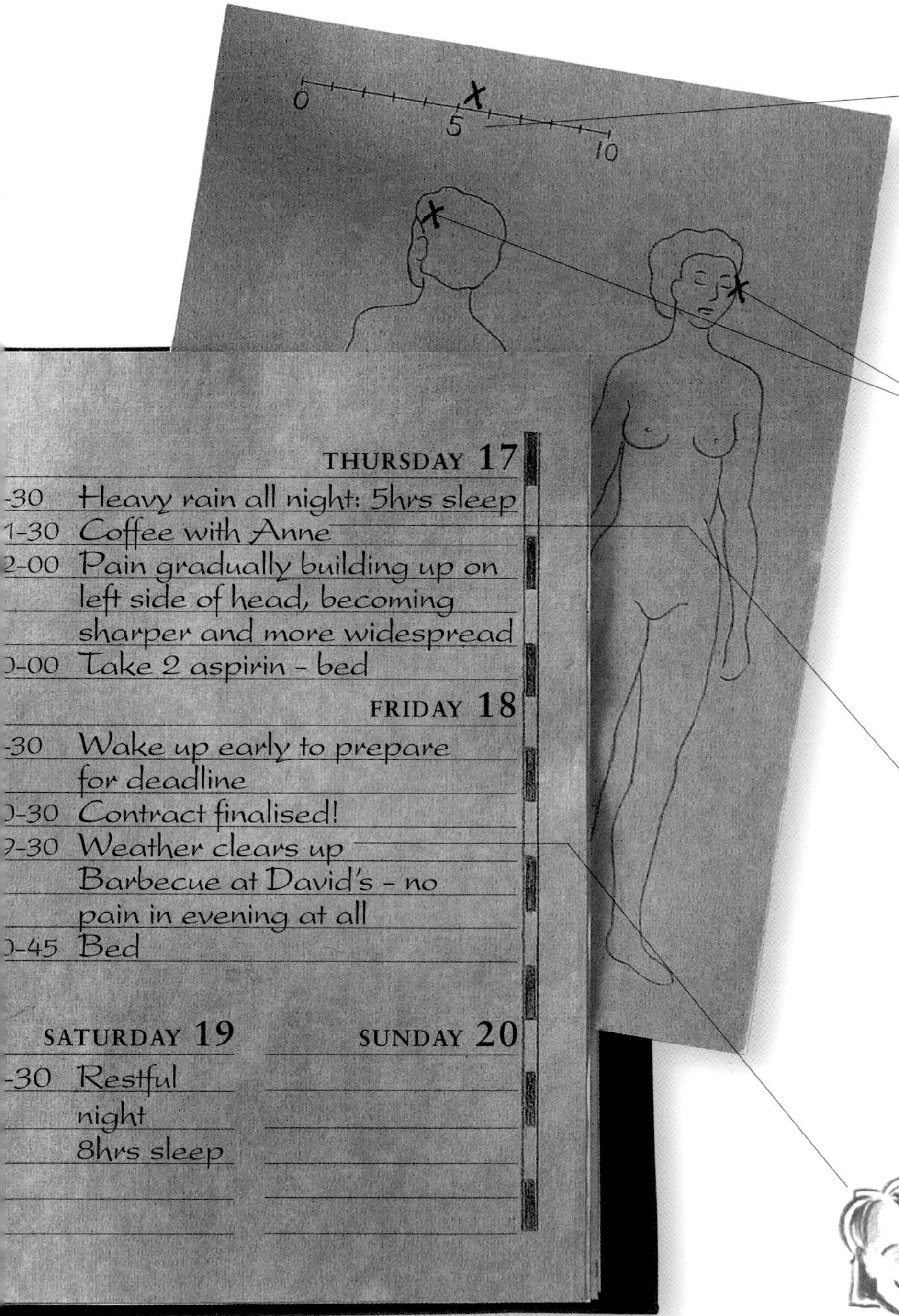

A pain scale (see pages 42–43) can help you to measure the intensity of your pain and any fluctuations in it on a day-to-day basis.

Marking the location of your pain on a diagram of the human body can help your doctor or alaternative practitioner to determine the underlying cause of the problem.

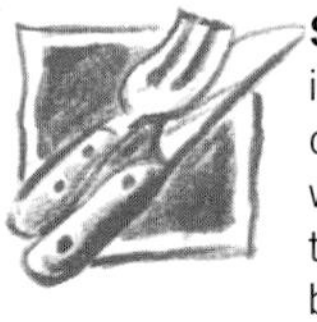

Some foods may trigger a more intense pain. Make a note of any changes in diet or appetite. This will help you discover whether there are certain foods and beverages that you should avoid. Also, note any conditions that make the pain worse, such as cold weather or bright lights.

Factors that seem to ease your pain should also be recorded. This will help you to see your pain patterns more clearly and enable you to plan ways to distract yourself from the pain.

THURSDAY 17

-30 Heavy rain all night: 5hrs sleep
1-30 Coffee with Anne
2-00 Pain gradually building up on left side of head, becoming sharper and more widespread
)-00 Take 2 aspirin - bed

FRIDAY 18

-30 Wake up early to prepare for deadline
)-30 Contract finalised!
?-30 Weather clears up Barbecue at David's - no pain in evening at all
)-45 Bed

SATURDAY 19   SUNDAY 20

-30 Restful
night
8hrs sleep

PAINKILLERS

A variety of herbal and medical painkillers are available to help relieve most pains. Whether bought over the counter or prescribed by a doctor, all should be used with care.

VERSATILE SPICE
The versatile medicinal uses of cayenne (red, or chili) pepper have long been known to American natives. The spice contains the painkilling ingredient capsaicin that can be used internally, to ease toothache for example, or externally, in a poultice for joint pain.

Herbal and medical, or pharmaceutical, pain-killers can be used to relieve many kinds of pain, ranging from mild toothache to arthritis flare-ups to the chest pains of a heart attack. Both types are available over the counter at pharmacies and supermarkets, and the herbal ones can also be found in health food stores.

In general, herbal painkillers take longer to become effective, and so are probably better suited to relieving chronic rather than acute pain, for which you want immediate relief. Because they cause relatively few side effects, it is generally safe to use them for an extended period. (Their use is further explored in the section on herbalism, page 86.)

Conversely, even nonprescription analgesics, pain-relieving drugs, are fast-acting, usually taking effect within an hour. However, using these pain relievers over a long period may cause undesirable side effects such as bleeding in the stomach and liver damage. If you have been taking over-the-counter painkillers like aspirin or acetaminophen for 48 hours and symptoms still persist, you should consult a doctor as soon as possible. He will advise on further treatment, which might include stronger drugs available only by prescription.

HERBAL PAINKILLERS

The healing properties of plants and herbs have been recognized since ancient times. Even today much of the world's population relies on herbal medicines for treatment of aches and pains. They can be particularly effective for relieving the pain of rheumatic conditions and headaches.

Two of the time-tested remedies for headache are teas made from lavender or peppermint. Catnip and valerian teas are touted as relief for headaches, particularly the stress-related kind, because they have a mild sedative effect. Feverfew is a popular

---

HERBAL PAINKILLERS

A variety of natural ingredients can be used to relieve a range of painful disorders. Many of these natural painkillers consist of kitchen herbs that are easily grown at home. For more information on the use of natural pain relievers for specific conditions see Chapters 5 to 8. For more information on herbalism see page 86.

PAIN	NATURAL PAINKILLER	TREATMENT
Rheumatic pain	Camphor from *Cinnamomum camphora* Chamomile from *Chamaemelum nobile*	Apply camphor oil to painful area; drink camomile tea. Take in tablet form or drink tea made from leaves.
Chilblains	Wintergreen from *Gaultheria procumbens* (pure oil may cause an allergic reaction)	Make poultice from leaves and apply to chilblain, or soak cloth in wintergreen oil and place on chilblain.
Migraine	Feverfew (*Chrysanthemum parthenium*) Lavender (*Lavandula angustifolia*) Capsaicin from *Capsicum frutescens*	Drink tea made from feverfew leaves (avoid if pregnant). Drink tea made from lavender flowers. Take capsaicin internally in powder or tablet form.
Cramps	Cramp bark (*Viburnum opulus*) Rosemary (*Rosemarinus officinalis*)	Drink tea made from bark. Apply rosemary oil externally.
Indigestion	Peppermint (*Mentha piperita*)	Drink tea made from mint leaves.

remedy for migraines. A few leaves eaten fresh or in capsule form on a daily basis can help prevent them. However, feverfew is not recommended for pregnant women. Ginger (between ½ and ¾ teaspoon of the powdered root in a glass of water) may also work against migraines, perhaps by inhibiting prostaglandin synthesis. If nothing else, ginger helps mitigate the nausea of migraine.

Breathing in the scent of essential oil of peppermint is also effective for relieving a headache. A drop or two can be rubbed directly on the forehead and temples. Or a few drops can be added to unscented hand cream and then rubbed into the skin.

For people who don't normally consume beverages containing caffeine, this stimulating substance can ease a headache by relaxing swollen blood vessels in the head. It also increases the effectiveness of pain relievers such as aspirin, and is in fact an ingredient in some headache remedies. However, caffeine is only a short-term cure; in the long run, it can actually cause the muscle tension that sometimes triggers headaches, and in someone withdrawing from caaffeine use, it can cause a throbbing headache.

Arthritis sufferers have several herbal remedies to choose from. Particularly popular is capsaicin, the substance in cayenne (red) pepper that causes hot tingling on the tongue. Capsaicin reduces levels of a chemical compound that transmits pain signals to the brain. To use it, mix a few dashes of ground red pepper with 2 to 3 teaspoons of olive oil and apply the mixture to affected joints with gauze several times a day. It takes a week or more for desensitization to take place, and the first few doses will cause mild burning. Capsaicin ointment is also available in over-the-counter preparations.

An infusion, or tea, made with dandelion (root and leaves) or nettle (leaves), can also be effective for relieving arthritic pain when taken three times a day. Dandelion root is alsoavailable in capsules and as an extract. Evening primrose oil, in both capsule or extract form, has a significant effect on rheumatoid arthritis and morning stiffness.

PHARMACEUTICAL PAINKILLERS

Pharmaceutical painkillers can be broadly divided into two groups: non-narcotic and narcotic. A knowledge of the workings and effects of these painkilling drugs can help you to plan your treatment.

Origins

The active ingredient in white willow (*Salix alba*) has been known for its ability to relieve pain since Roman times. The healing properties of its leaves and bark were first brought to the attention of the medical world in modern times when an English clergyman, Edward Stone, wrote to the Royal Society in 1763 about his success in treating rheumatic fevers with willow. In 1826 two Italian scientists succeeded in isolating the active substance from willow bark and called it salicin. It was Heinrich Dreser (1860–1925) who discovered in the 1890s that acetylsalicylic acid, a compound derived from salicin, did not have salicin's side effects, and the drug was then marketed under the name Aspirin. Worldwide, more than 120 billion aspirin tablets are now taken every year.

WHITE WILLOW
In ancient times the leaves or bark were crushed in olive oil and applied externally.

Non-narcotic painkillers are effective for relieving mild pain and, except for acetaminophen, also at reducing inflammation. Narcotic painkillers are used for treating more severe pain. Almost all are related to morphine, which is derived from opium, and include such drugs as codeine.

NON-NARCOTIC DRUGS
Non-narcotic painkillers are generally used for treating moderate pains such as flu symptoms, headaches, muscle cramps, and toothache. They include acetaminophen and the nonsteroidal anti-inflammatory drugs (NSAIDs) such as ibuprofen, naproxen, and aspirin. For more severe pain a combination of a non-narcotic drug, such as aspirin or acetaminophen, and a narcotic drug, such as codeine, is commonly prescribed.

How non-narcotic drugs work
When the body is injured or becomes infected, chemicals known as prostaglandins are released. These chemicals trigger the transmission of pain messages to the brain and encourage inflammation of the damaged area. Non-narcotic painkillers (except acetaminophen) block the production of these chemicals, thus preventing pain signals from being produced, and

DO'S AND DON'TS OF TAKING PAINKILLERS

When using painkillers, follow instructions carefully to maximize benefits and minimize side effects.

▶ *Never take more than the recommended dosage.*

▶ *Don't use more than one over-the-counter painkiller at a time. They may contain similar ingredients, which could lead to an overdose.*

▶ *Tell your doctor if you use over-the-counter drugs, as there may be drug interactions.*

▶ *Consult your doctor before taking painkillers, if you have an ulcer or history of liver or kidney disease.*

▶ *Take with water or, for quicker absorption, half a cup of coffee or tea.*

▶ *Beware: some people feel drowsy after taking painkillers. If you are affected, don't drive.*

EASY RELIEF
Take painkillers with water while sitting or standing, so they don't become stuck in your throat.

HOW PAINKILLERS WORK

Non-narcotic painkillers, except acetaminophen, and narcotic drugs work differently. Non-narcotics are effective at controlling inflammation because they act at the site of injury, while narcotic medications and acetaminophen relieve pain by stopping pain messages at the dorsal horn.

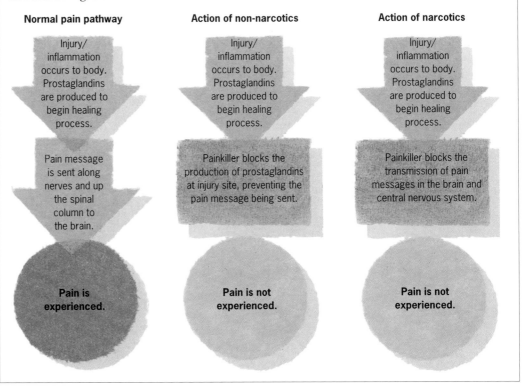

Normal pain pathway

Injury/inflammation occurs to body. Prostaglandins are produced to begin healing process.

Pain message is sent along nerves and up the spinal column to the brain.

Pain is experienced.

Action of non-narcotics

Injury/inflammation occurs to body. Prostaglandins are produced to begin healing process.

Painkiller blocks the production of prostaglandins at injury site, preventing the pain message being sent.

Pain is not experienced.

Action of narcotics

Injury/inflammation occurs to body. Prostaglandins are produced to begin healing process.

Painkiller blocks the transmission of pain messages in the brain and central nervous system.

Pain is not experienced.

stopping the pain while reducing inflammation. However, inflammation is not stopped completely, so the healing process can continue. Acetaminophen is also a mild painkiller but does not effect the release of prostaglandins or reduce inflammation. It is believed to work by blocking the transmission of pain messages in the brain and central nervous system.

Nonsteroidal anti-inflammatory drugs (NSAIDs)

NSAIDs are widely used to relieve pain, reduce inflammation, and lower body temperature. Over-the-counter preparations include aspirin, ibuprofen, and naproxen. Some of the prescription remedies in this category are diclofenac, ketoprofen, piroxicam, and sulindac. All of these drugs are particularly effective at reducing inflammation of muscles (caused by strains) and joints (caused by arthritis and gout). Foremost among NSAIDs is aspirin, which not only is effective at relieving moderate pain and reducing inflammation, but

also, when taken in small daily doses, can prevent heart attacks by keeping blood clots from forming.

Aspirin causes stomach upsets and nausea in many people, but it's possible to avoid these side effects by using coated (enteric) tablets, which dissolve lower down in the intestine. If you take aspirin for more than two days and it fails to relieve pain, consult a doctor. Use of aspirin over a long period is not advisable, as it can cause bleeding in the stomach. You should not give aspirin to children except under medical supervision, because there is a slight risk of a rare disorder called Reye's syndrome, which can involve severe brain and liver damage.

Gastric irritation is common also with other NSAIDs, particularly if they are used over a long period of time. NSAIDs can also cause rashes, dizziness, and tinnitus, and, when combined with alcohol, damage to the liver or kidneys. You can minimize the risk of these effects by using them for a short period only and by taking them with food and milk. Side effects from NSAIDs can vary widely among different patients; many can tolerate one form better than another. If you experience abdominal pain or other symptoms after taking one type of NSAID, ask your doctor for advice.

Acetaminophen

Acetaminophen is particularly recommended for people who suffer frequent stomach upsets, because it doesn't usually cause stomach problems. However, since it does not inhibit prostaglandins, it doesn't reduce inflammation and is therefore not as effective as the NSAIDs for treating arthritis or injuries to muscles and ligaments. Acetaminophen is safe for children, provided it is given in the correct dosage.

If you take acetaminophen, never exceed the recommended dosage. It is highly toxic in large doses: as few as 20 tablets can cause fatal liver damage. If you have a weak liver, an alternative is the more expensive acetaminophen formulation that contains an antidote to its possible toxic effects.

NARCOTIC DRUGS

Weak narcotics such as codeine are used to treat cases of moderate pain. For example, codeine is incorporated in cough medicines and some antidiarrhea medications. Weak narcotics cause a heightened feeling of excitement, and if patients use them over a long period of time, they risk psychological or physical dependence on them. However, if the recommended dosage is taken for a limited period, there is little danger of the drugs becoming addictive.

Strong narcotics such as diamorphine, morphine, pethidine, and pentazosine are used to relieve the severe pain caused by serious injury, major surgery, or chronic disease, when other painkillers have proved ineffective. However, they are not so effective in treating nerve pain. This is usually because substances produced in damaged nerves prevent the action of these drugs, or because the nerve receptors themselves are damaged so that narcotics can't switch them on to help in the blocking of pain stimuli.

MEDICAL PAINKILLERS

Some painkillers can be bought over the counter (indicated below with an asterisk); others are available only by prescription. The first five drugs listed below are examples of non-narcotics while the others are classified as narcotics. If you experience any unpleasant side effects, consult your doctor.

DRUG	TIME TO TAKE EFFECT	SINGLE ADULT DOSE	MAX PER DAY	SIDE EFFECTS AND COMMENTS
Acetaminophen*	½–1 hour	500–1000 mg 4–6 hours	4000 mg	Safe for children, pregnant women and asthmatics but not for those with liver disease; high risk of overdose
Aspirin*	½–2 hours	300–900 mg 4–6 hours	4000 mg	Gastric irritation; stomach bleeding and ulcers; tinnitus; Reyes syndrome (children)
Ibuprofen*	½–1 hour	200–400 mg 6–8 hours	2400 mg	Few side effects: indigestion; stomach ulcers; confusion in elderly
Diclofenac	2 hours	50 mg 8–12 hours	150 mg	Indigestion; stomach ulcers; confusion in elderly; rash
Naproxen*	2–3 hours	500 mg (initially) 6–8 hours	1250 mg	Indigestion; stomach ulcers; confusion in elderly
Codeine	½–1 hour	30–60 mg every 4 hours	240 mg	Constipation; nausea; mildly addictive
Propoxyphene	½–2 hours	65 mg every 6–8 hours	260 mg	Sedation; constipation; nausea; mildly addictive
Morphine	½–1 hour	10–30 mg 4 hours	Not applicable	Sedation; constipation; itching; risk of addiction

Origins

Opium, a strong painkiller, is derived from the seed pods of a particular species of poppy, *Papaver somniferum*. It has been known since ancient times as an effective pain reliever. The Sumerians used it to soothe colicky children and the Romans treated a range of painful symptoms with it. Opium is also known for its ability to create a pleasant euphoric state. Since the last century, pharmacologists have attempted to modify opium to produce substances that are longer-lasting or have a shorter and more intense effect. The most well known of these drugs are heroin and morphine. They played a major part in the advancement of medical science in the 19th century because of their ability to relieve severe pain, such as that experienced after major surgery.

PAPAVER SOMNIFERUM
The first regular use of opium was in the Far East, where it was either smoked or eaten.

Patients taking strong narcotics experience drowsiness, mood swings and impaired mental activity in addition to very effective pain relief. Unpleasant side effects, such as nausea, constipation and itching, are also common. As patients may become dependent on these drugs, they cannot be used over a long period.

How narcotic drugs work

Narcotic drugs are powerful painkillers. Unlike NSAIDs, which block pain messages at the site of an injury, narcotics work within the brain and central nervous system to prevent the transmission of pain signals. Narcotic drugs combine at specific sites known as opiate receptors, located in the spinal cord and midbrain. They block the transmission of pain signals to the brain, thereby preventing the perception of pain.

Unfortunately, however, opiate receptors are also located at various sites all over the body, so when narcotic drugs are injected, they not only achieve the desired pain relief but also create other physiological effects. Some of these may be beneficial, particularly in the nervous system where the drugs produce a marked reduction in anxiety. Other side effects may be undesirable however, in particular, nausea, constipation, and potential addiction.

Antidepressants and anticonvulsants

You may be surprised to find that your doctor prescribes antidepressants for nerve pain or similar disorders. These drugs are usually used to treat mood disorders, but they are also effective in relieving pain. They can help to improve sleep, which is often disturbed in chronic pain sufferers. However, antidepressants do not provide fast pain relief: they generally take two to three weeks to work, and for the peak effect, four to six weeks. In addition, their use is often associated with a dry mouth and constipation, although some of these side effects may diminish over time. Not all antidepressant drugs have this pain-relieving property – the exceptions include some very common antidepressants such as fluoxetine (Prozac).

Anticonvulsants, commonly used to treat epilepsy, are also effective in treating certain types of nerve pain, especially sharp, shooting pains. They act on the nerve fibers and prevent them from firing pain messages without cause. Both antidepressants and anticonvulsants are effective only if used on a continual basis. Although antidepressants are not addictive, patients often suffer side effects such as drowsiness, dizziness, and memory impairment, which reflect the action of the drugs on the processes of the nervous system.

Corticosteroid drugs

Corticosteroids are a group of powerful drugs related to natural hormones produced in the body. They are effective at reducing inflammation, and so are often used to relieve intestinal disorders such as Crohn's disease (see page 112) and inflamed tendons and joints caused by such conditions as tennis elbow (see page 137). Corticosteroids act by reducing the production of prostaglandins and suppressing the immune system. Because of their potency, they should be used with extreme caution.

LONG-TERM DRUG TREATMENT

In the short term, drugs may provide relief from pain. However, for chronic pain many people choose to avoid the unpleasant side effects of conventional medications by trying alternative therapies (see Chapter 4). As well as helping to reduce the pain, many of these therapies employ manipulative techniques or suggest dietary and other lifestyle changes that may treat the underlying cause.

CHAPTER 3

STRATEGIES FOR PREVENTING PAIN

*The pain caused by some illnesses, especially
stress-related diseases, can in many cases be avoided
by looking after your mind and body. An active
and responsible attitude about your health, in
partnership with your doctor and other health
practitioners, is the first step toward preventing a
whole range of painful symptoms.*

IMPROVING YOUR LIFESTYLE

A stressful job, poor diet, incorrect posture and lack of exercise can all influence the onset of painful disorders. Improving your lifestyle may help you to avoid pain and illness in the future.

GETTING A GOOD NIGHT'S SLEEP

There are several ways you can help yourself to a good night's sleep:

▶ *Cut down on coffee, tea, and other beverages that contain the stimulant caffeine.*

▶ *Exercise regularly.*

▶ *Keep to a consistant sleep schedule.*

▶ *Have a milk drink and banana, or a snack of complex carbohydrates such as rice crackers before bedtime. These foods can stimulate brain chemicals that induce and maintain sleep.*

▶ *Take time to relax before bed by having a bath or reading a book or magazine.*

Your general health, diet, fitness, and psychological health can all influence your susceptibility to pain and the way you perceive it. With an understanding of your body's needs, you can improve your lifestyle and minimize pain.

TREATING YOUR BODY RIGHT

In considering how to deal with pain or how to minimize the potential threat of it, try to think of the body and mind as a whole and not just the parts of the body where pain occurs. The recognition that all aspects of one's lifes, including diet, fitness, state of mind, and spirit, contribute to well-being is known as the holistic approach to health. If you learn to treat yourself right, you may be able to avoid pain caused by an unhealthy or unsuitable lifestyle.

Your body is very effective at providing warning signs when you are run down: tiredness and aches and pains can all be telling you to take immediate action to change your lifestyle. Changing potentially harmful habits can prevent the development of more serious illnesses.

Eat a balanced diet

Many painful diseases and illnesses are directly linked to poor dietary habits. A diet high in saaturated fats, for example, is known to contribute to hypertension and heart disease. Understanding which foods are highest in these fats, such as fried potato chips and mayonnaise, can help you to make responsible decisions about what to include in a healthy diet. Well-balanced meals, containing adequate protein, complex carbohydrates, fiber, vitamins, and minerals in the right proportions (see pages 57–58) can improve your health by increasing the body's natural defence mechanisms and making you less prone to illness.

Exercise regularly

Regular exercise can help to prevent the pain caused by certain disorders such as angina. Specifically, exercise can reduce the risk of pain associated with heart disease by helping to reduce blood pressure and cholesterol levels. In general, exercising regularly will help maintain a healthy body weight and also relieve stress, a common culprit in heightening existing pain.

Get enough sleep

Regular sleep is important to functioning well and safely during the day. In the short term, sleep deprivation leads to irritability and a shortened attention span; over long periods, people find it increasingly difficult to concentrate and their energy levels deteriorate. Sleep deprivation may also lower the immune system, exposing sufferers to the risk of pain caused by low grade illnesses such as viral infections. Depression and fatigue due to lack of sleep can also exacerbate any existing pain. Although the amount of sleep required varies from one individual to another and changes with age, adults generally need between seven and eight hours of sleep a night.

Reduce your alcohol intake

Initially, medical advice on alcohol intake for optimum health may seem confusing. Moderate drinking is now thought to be beneficial to health, promoting higher levels of good cholesterol and a reduced risk of clogged coronary arteries. Current recommendations are that men can consume up to two drinks a day and women one drink (see below), with one or two alcohol-free days per week. Drinking too much on a regular basis can lead to mental and physical health problems. Hangovers with headaches and stomachaches are common. Long-term alcohol abuse can cause memory loss, chronic inflammation of the stomach, and, in more advanced cases of alcoholism, cirrhosis of the liver. Excessive alcohol intake can also weaken the heart muscle, reducing the efficiency of its pumping action.

Giving up smoking

Smoking is known to cause the development and/or aggravation of a range of painful diseases including emphysema and chronic bronchitis, heart disease, cancer, particularly of the lungs, and stomach problems such as ulcers and gastritis. There are indications that smoking may cause damaged tissues to take more time to heal because nicotine contributes to the narrowing of blood vessels, thus reducing the flow of blood into the tissues to start the healing process.

Women who smoke may also be more likely to develop osteoporosis, a painful condition common after menopause, in which the bones become brittle. It is also worth remembering that nonsmokers who are exposed to tobacco smoke have an increased risk of contracting cancer. Although stopping smoking requires great determination, the risks of developing serious disease begin to reduce as soon as you give it up.

STEPS TO GIVING UP SMOKING

The following methods may help to bolster your determination to give up smoking:

▶ *Set a date for quitting completely. Seek out a nonsmoking friend who can help you to monitor your progress.*

▶ *Write a list of the advantages of giving up. Put it in a prominent position, such as in your diary or in the kitchen, so you see it often.*

▶ *Develop new interests like a sport or hobby.*

▶ *Make time for relaxation to reduce stress, thus reducing the urge to smoke.*

▶ *Congratulate yourself frequently on your progress.*

▶ *Save the money you would have spent on cigarettes and buy yourself treats, such as some new CDs.*

LOOKING AFTER YOUR BODY

By making the right choices for your body, you can help to improve your emotional and physical health and also increase your life expectancy. Take steps to adopt a healthier lifestyle by eating a well-balanced diet, exercising regularly, giving up smoking, and keeping your alcohol consumption at moderate levels.

BALANCING YOUR DIET
A varied diet that emphasizes whole grains, fruits, and vegetables, includes adequate protein and no more than 30% fat, can help to improve the way you look and feel.

INCREASING EXERCISE
Regular exercise such as walking or jogging can help to keep joints flexible and prevent stiffness. It also improves blood circulation and reduces the risk of heart disease.

CUTTING DOWN ON ALCOHOL
A recommended daily maximum intake of alcohol is one or two drinks (1 drink equals about 12 ounces of beer, 4 or 5 ounces of wine, or 1½ ounces of 80 proof liquor).

KICKING THE SMOKING HABIT
Smoking is a major cause of diseases such as lung cancer and emphysema, so it makes sense to give it up. Secondhand smoke can also increase the risk of lung diseases.

MANAGING STRESS

A certain amount of stress can be good, especially when it stimulates and motivates people. However, in the long term too much or inappropriate stress can lead to many painful disorders.

When you feel that your ability to cope is being outweighed by the demands put on you, stress has reached the point where it can have a harmful effect. This kind and level of stress can actually cause physical damage to the body.

HOW STRESS AFFECTS PAIN
Stress can be induced by external pressures, such as the demands forced upon you by family, work, or study. It can also be the result of internal pressures, such as illness, pain, anxiety, or depression.

During stress the brain alerts the hypothalamus, a small part of the brain that controls body functions such as temperature, sleep, and appetite. The hypothalamus in turn triggers the release of a variety of hormones that cause some typical body reactions such as an increase in adrenaline, raised blood pressure, rapid heartbeat, sweating, and a faster breathing rate. While this response may be useful when you are faced with sudden danger, excessive long-term stress can lead to serious problems, including increased pain. In the early stages, stress may cause migraine, stomachache, indigestion, and nausea. Over a longer period it can contribute to heart disease and backache. Stress can even intensify existing pain, because the typical stress response includes heightened sensitivity to all stimuli and increased tension in the muscles. For all of these reasons it's essential to examine the level of stress in your life and develop techniques to manage it more effectively.

Identifying stress factors
The first step toward managing stress is to identify specifically what makes you feel . this way. The task is not necessarily as straightforward as it sounds, because certain symptoms of stress may be attributed to some other cause. The typical signs include headache; irritability; insomnia; teethgrinding; aching shoulders, neck, and back; nausea; ulcers; indigestion; shortness of breath; unexplained diarrhea or constipation; heart palpitations; cold hands and feet; and skin problems. If you are experiencing such symptoms, then you need to analyze how often and when they occur in relation to other events in your life. A diary may be useful for this purpose.

Dealing with environmental stress
Your environment can contribute to stress in your daily life. The pace of modern urban living, crowding, noise, rapid change—all can create stress. A common theme in environmental stress is a feeling of loss of control, a sense that the individual is powerless.

THE PAIN–STRESS CYCLE

A little stress helps to motivate, but too much can lead to a vicious spiral of stress-related problems, such as tension and insomnia, that increase perception of pain.

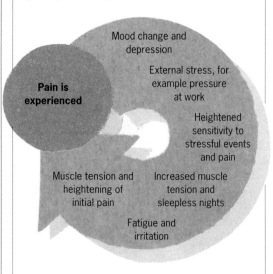

Pain is experienced

Mood change and depression

External stress, for example pressure at work

Heightened sensitivity to stressful events and pain

Muscle tension and heightening of initial pain

Increased muscle tension and sleepless nights

Fatigue and irritation

The Headache Sufferer

Many people regularly suffer headaches—perhaps once a week or more. A common type is the tension headache, caused by stress and exacerbated by lack of exercise and a poor diet. Painkillers may provide relief initially, but they do not address the symptoms in the long term. Learning to relax and improving your overall health can reduce or even eliminate these headaches.

John, a 31-year-old advertising executive, has suffered headaches for years, but since his promotion six months ago they have increased in frequency and intensity and are now occurring almost daily. The pain feels like a band of pressure around the head and down the neck. He has been taking painkillers but these are not really helping anymore.

John's doctor diagnosed that he is suffering from tension headaches, which are caused by stress and made worse by excessive drinking and smoking, poor diet, and lack of exercise. The doctor has advised John that the underlying causes of his headaches can eventually lead to more serious problems, such as heart disease, hypertension, and lung afflictions.

What should john do?

John should learn to do simple relaxation exercises, such as deep breathing, which can be done at work or at home and take only a few minutes. Relaxation books and tapes can also be helpful. In addition, he should give up smoking, cut down on alcohol and junk food, and start eating meals with high nutritional value.

He should also introduce some exercise into his daily routine. Short, daily walks will improve his circulation and reduce muscle tension.

Finally, John should try to ease pressure at work, for example, by delegating some work to other people, organizing his schedule more carefully, and not taking on more than he can handle.

Action Plan

Work
Delegate work to junior staff. Reorganize schedules, allowing time for a one-week holiday.

Exercise
Walk for half an hour every day and swim at least once a week. At work, get up from the desk regularly and move around.

Lifestyle
Start taking healthful lunches to work. Begin a program to stop smoking, and reduce alcohol to a maximum of two drinks per day. Learn relaxation exercises and practice them at least twice a day.

Lifestyle
Fast food, cigarettes, alcohol, and regular ;ack of sleep reduce the body's ability to deal with stress.

Work
Pressure at work to meet tight deadlines and employer's expectations can cause tension headaches.

Exercise
Insufficient exercise can contribute to high stress levels, increasing the risk of suffering from tension headaches.

How things turned out for john

John eased the pressure at work by rescheduling some deadlines. He has started to go for a 30-minute walk every morning and practices deep breathing exercises at work. He has cut down on smoking and alcohol and doesn't rely on fast food so much. An aromatherapy masseur showed him how to do self-massage on his neck and shoulders to ease tension. Overall, his headaches have eased and he feels much healthier generally.

Relieving stress with counseling

Many people find professional counseling can help them to cope with chronic stress symptoms. Counseling can take many forms, from assertiveness training to assist you in expressing your needs more effectively, to psychotherapy, which may help uncover and alleviate more deeply rooted causes of stress, such as emotional problems, poor self-esteem, anxiety, and depression.

STEPS TO COPING WITH STRESS

Recognizing and reducing harmful stress are important keys to minimizing or circumventing episodes of certain stress-related pain. It isn't possible or even desirable to avoid all the challenges in life that cause stress, but there are steps you can take to help you cope when stress begins to get out of hand.

▶ *Eat a well balanced diet. An inadequate diet will deplete your body of the resources it needs to deal with life's demands.*

▶ *Get adequate sleep. Sleep deprivation itself can cause stress, which in turn can cause insomnia.*

▶ *Exercise regularly. Physical activity helps to relieve tension and build up your general health, making you more resistant to illness and disease.*

▶ *Take time to relax. Schedule walking or gardening or other activitaies that bring you pleasure. Practice meditation or yoga on a regular basis.*

▶ *Learn visualization techniques. Imagining yourself in a pleasant setting can help promote feelings of relaxation. Visualizing a positive outcome to a problem that is causing stress can also help to reduce stress-related symptoms.*

▶ *Think positively. Try to distance yourself from experiences that induce feelings of anger and depression .*

To regain a sense of control over your environment, assess what elements cause you stress and consider how to avoid or reduce some of them. For example, if driving a car in heavy traffic makes you tense and anxious, explore options in public transportation. If external noise is an irritant in your home environment, look at the possibility of buying double-glazed windows, hanging heavy draperies, or even blocking external noise by playing background tapes. Recordings of new age music, Gregorian chants, or the sounds of waves can be very soothing.

Coping with stress in relationships

Juggling dozens of daily activities and trying to balance the needs of children, spouse, parents, and commitments to friends and community can be very stressful. The good news is, research shows that people who have many different activities or roles to play are better off. A good approach to achieving balance is to share more tasks with spouse and children and reassess commitments you have, keeping the ones that bring you the most satisfaction and discarding what you can, to allow more time for relaxing activities with family and friends.

Stress can also result from excessive demands on oneself. For example, a manager may become stressed by attempting to meet what she perceives as unreasonable expectations. If your job demands seem overwhelming, be as objective as possible about your performance. When you realize that you are doing the best job you can, accept that.

Stress is also caused by faulty communication. When personal relationships are conflicted, many people suppress their emotions instead of communicating directly how they feel. This can lead to physically painful symptoms, because anger, frustration, or distress, if not allowed direct and constructive expression, can often manifest themselves as headaches, nervous tics, palpitations, and hyperventilation. Communication is the first step toward overcoming stress in personal relationships. In the long term it is the most effective way to alleviate stress and bring about constructive change.

ENCOURAGING POSITIVE THINKING

I am feeling pleasantly relaxed

I feel good and I am giving up smoking

I am going to sleep well tonight

One way to encourage positive thinking is to bombard your mind with affirmative intentions. For example, telling yourself "I feel good and I am giving up smoking," is far more positive than the negative "I am not going to smoke any more." You can reinforce the message by writing out positive thoughts and placing them at eye level around the workplace and home. If you have made a conscious decision not to become tense during the day, put up messages such as "I am feeling pleasantly relaxed," and "I am going to sleep well tonight." Repeating these positive phrases to yourself even when stressed, helps to replace negative "what's the use?" self-sabotage thoughts. Thinking positively may help to counteract a pain problem before it escalates.

FOOD AGAINST PAIN

Many types of pain can be prevented by a diet rich in essential nutrients. Once good eating habits are a way of life, your body should become less susceptible to painful health problems.

A poor diet can contribute to many painful conditions, including heart disease, stroke, osteoporosis, stomach ulcers, shingles, migraine, and certain cancers. The pain of such conditions can often be alleviated or avoided altogether by eating the right foods in the right amounts.

EATING WELL TO FEEL GOOD
A well-balanced diet containing sufficient protein, complex carbohydrates, fats, minerals, vitamins, and fiber is essential for maintaining the body's natural mechanisms. For example, if you don't have enough fiber in your diet, you may suffer pain from constipation. Too much saturated fat (found primarily in animal products and palm and coconut oils) can aggravate or even bring on painful heart ailments such as angina. Many stomach complaints are caused by eating too many rich foods. Too much

sugar can cause tooth decay. Eating certain kinds of food can also make a significant difference to the management of a particular painful illness. For instance, evidence shows that polyunsaturated fats found in fish oils can have an anti-inflammatory effect on the joints of some arthritis sufferers. It also is possible to counteract other disorders by eating less of foods, such as dairy products, that can cause or aggravate a painful condition in some people..

Vitamins and minerals
Although your body needs only small quantities of vitamins and minerals, they play an important role in protecting you from pain caused by illness and disease. A lack of these nutrients in your diet can lead to specific illnesses and pain. For example, a deficiency of vitamin B_1 can cause fatigue, muscle weakness and nausea, while a deficiency of

---

CAPSULE FOR HEALTH

One of the best ways of promoting good health is to maintain a balanced diet by eating a variety of foods in moderation. Nutritionists recommend each day having 6 to 11 servings of breads, cereals, pasta, and rice; 3 to 5 servings of vegetables; 2 to 4 servings of fruits; 2 to 3 servings of dairy products; 2 to 3 servings of meat, fish, nuts, and dried legumes (totaling 6 oz); and spare amounts of fat, sugar, and salt. Fats should contribute no more than 30 percent of calories, saturated fats no more than 10 percent.

For a healthy diet eat these foods in abundance; the products on the right should be eaten in moderation.

FIGHTING PAIN WITH VITAMINS AND MINERALS

A healthy diet includes sufficient amounts of all the vitamins and minerals. Studies show that chronic pain sufferers are often deficient in some of these nutrients, because the stress of pain can deplete them in the body.

The table below shows the main sources of some vitamins and minerals and the Recommended Dietary Allowance (RDA). Do not take supplements that exceed the RDA without first seeking medical advice .

NUTRIENT	SOURCES	RDA: MEN	RDA: WOMEN	FUNCTION
Vitamin B_1	Whole-grain bread and cereals, beans, nuts, potatoes, pork, liver, heart, kidneys	1.5 mg	1.1 mg	B complex vitamins play a vital part in most processes in the body, including manufacture of red blood cells and release of energy from food. They are essential for healthy skin and correct functioning of the brain and nervous system. They may help to prevent the onset of nerve pain, and relieve menstrual pain and depression. Women need to take folic acid supplements (400 mcg) before conception and during early pregnancy to avoid neural tube defects like spina bifida in the developing fetus.
Vitamin B_2	Cereals, dairy foods, meat, fish, poultry, eggs	1.3 mg	1.1 mg	
Vitamin B_3	Rice, beans, meat, fish, eggs	17 mg	13 mg	
Vitamin B_6	Whole-grain bread, nuts, soy products, bananas, poultry, meat, fish, eggs	2.0 mg	1.6 mg	
Vitamin B_{12}	Cereals, dairy foods, meat, fish, eggs	2.0 mcg	2.0 mcg	
Folic acid	Whole-grain bread, cereals, nuts, beans, green leafy vegetables, liver	200 mcg	200 mcg	
Vitamin C	Citrus fruits, bell peppers, kiwi fruit, strawberries, potatoes	60 mg	60 mg	Antioxidant; is important to healthy teeth and gums; promotes healing of wounds.
Vitamin D	Dairy foods, oily fish, margarine, eggs (Also from action of sunlight on skin)	5.0 mcg	5.0 mcg	Heals bones; can help prevent osteoporosis and osteoarthritis.
Vitamin E	Wheatgerm, cereals, nuts, seeds, vegetable oils, sweet potatoes	10 mg minimum*	8.0 mg minimum*	Antioxidant; may relieve breast pain and leg cramps; may help prevent heart disease.
Calcium	Dairy foods, sesame seeds, green leafy vegetables, tofu, canned sardines with bones	800 mg	800 mg	Muscle and nerve function; healthy bones and teeth; can prevent osteoporosis, osteoarthritis.

Higher doses of Vitamin E may help reduce the risk of cancer and heart disease. Extra Vitamin E is often recommended for those recovering from heart attack.

vitamin B_2 can cause dry and cracked skin and sore lips and tongue. A calcium deficiency can lead to back pain and susceptibility to fractures. The table above shows the function of a number of vitamins and minerals. Vitamins can also help in pain recovery. For example, vitamin C may speed up wound healing and fight recurrent infections. It may also promote sleep, as it helps produce serotonin, a neurotransmitter that is involved in calming the mind.

Food allergies and intolerances

Some types of pain, such as migraine and abdominal cramps, may be triggered by eating particular kinds of foods. The most common triggers include cereals, dairy foods, caffeine-based products, yeast-based items, shellfish, and citrus fruits. You may be allergic to one or more of these foods or, more commonly, you may have a food intolerance. A food allergy is an abnormal response by the immune system to an otherwise harmless food substance. A food intolerance is also an adverse reaction to something in the diet, but it does not involve the immune system. For example, the body may lack an enzyme needed to digest a particular dietary substance. Sufferers from celiac disease have an intolerance to gluten found in wheat and other cereals. The condition damages the lining of the intestine. so that essential nutrients cannot be absorbed properly into the body.

Both conditions cause a range of symptoms, including headaches and indigestion, as well as chronic illnesses such as eczema and irritable bowel syndrome. The cause of a food allergy or intolerance is found by eliminating suspect foods from the diet, then reintroducing them one at a time while watching for adverse reactions. Such investigations should be undertaken with the supervision of a doctor or nutritionist.

EXERCISE AS PAIN PREVENTION

Exercise is vital for good health, helping to keep the body flexible and improve the circulation. By keeping active you can help to prevent painful illnesses and disease.

When the body is feeling pain, its natural instinct is to rest and resist activity. If you are suffering from an acute pain condition, such as severe joint inflammation, rest is generally advised because movement can aggravate existing damage. Likewise, if you are experiencing chronic pain, you may find it difficult to incorporate exercise into your life. However, because prolonged inactivity can be very harmful to your general well-being, it's advisable to reintroduce exercise as soon as possible. Unused muscles contract and become weak, and are more likely to go into painful spasm. Arthritis sufferers, in particular, need to keep their joints as mobile and flexible as possible. Lack of exercise in general can make you feel weak, fatigued, and breathless and can adversely affect your circulation. Inactivity over a long period can also lead to bone damage and weakening of muscles, making recovery from illness far more difficult.

In addition, exercise can stimulate the production of endorphins, the body's natural painkillers. Lack of exercise leads to low levels of endorphins in the bloodstream, in turn increasing the body's susceptibility to pain and compounding the problem by increasing the risk of depression.

What kind of exercise and how much?

There is a wide range of exercise options available. In the first instance you should consult your doctor or a physiotherapist as to how much and what kind of exercise to do to help alleviate your particular pain problem. For example, if you are suffering from osteoporosis, weight-bearing exercises may be just what you need, because they strengthen bones. On the other hand, if you

have a painful back or stiff joints that may become more stressed by weight-bearing exercises, another type of activity, such as swimming, might be more suitable. It may also be useful to think about less conventional forms of exercise. For example, t'ai chi (see page 75) and yoga (see page 74), can be very beneficial for back, neck, and shoulder pain. Both forms of movement strengthen muscles, improve posture, and aid in relaxation.

Most experts agree that the ideal level of activity for adults is 20 to 30 minutes of exercise that raises the pulse and respiration, at least three times a week, but preferably every day. Obviously the extent to which you are able to exercise will depend on the amount of pain experienced, but even small amounts of activity on a daily basis can make an enormous difference.

Going to a gym

Specific machines in a gym can be very useful for strengthening muscles and joints affected by particular pain problems. If you are attending a gym for the first time, see your doctor for a checkup before you go.

At your first session you will probably be asked about your medical history and current state of health. It is important to tell the instructor if you are taking any medications and if you have a medical condition or disability. The instructor will then work out an exercise program for you, which will be closely monitored and reviewed. He will also teach you about the benefits of the various exercise machines, how to use them properly, and also whether they are suitable for your needs and state of health. Your exercise regimen should ensure that both the time and intensity of effort you spend on a machine will build up gradually.

EXERCISING SAFELY
Exercise machines can be hazardous if not used properly. Always consult a trainer before using them.

Exercise bicycles and treadmills can be adjusted to your fitness level. Increase the level of difficulty as you improve.

Rowing machines provide an all-round work-out. If you have back, knee, shoulder, or neck pain, check with a doctor first.

Weightlifting is a great body strengthener and toner. Have a trainer show you proper techniques before you start.

Sedentary Lifestyle

Sitting in a chair—a car seat, armchair, or desk chair—for long periods, particularly with poor posture, puts pressure on the spinal discs so that they flatten and lose their cushioning action. This makes the back vulnerable to chronic pain.

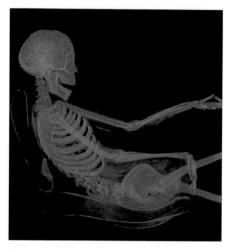

COUCH POTATO
Slumping on the sofa can do great damage to your back. Gradually it may become more curved, and the lack of support may cause your muscles to tense.

Sedentary lifestyles have become an increasing feature of modern society. Up to 14 hours a day may be spent seated—at home, at work, in the car or on a train. Such prolonged sitting can easily tire the back and make it vulnerable to problems when over-stretching or twisting. While a person sits in the same position for a long period, the back muscles become stretched. In particular, slumping in a chair without good support increases the risk of cramp and pain in the lower and mid back areas, and the neck and shoulders.

Driving for extended periods can exacerbate the problem, as the back muscles become tense and strained when going around corners and accelerating. In addition, bumps in the road can jolt the spine and cause bruising of the joints.

Action plan Try to change position frequently and get up to do tasks, rather than sitting still for long periods. If a long journey is necessary, plan regular short stops where you can walk around. Simple exercises like the ones below can relieve pressure, stretch the spine, and improve posture. These can be done in your chair or standing up. Always do exercises gently and stop immediately if they cause any pain.

CHAIR EXERCISES

There are several exercises you can do without leaving your chair. They will help you stretch your back, and also relieve tension and stress. Prepare by sitting up with your neck and shoulders relaxed and feet flat on the floor.

Roll your head down and up, and then to the left and right.

1 *Concentrate on your breathing while slowly rolling your head. Shrug your shoulders when finished.*

2 *Keep back and neck straight and clasp your hands behind the chair. Raise them a little way and look up.*

Be careful not to strain your muscles.

Pull in your stomach and sit tall.

3 *With palms facing outward, raise your arms above your head, breathing in at the same time, and clasp hands. Hold for a count of five.*

Avoiding injury when exercising

For those who haven't exercised for a long time, whether through choice or through immobility due to injury or illness, it is essential to seek a doctor's advice before beginning any exercise regimen and to build up a routine gradually.

If you have decided to start a new exercise program, remember to wear loose, comfortable clothing. Good choices are a tracksuit or lightweight cotton shorts with an aerated cotton top or shirt, which will allow the body to breathe. Women should make sure that they are wearing a well-fitted support bra. For active sports, use sturdy, nonslip trainers with cushioned soles that will reduce jarring of the knees, hips, and spine. They are also essential when jogging.

All exercise and sport routines require warming up and cooling down exercises (see page 27). A warm-up helps to prevent joint and muscle injuries, while cooling down afterward helps to lower the heart rate gently.

If your joints are stiff in the morning you can relieve the stiffness by taking a warm bath or shower before starting your exercise. After a bath or shower, relax stiff or sore joints by gently extending and flexing the joints as far as they can comfortably stretch. Lightly massaging painful joints and the back and neck areas with warmed olive oil can also improve your flexibility and enhance blood circulation through the muscles, thus helping to prevent muscle spasm and its ensuing pain.

EXERCISING AND YOUR LIFESTYLE

Regular exercise brings greater benefits than infrequent bouts of physical activity. Daily exercise performed without a break for just 12 minutes will make the body fitter by improving the efficiency of the heart and lungs. To build up a routine, try exercising at the same time each day, working up to 30 minutes or more per session. Choose a form of exercise that fits easily into your current lifestyle. It could be as simple as taking a brisk walk to your local shops for small items, rather than driving or relying on home delivery.

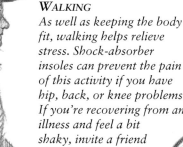

WALKING
As well as keeping the body fit, walking helps relieve stress. Shock-absorber insoles can prevent the pain of this activity if you have hip, back, or knee problems. If you're recovering from an illness and feel a bit shaky, invite a friend along until you feel fit enough to try the route alone.

CYCLING
Cycling can help to improve the functioning of the heart and respiratory systems, because the body continually takes in oxygen to meet the increased demands placed on the muscles. This type of activity is known as aerobic exercise. Start off with a small goal such as the end of the road, and as you feel more comfortable, increase the distance a little every day.

SWIMMING
Swimming is particularly suitable for people with joint disorders, such as arthritis, because water supports the body and limits stress on joints. If you suffer from back or neck pain, swimming on your back may be more comfortable. Before swimming always do warm up exercises at the side of the pool (see page 27).

CORRECT POSTURE

Many serious aches and pains result from poor posture. By improving your posture, you may be able to prevent severe and possibly long-term back and neck pains from developing.

LOAD CARRYING
Many posture problems develop as a result of poor lifting or load carrying. In some cultures heavy loads are carried on the head. This system avoids straining shoulders and back, and ensures good posture.

Look at any healthy baby or toddler sitting on the floor and you will see that his or her back posture is beautifully straight. Unfortunately, however, the posture of most persons deteriorates as they age. With our increasingly sedentary lifestyle, people can sit for hours at a time —often in poor seating—in the car, at home, in schools and colleges, and in the workplace. Over the years bad posture can lead to loss of muscle tone and ultimately severe back and neck pains, forcing sufferers to seek relief from physical therapists.

WHY GOOD POSTURE IS IMPORTANT

The human skeleton is covered with an interlinking system of muscles, which are connected to the bones by tendons. These act to lever and mobilize the body and to protect the inner organs. Ligaments provide extra support. The trunk is held up by a complex layering and interweaving of back and abdominal muscles which act as a sort of natural elastic corset when toned.

However, this complicated system is easily damaged, and any slight distortion of the posture can lead to limb or trunk stress and injury over time. This explains why ballet dancers, gymnasts, martial arts enthusiasts, and others who rely on having a fit body for their work, recognize the importance of good posture and work hard to build up strong trunk muscles.

Slouching or standing in awkward positions can put undue pressure on the muscles. The tendons and ligaments then have to compensate and work harder to support you, and you may start to feel an ache, perhaps in the back or neck, which in turn may lead to a headache. If bad posture is not corrected, over a long period of time these general aches can turn into acute muscle pain or even a slipped disc.

By consciously adopting a better posture, for example, by making an effort to sit without slouching, you can avoid incapacitating neck and back pain in the future.

Poor posture can also restrict the lungs and breathing capacity. The body needs a plentiful intake of oxygen in order to feel fresh and alert. But if the shoulders are hunched, breathing may become restricted, with the result that insufficient oxygen is taken in. Good posture encourages a relaxed diaphragm, which aids breathing.

Factors affecting your posture

Good posture has long been considered to promote a healthy body. Slouching, sitting and standing improperly, and walking stiffly are all recognized as potential causes of painful muscular problems.

Your posture can also be affected by your weight. For the body to work and move well, it is essential to maintain a reasonable and adequate weight for your height. If you are overweight, you may experience problems carrying around the extra weight, because your joints will be under greater strain. Being too thin causes different problems: your body may simply lack the stamina and strength to function effectively.

Injury and pain can also affect your posture. People with advanced rheumatoid arthritis, or with osteoporosis, for example,

---

CAUTION
If you have had recent surgery, a spinal or neck injury, a heart or thyroid problem, hypertension, a past severe head injury, also if you are diabetic, take sedatives or corticosteroids, or feel dizzy, check with your doctor before beginning a posture correction program.

Preventing Back Pain with

Improved Posture

Learning to walk, sit and stand with correct posture can be enormously beneficial for both the relief and prevention of back pain. Good posture can also help you to avoid injury when bending over or lifting.

Poor posture can be a cause of back pain. It can also exacerbate damage from other causes and lead to problems in other areas of the body. Before you can start to improve your posture, you need to assess the way you hold and move your body. The "wall test" (see right) can help you to establish a natural, comfortable posture that allows you to move and stand with a minimum of distortion and stress. Practice this for a minute or two every day, and try to visualize standing and walking with a relaxed posture. (See also Alexander techinque, page 76.)

Lifting is said to be the most common cause of back pain. The damage usually occurs when someone lifts without thinking or when they are under pressure. When people are in a hurry, they are more likely to twist when bending down or lifting and this puts the back at maximum risk. Always assess the situation before picking something up. Is it too heavy? Do you need help? When you do lift an object, make sure that you stoop and lift it in the correct fashion (see below), supporting the weight with your legs so that you protect the spine from damage.

THE WALL TEST

▶ *Stand against a wall with your feet slightly apart. Your head, shoulders, buttocks, and heels should touch the wall.*

▶ *Place one hand flat between the wall and your back. If there is no space you have a flat, possibly tight back. If there is lots of space your back is too curved. Ideally your back should be just slightly curved.*

▶ *Feel how you should adapt your posture to strengthen your back.*

LIFTING

When bending to lift things, breathe out and bend your knees. Keep your back straight and move slowly and carefully. Never flex the spine while bent over. Stand up slowly, holding your abdomen in to act as a corset. Keep the object close to your chest.

Keep your back straight

1 *Put your feet comfortably apart, on either side of the object to be lifted.*

Bend your knees

Hold in your abdomen

2 *Lift slowly and avoid twisting the body as you stand up.*

3 *Carry the object close to your chest and put it down on a clear surface.*

Keep the object as close to the body as possible

BUYING A BED

Spend time choosing the right bed to avoid such problems as chronic back pain. The following points are worth bearing in mind:

▶ *Make sure that the mattress is comfortable but provides firm support. Buy one of good quality, which will not sag with use (see below).*

▶ *Take into account your sleeping habits when choosing a bed— you take up more room if you sleep on your side, for example—and buy the widest that you can afford.*

▶ *If buying a double bed, make sure both you and your partner try it first.*

▶ *Make sure the bed is at least 6 in (15 cm) longer than you or your partner, whoever is taller.*

▶ *If there is a big weight difference between you and your partner, consider a pocket-spring mattress or twin beds—otherwise you will keep rolling together in your sleep.*

will find that their posture becomes distorted through no fault of their own. If you suffer from stress, you may notice that your head, stomach, and back become tense, causing pain. In response to the pain your body will tense even more, which over time can lead to general stiffness and distortion. Adopting a better posture can also help to relax cramped muscles.

Wearing comfortable shoes can make all the difference to freedom of movement and your body alignment when walking or running. High heels tip the pelvis forward and over-arch the back, affecting balance and causing an unnatural stance, which places strain on the back, knees, and feet.

Your clothes can also influence the way you move. Tight clothes or heavy outdoor winterwear can weigh the shoulders down, limit breathing capacity, and affect movement. Loose, light clothing is the least restricting to free movement. Even weather can affect your body posture: cold and windy conditions can cause you to tense and tighten your muscles and squash the lungs, by holding the body in to keep warm.

Adopting a good posture

Posture is developed without conscious thought from an early age. People rarely think about their posture unless the body begins to ache for one reason or another. Demonstrating how best to move, sit and stand with a relaxed, aware and stress-free musculature is far more complex. One of

the greatest difficulties in adopting better posture is in correcting entrenched physical misalignments. However, it's worth persevering to change bad habits.

You can take steps to help your body naturally into a better physical alignment. Always try to walk with your back straight, keeping your shoulders back and your stomach in, and lifting your chest and ribs. Whether walking, standing or sitting it may help to picture a string attached to the centre of the top of your head. Imagine that this string gently pulls the body up with every slight movement you make by lifting your chest and realigning the body. (See also Alexander tecnhique, page 76.)

Regular stretching and muscle strengthening exercises may help to prevent severe back or neck pain and tension headaches. Many injuries are caused by sudden movement after a period of inactivity. For example, lifting heavy items after sitting all day in a low chair can lead to back problems. Always warm up muscles sufficiently before any vigorous movement (see page 27).

A healthy posture relies upon the interplay between a relaxed mind and body. An angry or aggressive person has a totally different posture from someone who is laughing and happy. You can promote a more relaxed posture by decreasing your stress levels and reducing the tension in your life.

SLEEP AND POSTURE

Bad sleeping positions can cause severe chronic back and neck pain. You may think that the position in which you sleep is beyond your control, yet there are a number of changes you can make to prevent or ease pain.

Choosing the right bed

The first steps toward achieving a good sleeping posture are to get rid of your old mattress when it no longer provides adequate support and to buy a suitable new one (see left). A sagging mattresses can not only cause back pain but also make it worse, and you may wake up stiff and sore.

Waterbeds can provide firm support to the body and are often used in hospitals for patients who have painful joints and limbs or are suffering bedsores. Japanese futon mattresses are said to be effective for backache. However, they may be too hard for some people who have chronic back pain.

SELECTING THE IDEAL MATTRESS

A medium-firm to firm—but not too hard—bed is essential, as it allows the spine to relax and relengthen during sleep.

To prevent moisture from getting trapped in the mattress, place it on a slatted base or an open spring base.

NIGHT SUPPORT
A pocket-spring mattress gives excellent support to the whole body, as each spring moves independently. An innerspring base must be used with this kind of mattress.

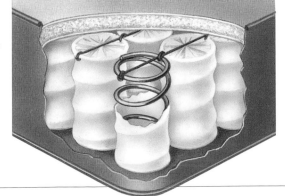

IMPROVING YOUR SLEEPING POSTURE

As roughly a third of your life is spent in bed, it is essential that you have a good sleeping posture. A bad sleeping position can lead to chronic back and neck pain. The following suggestions may help people who already suffer such pain.

Supporting the neck
Specially contoured pillows are available that give extra support to the neck. These pillows help to cushion the neck if it hurts to turn over in bed.

Improvising at home
If you find that your pillow doesn't cushion your neck enough, try tying a ribbon or some twine round the middle of it.

SUPPORTING THE BACK
If you often sleep on your back, you can avoid straining your lower back by lying with knees bent. so your feet are flat on the bed. You may find it more comfortable to slip a pillow under the knees for support.

SUPPORTING THE KNEES AND HIPS
If you have aching hips or knees or a painful back, placing a pillow or cushion between the knees or thighs may help you to sleep on your side. This position eases pain, because it keeps the pelvis from pulling on the lower back.

If you are sleeping with a partner, the mattress may start to dip in the middle and this can cause back pain. With a good bed base you should not have a problem. But if it does occur, or if you and your partner prefer different types of mattresses, you may find that twin beds or a split mattress will provide a good solution.

Adopting a good sleeping posture

To relax the body and promote a comfortable sleeping position, try breathing exercises before sleeping. Breathe in and out calmly and slowly to reduce tension in the back. Imagine that you can really feel your back letting go of any pain and tension. Visualize any pain draining away from your back, and you should feel more and more at ease. Gently wriggle your feet and toes and stretch both legs to aid circulation and to prevent stiffness.

If you suffer from chronic back pain, you may find it uncomfortable to lie on your back. However, by keeping your knees bent with your feet flat on the bed you can prevent additional strain and pull to the lower back when lying down.

Turning over in bed can present major problems for back-pain sufferers. A wide, soft fabric belt, or brace, with a velcro fastening offers extra support for the back when turning over or getting out of bed.

HELPING CHILDREN TO DEVELOP GOOD POSTURE

Encouraging school-children to stand and sit straight is not just a matter of basic discipline. Doint them properly is an important factor in avoiding back and neck pain later in life.

▶ *Make sure that your child's school bag is not too heavy. Check that his shoulders are relaxed and balanced when carrying the bag so that there is no strain on the back.*

▶ *If your child has a paper route, suggest that he or she use a bike to support the heavy newspaper bag.*

▶ *Watch your youngster's weight—being overweight can affect posture adversely.*

▶ *Check that your child's desk and chair are an appropriate size and are not leading to bad postural habits.*

▶ *Have a member of the school board evaluate the furniture in your child's school from a health and safety perspective.*

Massage Therapies

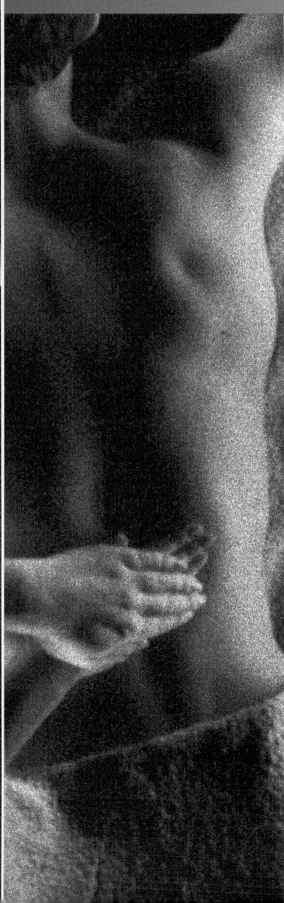

Massage, a relaxing and pleasurable way of dealing with pain, is widely available in a variety of forms, some based on Oriental medicine. The basic techniques of massage are easy to learn and can be used to give pain relief to family and friends.

MASSAGE

Massage (from the French word *masser,* meaning "to rub") is one of the oldest therapies known. It may have developed from the discovery that simply rubbing a sore area provides immediate relief. As it became evident that rubbing relieved not only local pains but also those in other parts of the body, the value of using the hands for healing must have been realized and more systematic approaches developed.

Method There are a great many forms of massage, but all aim to mobilize the natural healing properties of the body to help restore or maintain optimal health. Eastern styles, such as shiatsu, focus on balancing the body's vital energy as it flows in pathways known as zones, or meridians. Western style massage, such as Swedish, works toward relaxing muscles, improving circulation, and increasing mobility. It consists of gliding, kneading, tapping, and stretching strokes, along with deep circular movements and vibrations. This type of massage is particularly useful for alleviating pain and stiffness caused by sports injuries, and is often used in rehabilitation programs for patients who have had an accident or stroke.

Massage is also a convenient way to apply therapeutic substances to the skin and underlying tissues. Some massage therapists use warming or analgesic creams and oils, while others work with the essential oils of aromatherapy.

Result Many people have regular massage to help them relax and stay in peak physical condition. Those engaged in physically active pursuits, such as dancers and football players, find it particularly good for maintaining muscle tone. Massage has valuable preventative health benefits as well, because it improves the flexibility of muscles and connective tissues and enhances their blood supply; it also helps to boost the body's immune system.

HOW IT CAN HELP

Massage can help to relieve muscular pain as well as reduce stress and ease muscle tension. The treatment is useful for:

► Relieving neck and back pain

► Aiding relaxation

► Mobilizing stiff joints

► Improving muscle tone

► Stimulating release of endorphins, the body's natural painkillers

► Helping the healing process by improving the supply of oxygen and nutrients to muscles and connective tissues

► Improving drainage of waste products from the tissues

MASSAGE STROKES

There are four main types of stroke used in Western massage: friction, effleurage, percussion, and petrissage. They can be applied using light movements to provide gentle relaxing effects, or with deeper pressure to relieve tense, knotted muscles. A light oil, such as almond, helps to lubricate the skin and make the massage more effective.

EFFLEURAGE
This is a slow rhythmic stroke, applied with the fingers and palms.

FRICTION
The fingers and thumb are used for small circular movements.

PERCUSSION
This is a short, fast stroke applied with the side of the closed hand.

PETRISSAGE
This is a grasping and kneading action on fleshy areas of the body.

AROMATHERAPY

In aromatherapy, oils with healing properties, known as essential oils, are used in a compress or steam inhalation, added to bath water, or massaged into the skin. Essential oils are extracted from various medicinal plants by a process of distillation. They are highly concentrated so only a few drops are needed. For a massage, a few drops of one or more essential oils are added to a carrier, or base, oil such as almond oil.

Essential oils are absorbed into the body by inhalation and through the skin. They can have a localized effect and also pass into the bloodstream to reach other areas of the body. Some oils affect mood, by relieving tension or depression, for example. Aromatherapy is useful for treating stress-related disorders and chronic painful conditions like arthritis.

Method Essential oils are available at pharmacies and health food stores for use at home, but for treatment tailored to your personal condition, it is advisable to visit a trained aromatherapist. After a discussion of your condition, the therapist will select oils that you can use at home or will offer to apply them by massage. For relief of respiratory disorders such as sinusitis, a therapist will usually provide a combination of oils to be added to hot water for a steam inhalation.

Result As well as alleviating some specific disorders, aromatherapy aids relaxation and promotes the release of endorphins, thereby providing relief from conditions like anxiety and muscle and joint pain.

HOW IT CAN HELP

Aromatherapy can ease stress-related disorders and emotional states such as anxiety and depression. It is also helpful in alleviating:

▶ Nasal congestion and sinusitis (in a steam inhalation)
▶ Muscular tension
▶ Chronic neck and back pain
▶ High blood pressure
▶ Premenstrual symptoms
▶ Chronic bronchitis

MASSAGE OILS

You can buy massage oils ready mixed, or you can make your own by purchasing essential oils and mixing a few drops with a base oil such as almond or hazelnut. Essential oils should be kept in cool, dark surroundings but not in a refrigerator, as cold can degrade their quality.

ESSENTIAL OILS
Keep essential oils in glass bottles with tight-fitting stoppers.

Energy Therapies

Many treatments are based on the theory that energy pathways in the body play a part in health and well-being. Any blockages, deficiencies, or imbalances in these pathways cause symptoms. Treatment aims to restore the energy flow to a state of harmony.

ACUPUNCTURE

Acupuncture and several other Oriental disciplines, such as shiatsu and acupressure, are based on the traditional Chinese theory that pain and illness are the result of an excess or deficiency of energy, *chi* or *qi*, in the affected area of the body. The body's energy flows through a network of channels, or meridians, that are said to lie just below the body's surface. These meridians connect specific organs and systems and have a wider sphere of influence in the body. Acupuncturists focus on special points on the meridians to correct imbalances in the energy flow and thus relieve pain and illness.

In China acupuncture is often used as an anesthetic during surgical operations, providing complete pain relief while the patient remains awake. It is becoming a widely popular method of pain relief during labor, as it has no effect on the baby and allows the mother to remain alert throughout the birth.

Method The principal tools of acupuncture are fine stainless steel or silver alloy needles, which are inserted into the skin at specific acupuncture points. This procedure is painless, the only sensation being a slight tingling as the needle reaches the chosen point. The needles may be inserted in a variety of ways from vertically to almost horizontally. The acupuncturist may rotate or

HOW IT CAN HELP

Acupuncture is effective at easing chronic pain and also for alleviating stress-related conditions. It is particularly suited to the treatment of:

▶ Arthritis

▶ Rheumatism

▶ Angina

▶ Digestive disorders

▶ Fatigue

manipulate the needles to give added stimulation to the point. Sometimes a mild electric current is sent through a needle to achieve the same effect.

The acupuncturist may also burn a small cone of a dried herb, usually mugwort (*Artemisia vulgaris*) or moxa (*Artemisia japonica*), over the point or hold the glowing end of a moxa stick close to it. Or she may place a piece of moxa on the head of the needle and light it. The smouldering moxa imparts a gentle heat down the shaft of the needle into the energy channel.

Result Pain relief through acupuncture can be almost instantaneous; with some conditions improvements may be felt after several sessions. Acupuncture has often proved particularly effective for the relief of pain caused by arthritic joints and stiff muscles.

ACUPRESSURE

In this therapy gentle pressure is applied to acupuncture points with the fingertips or a blunt probe. Acupressure follows principles similar to those of acupuncture but may, in fact, predate it. It is likely that acupuncture points were first discovered by massaging and pressing tender areas on the body. The earliest medical tools discovered at archaeological sites in China are blunt-pointed pebbles, known as bian stones, which might have been used before the advent of needles. Acupressure is safe to use as a self-help treatment for many common ailments such as travel sickness.

Method Acupressure has the same aim as acupuncture, to restore the flow of energy along the meridians and to release any blockages. Treatment consists of sustaining firm pressure on selected acupuncture points for up to a minute or more, or stimulating the points using a circular, kneading movement. Pressure is usually applied with the fingertips or thumbs but can also be done with a rounded probe such as a pen top.

Result Many people have reported relief from a range of symptoms, including arthritis, back pain, and digestive and circulation problems. It has also proved effective in the self-treatment of conditions like migraine and tension.

HOW IT CAN HELP

Acupressure is an excellent preventative treatment. It is also useful for specific painful ailments such as:

▶ Migraine and other headaches
▶ Backache
▶ Digestive problems
▶ Chronic stiffness
▶ Sports injuries

REIKI

Reiki aims to rebalance the energy in the body to stimulate the body's natural healing systems and achieve greater well-being. It was developed in 19th-century Japan by a spiritual master, Dr. Mikao Usui, to harmonize body energy with the energy of its surroundings. The term *reiki* is Japanese for "universal energy."

Method Reiki is really a form of meditation based on the concept that the body radiates a vital life force or energy. Reiki healers must first be attuned to this life energy by a reiki master, to gain the ability to heal others. Once attuned the healer then learns a range of hand positions to use for self treatment, the treatment of others, and for group healing.

At a healing session the patient will be asked to lie on a massage table. The therapist will then place his or her hands over the body at points believed to be emitting weak energy. The hands are held palms down, with the fingers and thumbs extended and held together. The treatment is gentle but powerful, stimulating the body's self-healing ability.

Result After receiving reiki therapy, the patient usually feels a relaxing warmth and sometimes even a pleasant tingling sensation. It can also help people bring deep-seated emotional problems to the fore so that they can be resolved.

GROUP HEALING
Traditional Japanese Reiki healers work in teams, which makes the healing session much faster because several hand positions can be performed at once. A team may consist of as many as eight or nine healers.

HOW IT CAN HELP

Reiki is said to be of benefit in a wide range of disorders. It is effective at calming the nervous system and is often used in combination with other techniques as part of a pain management program. It is particularly useful for easing the pain associated with:

▶ Stress-related disorders
▶ Chronic neck and back pain
▶ Menstrual pain
▶ Chronic joint disorders

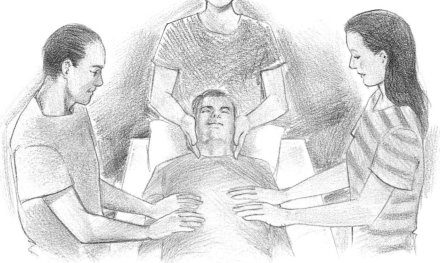

KINESIOLOGY

Kinesiology was developed by Dr. George Goodheart, an American chiropractor. Its original aim was to treat muscular imbalances, which can result in poor posture and pain. It is widely used by chiropractors and osteopaths, some of whom have evolved their own variations to diagnose and treat many health problems. Some practitioners practice kinesiology exclusively, while others use it as an adjunct to osteopathy or chiropractic work.

The principle behind the standard form of kinesiology is that weakness of specific muscles, with the consequent changes in posture, are responsible for causing pain. Practitioners believe that the weak muscles create an imbalance in the body's energy channels, or meridians. Certain "indicator" muscles are said to be linked to these meridians and can provide information about the whole body.

Method A kinesiologist will first check your posture and then examine you in standing and sitting positions, looking for muscular imbalances. There may, for example, be a tilt of the head or a dropped shoulder on one side. The practitioner will then carry out tests on individual muscles, while you are standing, sitting, or lying down, by applying light pressure to their normal action for a few seconds and gauging their relative strength.

The way in which the muscles respond to the tests reveals to the practitioner how the body is functioning. For instance, strong resistance is a sign of health, and poor resistance indicates weakness. These tests rely on the practitioner's knowledge of the muscles' actions and relationships. Strong muscles that weaken after a certain food is eaten can be used as indicators of food intolerance.

HOW IT CAN HELP

Kinesiology is best suited for locating and correcting physical disorders and thus is most effective in treating or preventing:

▶ Muscular and joint pains due to distorted posture

▶ Joint inflammation

▶ Migraine and other headaches and neuralgia

If a problem area is identified, the kinesiologist will use the fingertips to gently massage the acupoints, or trigger points, in the muscles, which will help revitalize the area.

Result Kinesiology provides a picture of a person's general state of health. Many patients report increased vitality and energy after treatment. The technique is also useful as a preventative measure.

SHIATSU

Shiatsu is a Japanese therapy, with roots in Chinese medicine, which is based on the belief that stimulating points on the surface of the body can influence the functioning of organs deep inside. Like acupressure, shiatsu works by the application of pressure to acupuncture points, in order to stimulate the body's energy flow and remove any blockages from the energy channels, or meridians. It also incorporates massage techniques to treat a wide range of disorders. The pressure points are located along the meridians at places where the energy channels lie close to the skin.

Method The name shiatsu comes from the Japanese for "finger massage." The practitioner uses circular motions and firm pressure applied with the fingertips and thumbs at specific energy points or along the course of the energy channels. Sometimes practitioners use the heels of their hands, their elbows, knees, and even their feet to apply suitable pressure. The strength of the pressure depends on the location and on whether the aim is to stimulate or sedate the energy flow. Light stroking techniques are used where energy is congested, and sustained or stronger pressure is applied to stimulate the skin.

Where there is pain in a specific area, such as the knee, the energy flow may be sluggish, so the aim of treatment is to clear the obstruction. For a painful joint the practitioner will focus not only on the joint itself but also on points along the energy channels that pass through the affected area. These may actually lie some distance from the exact location of the pain.

HOW IT CAN HELP

Like acupressure, shiatsu is an effective preventative treatment and is helpful for specific painful ailments such as:

▶ Migraine and other headaches

▶ Musculoskeletal disorders

▶ Digestive problems

▶ Bowel disorders

▶ Sports injuries

Result Shiatsu has proved most effective for the relief of tension and other stress-related conditions, and musculoskeletal disorders such as chronic neck and back pain. Patients often report an increased vitality and release from depression and insomnia. Shiatsu is also believed to prevent disease by strengthening the body's immune system.

REFLEXOLOGY

Reflexology involves fingertip pressure on areas of the feet called reflex zones, in order to relieve pain in other parts of the body. The technique is thought to have originated in China over 5,000 years ago. Reflexology was revived and further developed by a New York therapist, Eunice Ingham, in the 1930s. She discovered that certain points, mainly on the soles of the feet but also on the hands, correspond to certain organs and regions of the body. Tenderness of individual foot zones coincide with disturbance of the corresponding organ. Pain in an area of the body such as the head or abdomen can be relieved by working on the corresponding foot zone. Reflexology is now widely practiced in conjunction with other therapies, and many people have learned it in order to help family and friends.

Method The reflexologist uses the thumb and fingers to stimulate the reflex points. If the person receiving the treatment has a serious health problem, applying even a little pressure can sometimes be painful. Sessions of reflexology treatment generally last about an hour.

Result Patients often report that a session with a reflexologist provides a huge energy boost, as well as

relaxing the body and bringing it back into balance. It is possible to practice the techniques at home, but for best results, patients should seek the advice of a practitioner before treating themselves.

HOW IT CAN HELP

Reflexology is better suited for minor disorders and stress-related problems than for specific illnesses. It is useful for:

▶ Migraines, tension, and fatigue

▶ Digestive problems such as constipation

▶ Menstrual pain

TENS (TRANSCUTANEOUS ELECTRICAL NERVE STIMULATION)

The idea of using electrotherapy to alleviate pain dates back to Roman times when live electric eels were used to ease the pain of gout. TENS is a modern version of electrotherapy that spans both physical and energy approaches. It was developed as a result of the benefits observed from electro-acupuncture but, as its full name suggests, it works on the principle of stimulating the nerves.

Method Electrodes, connected to a portable transistorized stimulator, are placed on acupoints or over segments of peripheral nerves. The stimulator delivers a high frequency, low intensity current that induces a comfortable buzzing or tingling sensation, which can be sustained for 30 minutes or more. One of the advantages of TENS is its portability. A patient can carry his own unit, like a transistor radio, and switch it on whenever pain relief is required.

Result The brief, intense stimulus of the electric current travels by the faster "A" nerve fibers (see page 18), which block or disrupt the pain messages travelling in the slower "C" fibers. This disruption can outlast the actual stimulation, and relief may continue for some hours. Treatment can also induce a general feeling of well-being as well as reducing pain. TENS is often used as an alternative to long-term painkilling medication.

In 1975 Professor R. Melzack, one of the world's leading researchers into pain, reported having great success with the use of TENS: 75 per cent of peripheral nerve injuries, 60 per cent of phantom limb pain, and 62 per cent of shoulder and arm pain were relieved in experiments using TENS.

People who have had a heart pacemaker fitted should not use TENS, because it can interfere with the action of the pacemaker.

HOW IT CAN HELP

TENS is useful for alleviating cases of prolonged, intractable pain, particularly persistent nerve pain. It is not, however, a substitute for proper medical treatment of the underlying causes of pain. Specific problems it can help include:

▶ Sports injuries

▶ Lumbago

▶ Sciatica

▶ Phantom limb pain

▶ Shoulder and other joint pain

▶ Pain during childbirth

ELECTRICAL PAIN RELIEF
In TENS treatment, electrodes that deliver electrical impulses are placed on the surface of the body or implanted under the skin.

ZERO BALANCING

Zero balancing combines methods designed to restore harmony to the body's energy fields with manipulative body-working techniques. It was developed by Dr. Fritz Smith, an American osteopath and acupuncturist, who believed that working on the body's structure as well as its energy channels was the best way to stimulate the life force within the body and enhance the natural healing forces.

Unlike techniques such as acupuncture and shiatsu, which concentrate on energy pathways near the surface of the body, zero balancing focuses on the energy channels that pass through the bones deep within the body. Practitioners believe this energy flow is most easily evaluated at the joints.

Method In a zero balancing session you will be asked to lie fully clothed on your back. The practitioner will examine your joints to discover their flexibility and range of movement, and then use sustained stretches and finger pressure to encourage the release of tension accumulated in the body. Zero balancing treatment works with the whole body, usually through the legs and spine, and deals with each area of pain as it is uncovered. The treatment aims to create a feeling of deep relaxation, giving a person the opportunity to let go of stress, tension, and pain.

HOW IT CAN HELP

Zero balancing is a gentle therapy that is particularly helpful for:

- ▶ Neck and back pain
- ▶ Stress-related disorders
- ▶ Migraine

Result The practitioner applies only gentle pressure and stretching movements that are well within the tolerance of the individual. This makes zero balancing particularly suitable for cases in which more vigorous procedures, such as massage, might be too painful. Many people report increased flexibility as well as relief from pain.

THERAPEUTIC TOUCH

Therapeutic touch is the term used by Dr. Dolores Krieger, Professor of Nursing at New York University, to describe the "laying-on of hands" healing, which she sought to revive by training nurses in the art. According to Krieger it does not require professional qualifications; almost anyone can use their hands to help, if they are able to develop sensory skills.

Method In therapeutic touch, the hands do not usually touch the body but are held and moved an inch or two away from it. The treatment is founded on the belief that there is an energy field around the body and, with practice, it is possible to feel it. The healer passes the palms of the hands over the body to detect areas of congestion and pain. The aim is to unblock congested areas, so that energy can flow more smoothly.

Result Therapeutic touch can produce a deep relaxed feeling in the patient. Experiments with mice have shown that injuries heal faster when subjected to the energy of healing hands. You can learn to expand your own sense of energy and use it to help yourself, family, and friends.

HEALING HANDS
People who use the healing power of touch often report a feeling of warmth or tingling in their hands.

HOW IT CAN HELP

Therapeutic touch can be used for any type of illness as an adjunct to other treatments, but in particular, it can give considerable relief in the painful stages of childbirth. It may also be useful for alleviating:

- ▶ Neck and back pain
- ▶ Irritable bowel syndrome
- ▶ Chronic migraine

FAITH HEALING

Healing has long been associated with religion, indeed Christianity is founded partly on the belief in Christ's ability to heal. Faith healing is usually done in a religious setting, for example, during a church service or prayer-group meeting. Unlike other forms of healing, such as therapeutic touch, it is often carried out at a distance and need not involve touch or close contact.

Natural Medicine

Naturally occurring materials such as plant extracts can be used medicinally to alleviate pain. Herbs and plants contain a complex mixture of ingredients, some of which act on the body's chemistry and physiology to relieve painful symptoms.

HOMEOPATHY

The basis of homeopathy is to give a very diluted dose of a substance that, if given to a fit person at full strength, would cause symptoms akin to those of the illness being treated.

Method Homeopathic medicines are derived from plant, animal, and mineral compounds. A number of remedies are considered to have widespread application for painful disorders and can be obtained from any homeopathic pharmacy as well as drugstores and health-food shops. However, a qualified practitioner of homeopathy will prescribe a more individualized remedy, based on careful questioning about the nature of your pain and the various things that may influence its frequency and intensity. Pain resulting from cystitis, for example, might require different remedies in different patients, depending on various factors such as the degree and nature of the pain, whether the pain occurs before or after urination, and whether or not there is blood in the urine.

Result A homeopathic remedy that is well matched to your symptoms and other individual characteristics, such as your temperament or food preferences, will often be more effective in alleviating pain than a conventional painkiller. Homeopathic remedies do not cause any of the side effects associated with orthodox medications.

HOW IT CAN HELP

Homeopathy is effective for the treatment of a wide range of painful conditions including:

► Digestive complaints

► Migraine and other headaches

► Skin conditions such as eczema

► Premenstrual syndrome

► Joint ailments such as arthritis

HOW HOMEOPATHY WORKS

Homeopathic medicines are produced by repeatedly diluting the original active component, a process known as potentization. Each successive potency is signified by a number. The higher the number the more potent the remedy. Arnica 30, for example, is both more dilute and more therapeutically powerful than Arnica 6. Homeopathic remedies are usually taken in pill form.

A definitive explanation of how homeopathic medicines reduce inflammation or relieve pain has not been established. The amount of active ingredient in a remedy is so minute that it is not possible to detect any trace of it. Nevertheless, homeopathy has proven effective and is widely accepted.

HERBALISM

Throughout history plants have been used to treat painful disorders. Different traditions of herbal medicine have developed around the world, such as the Ayurvedic system in India, traditional medicine in China, and natural remedies of the Indians in North America.

Method Modern medical herbalists and experts in pharmacognosy (the study of the chemical actions of plants) have identified many plant compounds that are used for pain control in different parts of the world. The active ingredients of medicinal plants are attracted to receptors on the cells of organs and other tissues in the body. These ingredients fit into the receptors like jigsaw pieces, and then initiate chemical changes that modify the function of the organ. Herbal remedies may be taken internally in tablet form or as a tea, or used externally in a cream, lotion, or ointment.

Herbs can relieve pain in a number of different ways, depending on their individual properties. For example, red pepper (chili and cayenne) contains capsaicin, which inhibits the action of chemicals that relay pain messages to the brain. Marshmallow (*Althea officinalis*) has a high content of mucilage, a sticky substance that helps to prevent irritation and ulceration of the digestive tract. Red sage (*Salvia officinalis*) relieves pain of mouth ulcers and sore throats.

Result When used as recommended, herbal medicines usually produce few side effects. People who suffer from plant allergies, however, may have allergic reactions to certain herbs. It's advisable to use any new herbal remedy sparingly at first. Herbs are effective for many common illnesses and can also help relieve arthritis, migraine, and gastrointestinal disorders. Some are helpful in restoring general health as well.

Dang gui   Gou qi zi

Shi jue ming   Lugen

CHINESE HERBAL HEALING
Chinese herbalists have practiced their art for centuries. Western scientists are currently researching the healing properties of many potent Chinese herbs.

HOW IT CAN HELP

Herbalism is believed to be effective for a wide range of conditions. It is generally helpful in relieving pain or other symptoms associated with:

► Skin disorders such as eczema

► Stress-related disorders

► Joint disorders such as arthritis

► Digestive disorders such as stomach ulcer and irritable bowel syndrome

► Respiratory disorders

► Sleep disorders such as chronic insomnia

► Migraines and other headaches

SOME HERBS AND THEIR USES

The chart below shows a range of common pain problems that can be treated using herbs. Because many have potent chemical components, it is important to treat them with respect; consult a qualified medical herbalist who can advise about the proper dosage.

CONDITION	HERB	METHOD AND AIM
Sore throat, ulcers	Red sage *Salvia officinalis*	Use infusion or liquid extract as mouth rinse or gargle to soothe pain.
Toothache	Oil of cloves Chamomile (*Chamomilla*)	Apply oil of cloves on a cotton ball to the affected tooth. Use chamomile infusion as a mouth rinse.
Stomach ulcers	Liquorice (*Glychyrriza glabra*) Slippery elm (*Ulmus fulva*)	Drink liquid extracts of liquorice for pain. Use slippery elm tea or lozenges to soothe inflamed mucous membranes.
Colic, spasm, intestinal gas	Black hellebore (*Helleborus niger*); Wild yam (*Dioscorea villosa*; Ginger (*Zingiber officinalis*)	Drink liquid extracts to relieve and prevent muscle spasms. (Ginger assists action of other herbs; drink it as a tea.)
Cystitis	Uva ursi (*Arctostaphylos*); Marshmallow (*Althaea officinalis*)	Drink liquid extracts to soothe inflammation.
Muscles and joints	Oil of wintergreen (*Gaultheria procumbens*); Devil's claw (*Harpagaphytum procumbens*)	Massage oil of wintergreen into muscles and joints to soothe and relax them. Take devil's claw tablets.
Migraine	Feverfew (*Chrysanthemum parthenium*)	Eat leaves, drink tea, or take tablets to prevent and ease pain.
Neuralgia	Passionflower (*Passiflora incarnata*)	Drink liquid extracts to soothe pain.

NATUROPATHY

In naturopathic medicine numerous alternative approaches are used to relieve pain and restore and promote the body's healing powers. To achieve longterm health and well-being, naturopathy often requires a change in diet and other lifestyle factors to deal with whatever is causing the underlying condition.

The term "naturopathy" came into use during the 19th century. But the principles on which it is based go back to the Greek physician Hippocrates (*c.*460–*c.*370 BC), who maintained that simple therapies such as diet could help the body heal itself.

Modern naturopathy was pioneered in Germany and was brought to the U.S. in 1902 by a German healer, Benedict Lust. He railed against such bad habits as overeating, and use of alcoholic drinks and advocated corrective breathing, regular exercise, and a wholesome mental outlook. Today's naturopaths emphasize the responsibility of each individual in following a sensible diet and a prudent, healthful lifestyle.

Method Treatment might include soft tissue massage and relaxation techniques, plus nutritional therapy and herbal remedies. Some naturopaths also recommend various forms of hydrotherapy, such as hot and cold compresses, sprays, and baths to stimulate circulation to inflamed joints and other areas.

Result Naturopathy has proved beneficial for a range of conditions. For example, it can ease chronic disorders like arthritis and reduce the need for painkillers. If you incorporate elements of naturopathy into your lifestyle, it can have a dramatic effect on your health.

HOW IT CAN HELP

The holistic approach of naturopathy is suited to a wide variety of medical problems, but particularly stress-related ailments. It is generally helpful in relieving pain associated with:

► Arthritis
► Inflammation
► High blood pressure
► Stomach disorders
► Anxiety
► Fatigue
► Menstrual pain
► Respiratory disorders

DIETARY AND NUTRITIONAL THERAPY

Major tools in naturopathic medicine are dietary measures to support the body's self-healing mechanisms. Naturopaths were among the first to maintain that a healthy diet is one that is low in salt, saturated fats, and processed foods.

In treating disorders, for example, inflammation or pain in the digestive or respiratory system, a naturopath might recommend a juice fast, to cleanse the system, or a special diet. The aim always is to help the body direct its energies into resolving the underlying causes of medical problems.

A naturopath might advise on foods to avoid for certain painful conditions, for example, eschewing coffee and chocolate, which can trigger migraines in susceptible individuals. Some naturopaths also prescribe vitamin or mineral supplements to modulate body chemistry, usually after doing tests to check for deficiencies.

HOME HYDROTHERAPY FOR PAINFUL CONDITIONS

You can treat painful conditions by applying hot or cold water as a spray or a compress. To make a compress, soak a large handkerchief or small towel in hot or cold water. Wring out, fold to size, and place on the painful part. You can tie it in place with a scarf or bandage.

PAINFUL CONDITION	METHOD
Headache	Apply hot and cold poultices to nape of neck—2 minutes hot, 1 minute cold. Apply cold compresses to forehead; repeat frequently.
Sinusitis	Apply hot and cold sprays or sponge to face—2 minutes hot, 1 minute cold.
Sore throat, pain in swallowing	Apply cold compress to throat for 2 to 3 hours or overnight.
Painful cough	Apply hot and cold compresses to chest—3 minutes hot, 1 minute cold.
Pain or colic	Apply hot compresses to abdomen; repeat frequently.
Back, neck, or shoulder pains	Apply hot and cold poultices to the painful area—3 minutes hot, 1 minute cold, for 20 to 30 minutes, once or twice daily.
Knee, wrist, or ankle injuries or pain	Apply cold compresses to the painful area for 1 to 2 hours or overnight.

Mind Therapies

Many therapies focus on calming the mind in order to reduce the perception of pain, or visualize it in a form that makes it easier to manage. Others attempt to resolve psychological conflicts and anxieties that are often associated with pain and its causes.

AUTOGENIC TRAINING

Autogenic training is a system of self hypnosis in which special mental exercises are used to switch off stress reactions of the body and replace them with restful, relaxed states. It can help to relax the body prior to sleep, make the mind more receptive to change—for example, to stop bad habits—or to relieve painful illnesses. Autogenics literally means "generated from within" and was first developed by neurologist Dr. Johannes Schultz in the 1920s.

Method Autogenics is based on the principle of "passive concentration." With practice, subjects develop a state of deep relaxation so they can give themselves positive suggestions designed, for instance, to relieve tension, ease pain, or stop smoking. There are six basic exercises that can be done anywhere, whether sitting or lying down, to achieve a state of deep relaxation. These are taught over a series of sessions into which "intention exercises" are gradually introduced. Autogenic exercises are tailored to the individual and may entail a period of concentration on the area causing the trouble. For example, you might be asked to imagine that your arms are heavy or your legs are hot. By concentrating on specific bodily sensations you can create a state of deep relaxation and learn to focus your attention inward.

HOW IT CAN HELP

Autogenic training is effective for easing the pain from stress-related disorders. It can also relieve:

► Migraine
► High blood pressure
► Fatigue
► Stomach disorders
► Menstrual pain
► Menopausal pain

Result It is believed that release of muscular tensions and even repressed emotions such as anger and grief may account for the effectiveness of autogenics. Some patients experience dramatic reactions to the therapy when repressed emotions are released.

RELAXING AT HOME
The relaxation techniques can easily be performed in the workplace or at home.

PSYCHOTHERAPY

Psychotherapy is a term that covers a wide range of approaches to the mental and emotional experiences of pain. It involves talking and problem solving, either on a one-to-one or group basis. Pain is the perception of a signal from the nervous system. Suffering is the negative reaction that complicates it. Psychotherapy offers help with these emotional components, which can either be a result of the pain or can actually cause it.

Method Most psychological pain therapy is conducted by a trained therapist on a one-to-one basis. In group therapy people with common problems share their insights and experiences, with sessions usually monitored by a therapist. Any psychotherapeutic help must be used in conjunction with proper attention to the physical causes of the pain.

Counseling varies from the guidance provided by priests and religious leaders to the more structured interviews with specially trained psychotherapists. In either case the opportunity to express fears and anxieties about pain and its causes can release some of the physical tensions associated with it.

Result The question of whether psychotherapy can make a significant difference to the management of pain has for many years been a popular subject for research. Back in 1959 the British Journal of Medical Psychology reported a study in which therapy was used on a group of patients with musculoskeletal pain who also received physical therapy. A similar group received physical therapy only. Results showed that almost twice as many patients in the group receiving psychotherapy became pain-free compared with those in the control group.

HOW IT CAN HELP

Patients who have painful disorders caused by some deeper underlying emotional or psychological problem can benefit from psychotherapy. Tension, insomnia, and phobias may all be caused by psychological stresses. This approach can also be useful for physical ailments such as:

▶ Cardiovascular disorders, including high blood pressure and angina

▶ Stomach disorders

▶ Bowel problems

▶ Migraine and other headaches

BEHAVIORAL AND COGNITIVE PSYCHOTHERAPY

Faulty patterns of behavior, such as using pain as a way of seeking attention, can often reinforce the likelihood of pain becoming chronic. The aim of behavioral psychotherapy is to break such damaging thought cycles, reinforce positive behavior patterns, and teach people some coping mechanisms to help them deal with their pain.

Cognitive therapy is also commonly used in pain management. It is based on the notion that a person's thoughts, perceptions, and private interpretations can add to the distress of the physical symptoms he is experiencing. The major focus of this approach is to help patients change their thought patterns and plan and achieve goals for change.

HYPNOTHERAPY

Hypnotherapy was developed as part of psychotherapy to provide faster results and help in making an accurate analysis of a patient's problems. A candidate suitable for hypnosis is placed in a trance, to provide a therapist with greater access to his or her unconscious mind. With probing questions the therapist hopes to uncover emotional blocks that are preventing the patient from dealing with important life issues. These obstacles to free expression may be causing tension and stress-related problems such as headaches and chest pains.

Method While the patient is in a trance the therapist will suggest positive mental images that will help the patient to gain control over his or her physical condition. The practice of autosuggestion, or self-hypnosis, can also be taught to patients so that they can repeat the exercises at home. In some treatments, the therapist may explore the patient's subconscious mind in order to discover possible psychological causes of pain.

Result Hypnotism is effective at suppressing painful symptoms, but not necessarily the causes. With

HOW IT CAN HELP

Hypnotherapy is suitable for disorders that have a strong psychological element, such as phobias. It is also helpful in treating psychosomatic disorders and stress-related conditions.

hypnotherapy relief from pain is usually temporary and the patient should consider other ways to treat the cause. The main benefit for the patient may be the realization that the mind can play a significant role in the perception of pain.

VISUALIZATION

Visualization is based on the belief that the brain has a subconscious ability to heal, dating from primitive times in human development, which it cannot make use of on an intellectual level. By visualizing positive images it is possible to access this latent skill to modify, for example, nerve pathways that pass pain messages to the brain.

Using the close link between images and physical sensations, a patient can be trained to exercise his imagination so that he can increase the input of positive impulses to his brain. It is suggested that these impulses can close the pain gate to prevent pain messages from being transmitted—a mechanism similar to that involved in transcutaneous electrical nerve stimulation or TENS.

Method Visualization can be difficult to do at first, so it is better to learn the techniques from an expert and then practice them at home. The imagery that a therapist uses will depend on the nature of your pain. For example, if you feel a hot, burning sensation, your therapist might choose cool images of water or ice flowing over the affected area, or you might picture heat draining away like volcanic lava. Pain induced by cold or damp conditions may need the imagery of warmth and sunshine bathing the area.

Result Visualizasation therapy for cancer patients was developed by Dr. Karl Simonton. Simonton found that patients undergoing radiotherapy for cancer made better progress when they practiced a form of visual imagery of the body's defences overcoming the tumors.

The therapy is most effective when the imagery chosen by the patient is something with which the individual can identify, such as a sports team beating its opponents. Visualization is an integral part of many meditative and psychotherapeutic approaches. It is particularly effective when used in combination with deep breathing and relaxation exercises.

HOW IT CAN HELP

Visualization is suitable for almost any kind of physical or emotional problem. It is particularly helpful for relieving pain caused by:

► Cancer

► Angina

► Asthma

PRACTICING VISUALIZATION AT HOME

Visualization can help manage pain. The following are two examples of the method, but you will need to find images that work for you specifically:

▸ *Imagine that the pain is a fierce beast. Slowly build a wall around yourself to keep the beast away. Feel the pain ebb as the wall grows.*

▸ *See the pain as a shark. Surround yourself with dolphins to drive the sharks away. Feel the pain recede.*

MEDITATION

Meditation embraces various contemplative practices, both religious and secular, as well as the more dynamic forms of ritual dance and movement. Vigorous dances designed to induce trance-like states are performed to rapid drum beats, often as a prelude to impressive feats. For example, fire walkers can walk or run over a pit of burning embers, apparently without injuring their feet. The more accessible forms of meditation are those used in spiritual retreats for Christian and Buddhist contemplation and in disciplines, such as yoga, that have origins in Eastern mysticism.

Whether dynamic or contemplative, meditation has been shown to lift the brain into the alpha rhythm state, that is, a state of relaxed awareness somewhere between full consciousness and sleep. In this state pain impulses are likely to be less intense. Meditation is often used as a prelude to more focused approaches such as visualization.

Method You can meditate alone but may find it easier to get started if you practice with a group. Most people prefer a silent room, but if there is unavoidable background noise, playing tapes of music or sounds of nature may create a more conducive atmosphere. Your meditation teacher may give you a mantra, a personal image or word on which to focus. As you concentrate on your breathing, your mind will enter the alpha rhythm state. Try to meditate for about 10 minutes at a time.

Result Meditation can provide relief from stress and, when practiced on a regular basis, can lead to long-lasting effective pain relief.

HOW IT CAN HELP

Meditation is particularly effective at relieving chronic pain and discomfort caused by high levels of stress. It can also help to alleviate pain caused by:

► High blood pressure

► Circulation problems

► Chest complaints such as asthma

► Migraine

Relaxation Therapies

*Releasing muscular tensions and reducing mental ones
are essential to the management of pain. Rhythmical
breathing and other techniques not only relieve pain but
tap into the healing powers of relaxation.*

PROGRESSIVE MUSCULAR RELAXATION

Rhythmical breathing to relax the
muscles is the basis of most
relaxation therapies. It is an integral
part of yoga and other meditation
techniques as well as of autogenic
training. Many people use a
meditation-like imagery to heighten
the response, but often the process
of focusing on different areas of
the body or particular muscle
groups to relax them is enough to
concentrate the mind.

Method As with all relaxation
therapies it is important to find a
comfortable position. Lying flat on
your back with all joints free from
pressure or restriction is usually the
most suitable position. The nape of
the neck and the knees can be
supported with low pillows.
Alternatively, relaxation therapy
can be practiced in a sitting

*RELEASE OF TENSION
Muscular relaxation
techniques can be
used to provide
emergency stress
relief.*

HOW IT CAN HELP

*Progressive relaxation is useful as
part of pain management programs
and stress relief. It has been found
particularly effective in relieving
the chronic pains that often
accompany spinal injury.*

position, even at work, although it
will not be possible to let go quite
so completely.

It is best to learn relaxation
techniques from a professional
therapist and then practice at home.
A therapist will usually start by
encouraging you to establish a steady
breathing rhythm. You will then be
asked to focus the mind for a few
breaths on one area of the body, such
as the feet and legs, before moving
up through the body a little at a time.

Some therapists use alternate
tensing and relaxing techniques
in which the muscle groups
visualized are actively
tightened and then released
as the breath is forcefully
exhaled. Patients are trained
progressively in the use of such
techniques until they are able to
apply them on a daily basis at home
or in the workplace.

Result Patients who use this method
report a greater awareness of the
body and more feeling of control.

BIOFEEDBACK

Biofeedback training allows a person to gain a measure of control over bodily functions that are usually automatic, or involuntary—for example, heartbeat, blood pressusre, skin temperature, even brain-wave patterns. Electronic monitors used to measure these responses produce visible or audible signals. During the training, a person learns how to alter the electronic signals and, in the process, change an involuntary bodily response.

Method The therapist will attach biofeedback electrodes to the skin, or alternatively the patient may be asked to hold the electrodes. Biofeedback instruments can work in a number of ways: some measure blood pressure or brain waves, others detect changes in pulse or skin temperature, the latter indicating shifts in blood flow. These changes are usually indicated by a sound that changes in pitch or intensity or by a needle or dial that rises or falls. As the person relaxes and tension is released, the sound diminishes or the needle moves back. This is known as feedback and gives users a clear sign

that they are achieving a measure of control over a particular bodily function or a more relaxed state. In time, patients learn to achieve this control or state without the aid of a biofeedback monitor.

Biofeedback is valuable as a tool for learning general relaxation techniques and can be used in a more focused way in specific pain areas. For example, some biofeedback monitors can be used to teach patients how to reduce their blood pressure, which is a vital to managing stress-related heart conditions. Others can help migrain sufferers to redirect some of the blood flow from constricted blood vessels in the head to their hands, and thus reduce pain.

Result Biofeedback has been found to be more effective in the management of head and neck pain than back pain. Some studies have shown that, over time, biofeedback tends to be more useful for easing nervous tension than reducing muscle tension. But overall, biofeedback helps patients become more active participants in their own treatment.

HOW IT CAN HELP

Biofeedback is particularly useful for achieving long-lasting relief from pain associated with nervous disorders such as fibromyalgia. It has also proved effective at reducing pain caused by stress, but is less effective in the treatment of depression-related ailments. If used in conjunction with yoga or other relaxation techniques, it can help to alleviate pain associated with:

▶ High blood pressure

▶ Migraine

▶ Heart disease

▶ Childbirth

BODY MONITORS
Biofeedback monitors detect unconscious body processes such as pulse, blood pressure, and sweat.

FLOTATION AND SENSORY DEPRIVATION

A flotation tank is an enclosed chamber in which the patient floats in water at skin temperature and in total darkness and silence. This sensory isolation tank gives complete freedom from external stimuli and enables the thoughts to focus inward. It is said to help the user gain greater control of the body and reduce blood pressure or pain.

Method The tank contains 10 to 12 in (25 to 30 cm) of water at 93.5°F (34.2°C), in which Epsom salts and other minerals have been dissolved to give buoyancy. You will be asked to take a shower before entering the

tank. The therapist will give you earplugs, to prevent irritation from the minerals, and an inflatable pillow to support your head. You will then be left in total darkness to float in the water for 15 to 30 minutes. If desired, you can have soothing music tapes played to aid meditation and visualization while in the tank.

Result An hour in a flotation tank is said to be the equivalent of 4 hours' sleep and can produce a state of deep relaxation. The method is an excellent stress reliever, and the benefits can last up to four days.

HOW IT CAN HELP

Flotation is effective at inducing a deep feeling of relaxation and can help to minimize pain resulting from stress-related ailments. Recent research into the reasons for its effectiveness at relieving pain suggests that floating somehow stimulates the release of the body's natural painkillers, endorphins.

▶ High blood pressure

▶ Heart disease

▶ Digestive ailments such as irritable bowel syndrome

▶ Migraine

▶ Sleep disorders, such as insomnia

CHAPTER 5

HEAD AND THROAT PAIN

Many painful conditions that affect the head, neck, and throat can be successfully treated at home with natural therapies. Most ailments produce distinctive symptoms, and with a knowledge of how these match the types of pain affecting an area of distress, you can learn to distinguish when it is possible to deal with pain safely at home and when you should consult a doctor.

HEADACHES

Most headaches emanate from tension, stress, or a minor illness or disorder, but occasionally they can act as a warning of a serious condition and should be investigated by a doctor.

MIGRAINE TRIGGERS
Eating cheese, chocolate, or citrus fruits, or drinking red wine can trigger migraine attacks in some people. Other triggers include waiting too long between meals, being overtired, or having too much or too little sleep. Stress and such emotions as worry and excitement have also been linked to migraine. Although depression can trigger migraines in susceptible individuals, research has shown that people who suffer from migraines are not as a group unusually anxious or depressed.

Pain in the head may have a variety of causes, among them, muscle spasm, nervous tension, or a trapped nerve caused by a crick in the neck. When the muscles in the head, face, or neck go into spasm, the blood vessels surrounding them become over-constricted and then compensate for the constriction by dilating. Nerve fibers respond to the stretching of the blood vessels by sending pain messages to the brain. The pain may be felt all over the head or it may occur in one part only. The sensation experienced can range from a superficial ache to a deep throbbing pain caused by blood rushing through the dilated arteries

By providing an accurate description of your headaches, including frequency and the pattern of occurrence, you can help your doctor to diagnose the problem and find the appropriate treatment. For example, a severe incapacitating headache that gets worse over time requires urgent medical attention, as it might indicate a dangerous brain disorder such as a tumor. However, most headaches are a reaction to unhealthful lifestyle traits such as irregular meals, poor posture, or relentless stress. Eyestrain, infection, an adverse reaction to particular foods, air conditioning, hangovers, lack of sleep, menstrual disorders, certain prescribed drugs, and dental problems can also be responsible. In these cases the headache can be safely and successfully treated at home with simple painkillers, herbal medicine, or relaxation. In the longer term a change in lifestyle is probably required to prevent the headache from recurring. More problematic are tension headaches and migraines, which are not life-threatening conditions, but they can disrupt a sufferer's life, causing persistent incapacitating pain, sometimes accompanied by nausea and sight disturbance.

Migraines

Migraines are severe headaches that can last from a few hours to several days. They are caused by changes in the brain stem, which cause the blood vessels to constrict. Blood flow then becomes reduded to some parts of the brain, and the constricted arteries start to dilate and stretch the sensitive nerve fibers around them, causing intense pain. Migraines almost always affect just one side of the head, and the pain is severe and throbbin, and often accompanied by nau-

---

PROCESS OF A MIGRAINE

Migraines may be caused by tension, triggered by factors such as fatigue or stress. This sets off a sequence of events leading to pain. Many women are prone to migraines just prior to menstruation, because of hormonal changes.

| Changes occur in the brain stem. | Blood vessels around the brain become constricted. | Supply of oxygen to the brain is reduced. | Blood vessels respond by dilating. | Nerve endings respond to stretching by sending a pain message. |

sea, vomiting, and hot flushes that alternate with shivering spells. As the hours pass, the pounding pain becomes a steady ache, but after a period of sleep it often subsides.

Although migraine pain can sometimes be relieved with painkillers, the possibility of side effects make this treatment less desirable. Strategies for managing migraines should focus more on preventing their occurrence than the use of drugs. Migraines may be triggered by a number of factors including stress, certain foods, and changes in routine and environment. Note down what you eat and drink and any resulting headache in a pain diary (see page 44). This may help you to pinpoint a trigger factor, such as red wine or too little sleep.

Treatment For many migraine sufferers, lying in a darkened room may be the only way of dealing with an attack. The herbal remedy feverfew (*Tanacetum parthenium*) has been shown to be effective in many cases, but only if taken every day as a preventative; once a headache starts it is of little value. The recommended dosage is a daily supplement of 125 milligrams, containing at least 0.2 percent of the active ingredient parthenolide. You can obtain

HEADACHE REMEDY

Whenever you feel a headache coming on, try brushing it away, using a moderately stiff hairbrush or your fingers to massage the scalp and relieve muscle tension:

■ *Starting above your eyebrow, draw the hairbrush over your scalp, back above the ear, and down the back of the neck.*

■ *Go back to the top of the eyebrow and repeat the stroke again, starting an inch to the right of the previous stroke.*

■ *Continue with brush strokes until you have done the entire head.*

■ *Repeat every hour after pain relief to make sure the headache does not return.*

FIGHTING HEADACHES

Instead of using painkillers, you can adopt other strategies to help prevent headaches from recurring. Some you can practice safely at home; for others you will need to visit a practitioner of alternative medicine.

▶ *Research has shown that Transcutaneous electrical nerve stimulation, also known as TENS (see page 83), can be effective at easing migraine pain. Equipment that sends out a mild electrical current to relax muscles painlessly is available for home use.*

▶ *For headaches with pain at the side of the head, do acupressure with your thumbs; press underneath the base of your skull in the hollow areas on either side of the two vertical neck muscles. Tilt your head back with eyes closed and continue pressing for 1 to 2 minutes as you breathe deeply.*

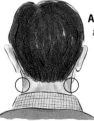

Acupressure You can apply acupressure to your neck yourself, or ask your partner or a friend to help you.

▶ *Exercise has the effect of dilating the blood vessels. This means that a brisk walk, swim, or bicycle ride can actually prevent blood vessels in the head from becoming constricted and sparking a headache. If you are already suffering a headache, exercise can help to return the blood vessels to their normal size and also stimulate the release of soothing endorphins. Regular walking, jogging, or swimming can help to prevent the build up of tension in the neck and shoulders. However, always consult your doctor before starting a new exercise program.*

▶ *Use your shower for hydrotherapy to relax your head and neck muscles. Adjust the water temperature as hot as is comfortable and direct the jet onto your back, neck, shoulders, and scalp for at least five minutes. Massage the muscles at the same time. Once you feel relaxed, run cool water over the same areas for several minutes.*

Hydrotherapy You can practice hydrotherapy in your own home quite easily, using a shower or shower attachment.

▶ *In a 1996 study by the Royal Danish School of Pharmacy, 81 per cent of migraine patients said they felt that reflexology had cured (16%) or helped (65%) their symptoms. Just under 20% said it enabled them to do without prescription medication.*

▶ *Aromatherapy can prevent the onset of a headache. When you feel symptoms coming on, mix 1 or 2 drops of lavender oil with 5 drops of olive oil and massage in a circular motion across your temples, behind the ears, and on the back of the neck.*

Herbal baths Ease tension by adding 3 drops each of lavender oil, marjoram, and chamomile essential oils to a bath.

TEETH CLENCHING

Some studies have suggested that prolonged periods of teeth clenching can trigger the release of substances called neuropeptides, which in turn can start a migraine. Current research indicates that if you can control teeth clenching, you may be able to prevent migraine attacks.

▶ *When not chewing, aim to keep the teeth slightly apart.*

▶ *Try chewing sugar-free gum to help kick the habit.*

▶ *Prevent clenching during sleep by doing relaxation therapies before bedtime (see page 91).*

▶ *If you have a serious problem, your dentist can provide you with an appliance to prevent teeth clenching. This fits over the lower teeth and is worn at night.*

> **WARNING**
> Consult a doctor immediately if a headache comes on suddenly for no apparent reason and occurs with any of these symptoms:
> ▶ *weakness, numbness, or tingling in the limbs*
> ▶ *partial loss of consciousness*
> ▶ *a high fever*
> ▶ *skin rash*

feverfew tablets from health food stores. You can also drink it as infusion. by pouring boiling water over freshly picked leaves.
▶ see also manipulative, massage, energy, natural, mind, relaxation therapies

Temporomandibular disorder (TMD)

The temporomandibular joint connects the lower jaw bone with the temporal bone of the skull. When this joint and the muscles and ligaments that support it fail to function properly, the result can be pain in the head, jaw, and face. grinding the teeth together constantly and tensing the jaw muscles frequently are two major causes of TMD. Patients typically complain of a stiff jaw or difficulty in opening the mouth, tenderness over the jaw joint, and a clicking sound. Sufferers often mistakenly believe that the pain is coming from the ear or that the joint is damaged. Although TMD can lead to arthritis of the temporomandibular joint, this is a rare occurrence.

Treatment This depends on the severity of the problem. Painkillers can be helpful, also a hot compress applied to the painful area, jaw exercises, a soft diet, TENS (see page 83), and physiotherapy. Teeth covers can also be effective (see far left).
▶ see also manipulative, movement, massage, energy, relaxation therapies

FACIAL PAIN

Pain in the face may be due to a variety of causes, such as injury or infection, but frequently it may occur for no apparent reason. Pain may originate in the face itself be referred to the face from other parts of the body. The nerves supplying sensation to the face, including the sinuses, teeth, and surfaces of the eyes, nose, and skin, are all branches of the trigeminal nerves. One of these main nerves supplies the right side and another supplies the left. This means that if there is damage to one part of the face served by a trigeminal nerve, it may be felt in another branch of the same nerve. For example, a patient may feel certain that the pain is from a tooth, when in fact the pain may be referred to the tooth from a sinus problem on the same side.

In addition, an individual's psychological state can influence facial pain by mechanisms that are not fully understood. It is estimated that 10 per cent of patients who are depressed also suffer from facial pain.

Sinus pain

In the skull and face there are 14 sinuses, or air-filled cavities in the bones. Infections, blockages, local growths, or tumors can all

---

SINUSES

The word sinus is used generally to describe the air-filled cavities in the bones surrounding the nose (see right). These sinuses are lined with membranes that can become inflamed and cause pain. Known as sinusitis, this condition may be due to bacterial infection or, in some cases, a tooth abscess.

THE SYMPTOMS OF SINUSITIS
Typical symptoms of sinusitis are a sensation of tightness in the affected area, which may develop into a throbbing pain, fever, a blocked nose, and loss of the sense of smell.

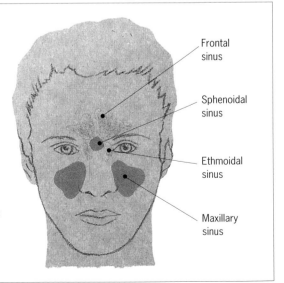

Frontal sinus

Sphenoidal sinus

Ethmoidal sinus

Maxillary sinus

give rise to problems with the sinuses. Most commonly, sinus pain is caused by an acute bacterial or viral infection such as the common cold. Infection spreads from the nose inflames the membrane lining the sinus. Chronic sinus problems may be caused by small growths in the nose, smoking, irritant fumes and smells, and common respiratory and food allergies.

Treatment To open up the air passages and help drain excessive mucus from the sinuses, try aromatherapy oils or steam. One good remedy is to place a few drops of eucalyptus oil on a hankie and inhale deeply. To relieve pain, sponge the face and sinus areas with hot and cold water alternately (2 minutes hot and 1 minute cold).

If you feel a dull ache in your forehead, a simple acupressure technique may be helpful. Place the thumb and index finger of your left hand on either side of the bridge of the nose near the eyebrows. With the fingers and heel of your right hand grasp the muscles on either side of the spine at the back of the neck. Put pressure on all four points simultaneously while you breathe deeply for 1 minute.

If symptoms persist your doctor will usually prescribe antibiotics to clear up the infection. In more severe cases surgery may be required to prevent further blockage.

▶ *see also manipulative, massage, energy, natural, relaxation therapies*

Trigeminal neuralgia

Trigeminal neuralgia (TGN) is a painful disorder of one or both of the trigeminal nerves (see opposite page), a condition that mostly affects people over the age of 40. Sufferers complain of a severe incapacitating pain, which normally lasts for just a few seconds and is often described as lancinating, or like an electric shock. The pain can affect any area served by the trigeminal nerves but most commonly is felt in the midface region.

Treatment Acupuncture, acupressure, and hydrotherapy can be effective at treating TGN. If you feel facial pain coming on, it may help to press the end of your eyebrow near your nose with your finger. Alternating hot and cold compresses to the area can also be effective: use a hot compress for 3 minutes and a cold compress for 1 minute, for a total of 20 minutes. As stress may be a contributing factor to the pain, relaxation therapies may be particularly useful. To relax

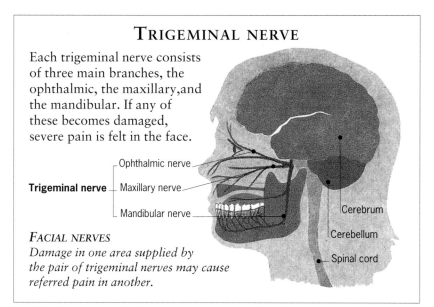

TRIGEMINAL NERVE

Each trigeminal nerve consists of three main branches, the ophthalmic, the maxillary, and the mandibular. If any of these becomes damaged, severe pain is felt in the face.

Trigeminal nerve
- Ophthalmic nerve
- Maxillary nerve
- Mandibular nerve

Cerebrum
Cerebellum
Spinal cord

FACIAL NERVES
Damage in one area supplied by the pair of trigeminal nerves may cause referred pain in another.

the nervous system, add 2 drops each of essential oil of lavender and basil to a steam inhalation, a bath, or a massage oil. Some sufferers have found relief by taking up to 600 mg daily of vitamins B_1, B_6, and B_{12}. These can help to improve nerve function.

The conventional treatment for trigeminal neuralgia is carbamazepine. If this drug fails to control the pain or causes serious side-effects, surgery is usually recommended.

▶ *see also massage, energy, natural therapies*

Atypical facial pain

Atypical facial pain (AFP) is a condition that most commonly affects middle-aged women. Sufferers usually complain of constant pain over a bony area on one side of the face. If you suffer from this type of pain, it is essential to consult a doctor so that he or she can perform tests to rule out the possibility of serious bone or sinus disease.

Treatment Depression sometimes contributes to AFP in these cases meditation and hypnotherapy may help limit the recurrence of attacks. Therapies that work on the body's energy pathways, such as shiatsu, acupuncture, acupressure, and TENS may also be effective. Conventional treatment also addresses the emotional aspects of the pain, and so antidepressants are commonly prescribed for AFP. However, a lower dosage is given than that for patients who suffer from clinical depression. Treatment is generally successful, although the drugs may be prescribed over months or even years and must be taken daily throughout this period.

▶ *see also massage, mind, relaxation therapies*

97

EAR, MOUTH, AND THROAT PAIN

Problems with the ear, mouth, and throat can usually be diagnosed quickly and treated successfully, but dental treatment or special tests may sometimes be necessary.

The ears, mouth, and throat are among the most sensitive organs in the body and consequently are susceptible to a variety of disorders. Many of the commonest conditions are easily treated at home.

EARACHE

Earache is an extremely common problem, particularly in children. The most prevalent cause is infection, which can affect one of three parts of the ear: the outer, middle, or inner section. Occasionally, pain may feel as if it is in the ear when in reality it results from problems in the neighboring neck or throat areas, which are served by the same nerves as the ear.

Problems of the outer ear

Soreness and inflammation, with scaly skin surrounding the area and sometimes a slight watery discharge, are generally signs of problems of the outer ear. These symptoms may indicate a common condition, otitis externa, which is essentially a skin problem. There may also be a strong desire to poke the ear with anything that might be available, such as a matchstick or pen, but this could damage the eardrum. Excessive ear wax, a secretion produced by glands in the outer ear, can also cause irritation. Boils in the ear canal, which can produce considerable discomfort, require medical attention.

Treatment Warm almond oil applied with a cotton ball can relieve minor skin problems affecting the outer ear and also soften ear wax so it can be removed more easily. However, if problems persist you should consult a doctor, because it may be necessary to clean the ear canal. This should not be attempted at home, as the use of cotton swabs or other implements may simply push the ear wax deeper into the canal.

THE EAR

The most common disorders of the ear occur in the middle section, which includes the eardrum, malleus, incus, stapes, and eustachian tube. In most cases earache is due to infection.

EAR CARE
The ears are delicate organs vital for balance and hearing. They should be safeguarded from excessive noise.

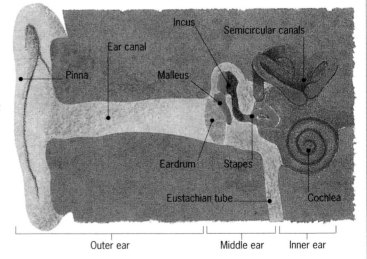

Problems of the middle ear

If earache is associated with impaired hearing, the problem is usually in the middle ear. This type of earache is often experienced during an airplane flight (see right). Pain in the middle ear due to infection is common in children. The reason is that their eustachian tubes, which regulate air pressure in the middle ear, are shorter, so infections can easily spread from the throat. When there is inflammation and a build-up of fluid in the middle ear, this a condition called otitis media. If pressure builds up behind the eardrum, severe earache ensues and the eardrum may rupture, relieving pressure and easing pain. The eardrum soon heals and there is normally no lasting damage.

Treatment Otitis media is usually treated with antibiotics. In cases of chronic otitis media, a small tube, or grommet, may be inserted into the eardrum to allow fluid to escape and prevent a build-up of pressure.

Problems of the inner ear

If you experience ringing in the ears, dizziness or disturbance of balance, you should consult your doctor, as these symptoms could indicate Ménière's disease, a disorder of the inner ear that can lead to hearing loss.

MOUTH PAIN

The mouth has a complex structure, reflecting its important role in eating, drinking, and speaking. As many diseases caused by bacteria, viruses, or fungi can be transmitted orally, it is very vulnerable to infection.

Mouth ulcers

A mouth ulcer is a break in the lining of the mouth. Most common are aphthous (pronounced apthus) ulcers which occur alone or in groups on the inside of the lips, the cheeks, or underneath the tongue. Affecting about 1 in 5 of the adult population, minor aphthous ulcers are recurrent and heal in about two weeks. The commonest cause is a deficiency in minerals and vitamins, particularly iron and some of the B vitamins. Stopping smoking often leads to aphthous ulcers for reasons that are unclear. Biting the lip or tongue can also trigger these ulcers in susceptible individuals.

Treatment Research has shown that 40 per cent of aphthous ulcer patients have low levels of vitamin B_2 and B_6. If you suffer from aphthous ulcers, taking supplements of these vitamins for four weeks may help prevent further outbreaks. The recommended dietary allowances for adults are 1.3 to 1.7 mg of vitamin B_2 and 1.6 to 2 mg of vitamin B_6 per day.

If you continue to suffer from aphthous ulcers and you don't respond to vitamin B_2 and B_6 therapy, it is worth considering other factors such as a food allergy. The main food substances that trigger aphthous ulcers are benzoates (food additives), cinnamon, and chocolate. Benzoates are found principally in carbonated drinks, particularly diet sodas. (Regular and diet 7-Up contain no benzoates.) Cinnamon is found in curries, cakes, cookies, and tartar control toothpastes. If products containing these substances are avoided, aphthous ulcers tend to heal quickly and not recur.

▶ *see also energy, natural therapies*

Cold sores

Cold sores are small blisters that form around the mouth. They are caused by a herpes virus (*herpes simplex*) often acquired in childhood. The initial infection can produce widespread mouth and lip ulcers. After the first outbreak the virus hides in the nerves that supply the lips and facial region, and if it is reactivated, causes new cold sores. Among the conditions that can trigger cold sores are sunlight, menstruation, a cold, trauma, or stress, or they may appear for no apparent reason. Cold sores are highly infectious when the blisters are moist, and sufferers can transfer the virus to other sites on their own body, such as the nailbed or the eyes. The virus can also be transmitted to other people by direct contact, for example, during kissing or oral sex.

Treatment The conventional treatment for cold sores is an ointment like acyclovir cream, which effectively reduces the severity and duration of an attack. Note that ointments and creams are more effective if applied as soon as the first tingle of a developing cold sore is experienced. It is also important to spread the cream over a much larger area than the tingle seems to cover.

Applying an ice cube to a lesion for an hour or so when it first appears can help inhibit the virus and speed healing. Dipping a cotton ball in cold milk, geranium oil, or lemon juice and applying it to the sore has the same effect. These remedies can also help relieve pain.

EASING AIRPLANE EARACHE

Both adults and children can experience earache during an airplane flight. This is brought on by rapid changes in barometric pressure as the plane takes off and descends for landing. Following are some things you can do to ease the discomfort.

▶ *Take a deep breath, pinch your nose shut, close your mouth, and try to breathe out but don't do so. Swallow at the same time.*

▶ *Suck a hard candy or chew gum on take off and landing to encourage vigorous swallowing.*

▶ *When flying with a baby, breast or bottle feed the infant during takeoff and landing. The sucking action and swallowing will help to equalize air pressure in the baby's ears.*

SORE THROAT ANTIDOTES

To ease the pain caused by a sore throat, try any of the following:

■ *Twice daily gargle with an infusion of red sage or thyme, made with 2 teaspoons of leaves steeped for 10 minutes in ¾ cup (6 fluid ounces) of boiling water.*

■ *Sip chicken broth to help ease congestion.*

■ *Eat foods rich in zinc, such as meat and fortified cereals, or suck on zinc lozenges, to assist your immune system in the healing process.*

■ *Mix 2 drops each of eucalyptus and peppermint oils with 2 teaspoons of carrier oil and apply to the chest and throat area.*

To prevent the recurrence of cold sores, it may help to take tablets of L-lysine, an amino acid that counteracts arginine, another amino acid on which the herpes virus thrives. Other natural remedies include garlic pills and echinacea tablets (to stimulate the immune system) and yogurt or pills that contain acidophilus. Avoid salty and acidic foods until the lesion heals completely.

▶ *see also massage, energy therapies*

SORE THROATS

A sore throat may be the first symptom of a cold, the flu, or laryngitis, as well as many childhood illnesses such as chickenpox and mumps. In most cases the condition lasts only a few days and, provided the sufferer has an adequate fluid intake and no other symptoms emerge, it is usually not serious enough to warrant a visit to a doctor.

Treatment Try gargling with a soluble painkiller such as aspirin or acetaminophen before swallowing it. Alternatively, gargling with salt or an herbal mixture such as sage or thyme (see left) or 2 drops of essential oil of lemon and sandalwood mixed with warm water will help soothe the throat.

Acute tonsillitis

Tonsillitis is an inflammation of the tonsils due to infection. This highly infectious condition can be distinguished from a general sore throat by looking at the back of the throat. With acute tonsillitis the throat is inflamed and there are white spots on the tonsils. Often it is accompanied by fever.

Treatment If acute tonsillitis is suspected, it is probably best to stay at home and rest.

Gargling a warm infusion of sage or soluble aspirin can help. Antibiotics can shorten the duration and severity of tonsillitis caused by bacteria (strains of streptococcus are the most common culprits). With viral tonsillitis, the condition usually clears up on its own within a few days.

TOOTH AND GUM PAIN

The gums are the soft tissue surrounding the teeth. When healthy, they are firm and pink or brown. Gum disease causes the gum tissue to become inflamed. If this happens to you, blood may appear on your toothbrush or on an apple you've bitten into.

Infected gums

Gums are particularly susceptible to the infections gingivitis and periodontitis. Of the two, periodontitis is the more serious and is a leading cause of tooth loss in adults. These conditions are caused by bacteria, but the bacteria responsible are different from those that cause tooth decay. Incomplete brushing allows plaque and tartar to build up on the teeth. Also known as calculus, tartar is formed when existing plaque becomes calcified from minerals in the saliva. This causes the gum around the margin of the tooth to become inflamed and reduces the periodontal ligament, which anchors the tooth in the bone, so that the gum bleeds easily during brushing or flossing.

Always attend to gum problems immediately. If you don't, inflammation around the tooth will increase and more of the periodontal ligament will be lost. Eventually, the bony support of the tooth will erode, leading to bad breath and tooth loss. This process, which takes many years, is painless and occurs even when gums look healthy.

Treatment To maintain healthy teeth and gums, eat a well-balanced diet that includes foods containing calcium (good sources are dairy products and leafy green vegetables) and whole grains, nuts, and raw vegetables. These last three stimulate saliva production, which is a natural defense against decay caused by plaque. Equally important to good dental health are careful brushing of the teeth, using a soft toothbrush, for at least two to three minutes twice a day; flossing at least once a day; and having a dental check-up and cleaning every six months.

Some people report that chewing cardomom seeds helps to keep gums healthy.

TEETH AND GUMS

The pulp, the most sensitive part of the tooth, contains nerves and blood vessels and is protected by dentine and enamel. The periodontal ligament acts as a shock absorber, cushioning the teeth and jaw when food is chewed.

TEETH CARE
Regular cleaning by a dental hygienist helps control plaque and prevent gum problems.

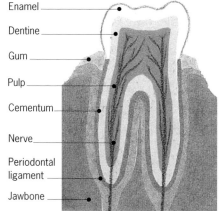

Enamel
Dentine
Gum
Pulp
Cementum
Nerve
Periodontal ligament
Jawbone

TOOTH DECAY

If the protective enamel coating of a tooth becomes weakened, it may become eroded. Cavities soon start to form and sweet or very hot or cold food and drink then have access to the inner dentine layer and can cause sharp pain. Bacteria enter the cavities, leading to an infection that can spread through the tooth.

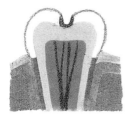

Acids formed from the breakdown of food wear away areas of enamel.

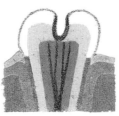

Bacteria enter cavities in the enamel and attack the underlying dentine.

Decay spreads to the pulp at the center of the tooth, causing toothache.

The pulp is destroyed, the tooth dies, and infection may spread. Pain subsides.

PREVENTING TOOTH DECAY

You can help to prevent painful tooth problems with a few simple measures:

▶ *Limit sugar intake. The more frequent the sugar intake, the more frequently teeth are exposed to an acid environment.*

▶ *Brush teeth twice daily and use floss every day.*

▶ *Have a dental check-up and cleaning every six months.*

▶ *Consider using fluoride supplements, treatments, and/or toothpastes. Fluoride can toughen a tooth against acid attack by strengthening the mineral composition of the enamel. However, too much fluoride can cause fluorosis—a dark mottling of the teeth. Children should use a very small amount of toothpaste that contains fluoride and should not be given fluoride tablets without first consulting a dentist.*

Also, a mouthwash made with 5 to 10 drops of myrrh in a cup of warm water helps control mouth bacteria. For bleeding and inflamed gums, rinse your mouth for 1 minute with several mouthfuls of a 0.1 per cent solution of folic acid and then swallow.

▶ see also *massage, energy, natural therapies*

Teeth problems

The main problem affecting teeth is decay caused by plaque—food, saliva, and bacteria, which coats the teeth and turns sugars into acids. These acids bleach minerals from the teeth in a process called demineralization. Initially, the outer surface of the tooth enamel remains intact but the demineralization shows up as a white spot. At this stage, the tooth decay is painless. If the process continues, however, bacteria can invade the inner dentine layer and pain will develop.

If the condition is left untreated, the infected pulp will die, often leading to a dental abscess. This is a pus-filled sac that forms as infection spreads into the tissue around the root of the tooth. The tooth aches constantly, the surrounding gum becomes red, swollen, and tender, and chewing is very painful. The abscess may spread through the tissues and into the jaw bone, causing inflammation and swelling in the face and neck. A serious infection can destroy bone around the root area.

Treatment Minor tooth decay can be treated by a simple dental filling. However, if the pulp of a tooth is affected, as in irreversible pulpitis, it must be removed and the tooth filled. If an abscess forms, your dentist may prescribe antibiotics to treat the infection. The dentist will need to drain the abscess to release the build-up of pus, before extracting the tooth. After a tooth has been removed, blood fills the tooth socket and clots; over a period of several weeks the area will heal up completely. Occasionally, and particularly in the case of lower molar teeth, the blood clot does not form properly, causing a painful condition known as dry socket. This can be relieved with a zinc oxide dressing from the dentist. Alternatively, for any tooth pain, oil of cloves applied to the painful area provides short-term relief.

▶ see also *massage, energy, natural therapies*

Other causes of toothache

Your dentist may take X-rays of the teeth, jaws, and sinuses to discount other causes of pain such as sinusitis (see page 96). Irritation of the sinus linings can stimulate the nerves in the teeth and mimic toothache, because the roots of the upper teeth project into the maxillary sinuses, This condition is usually easy to distinguish from the pain associated with tooth decay because it affects several teeth at the same time.

Toothache may also be due to receding gums, which expose the cementum, the layer that covers the root. Tooth-brushing can wear away the cementum, thus exposing the underlying dentine and making the tooth susceptible to pulpitis. Receding gums may be treated by sealing off the dentine with dental adhesive. Rarely, toothache may indicate a problem with the facial bones such as misalignment of the jaw.

THE EYES

The eye is a complex organ that converts images into nerve signals and sends them to the brain for analysis. Most pain in the eyes is minor, but in serious cases the sight may be at risk.

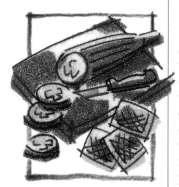

TREATING YOUR EYES

To ease tired, aching eyes, take time to give them a special treat:

■ *For sore eyes, bathe them with a mixture of juice from an aloe vera plant and warm water.*

■ *For swollen, baggy eyes, place cold used tea bags or cucumber slices over each eye.*

■ *For dry tired eyes, bathe them with a solution made by boiling a pint of water with a pinch of baking soda. (Cool the solution first.)*

Minor disorders of the eye and the area surrounding it can be safely treated at home, either with conventional or alternative health-care methods. More serious conditions must be treated by professionals. Although painful eye problems are often accompanied by loss of vision, many serious progressive conditions are painless, making self-diagnosis difficult. You can help to avoid serious eye problems by reporting the onset of any symptoms promptly to your ophthalmologist. You should rest your eye muscles at regular intervals during concentrated use and wear protective eye gear when doing potentially harmful activities such as working with a drill or blowtorch.

Preventing eyestrain

If your work involves concentrated use of the eyes, such as for reading or using a computer, rest your eye muscles every half hour. You can do this by focusing on an object in the distance. Without taking your eyes off the object, gently sway from side to side.

If you wear contact lenses, keep your lense containers as clean as possible to prevent infection (using distilled water or boiled tap water). Eat plenty of green and yellow vegetables for vitamin A, the essential vitamin for healthy eyes. Wear optical quality sunglasses in the snow and in bright sunlight to avoid damage from ultra violet light.

Chronic glaucoma

Chronic glaucoma is a potentially blinding condition, but is completely treatable if diagnosed early. Affecting 1 in 200 of the population over the age of 40, this common condition is caused by damage to nerve fibers from excessive pressure of the fluid in the eye. Although glaucoma is often painless in the early stages, if not detected it can cause severe pain in and around the eye and loss of vision in the later stages. The condition is detected by measuring eye pressure, and should be done as part of a routine examination by an ophthalmomogist. You should see an eye doctor immediately if you experience unfamiliar pain in the eyes, loss of peripheral vision, or blurring of vision.

Treatment Most forms of glaucoma can be controlled by taking regular medication, usually eye drops, but sometimes tablets or capsules. In some cases, minor eye surgery is needed to reduce fluid pressure in the eye.

MAKING AN EYE BATH

To make a soothing eye bath, add 1 teaspoon of eyebright to a teacup of boiling water. Cover and leave to cool, then strain through coffee filter paper and use the solution to bathe the eyes.

USING AN EYE BATH
To bathe the eye, half fill an eye cup, hold it against your eye, and tilt your head back.

CAUTION
If you experience any of the following symptoms consult a doctor: redness of the eye, sudden loss of vision, black spots that obstruct vision, flashing lights, double vision, excessive watering of an eye accompanied by pain.

CHAPTER 6

CHEST AND ABDOMINAL PAIN

From heartburn to heart attack, from indigestion to appendicitis, pain may occur in the chest or the abdomen for reasons that vary hugely in seriousness. A knowledge of the different kinds of pain and their underlying causes can help you decide whether your symptoms indicate a minor problem or a serious condition that requires urgent medical investigation.

CHEST PAIN

Many people panic unnecessarily when they experience chest pain. Very often problems are minor and easily treated. Some kinds of chest pain, however, require careful monitoring.

PREVENTING HEARTBURN

Heartburn is often associated with overeating or with rich and spicy foods. By paying careful attention to your diet and general health you can help to prevent the condition.

▶ *Eat small meals.*

▶ *Avoid fatty foods, including those with hidden fat such as pastry.*

▶ *If you are overweight, go on a reducing diet.*

▶ *Wear loose clothing and avoid tight belts.*

▶ *Relax before and after eating.*

▶ *If you get heartburn at night in bed, raise the head end of the bed or use additional pillows to elevate the upper part of your body.*

▶ *Avoid stooping at the waist.*

▶ *Stop smoking. This habit reduces the effectiveness of the cardiac sphincter (see right).*

Many chest complaints are caused by minor problems such as a strained muscle or heartburn. In some cases, however, chest pain may indicate a condition that needs urgent medical investigation—a heart attack, for instance. Several causes of chest pain are outlined below, along with self-help treatments and guidance on when to seek medical advice.

Heartburn

Heartburn is a common complaint, usually described as a burning sensation behind the sternum, or breast bone. It is caused by a backflow of acids from the stomach into the gullet, or esophagus, the tube that carries food to the stomach. This usually occurs because of a failure of a ring of muscle called the cardiac sphincter, which separates the esophagus from the stomach. When functioning normally, this muscle opens to allow food through and then closes to keep it inside the stomach (see below). Heartburn is often brought on by overeating, or by eating spicy or fatty foods, which relax the sphincter. Certain beverages such as coffee, cola, and beer can intensify the pain of heartburn because they increase the acidity of stomach juices. Lying down or bending over, can also precipitate the pain. Mild, infrequent heartburn does not usually require medical investigation, but if it gets worse or cannot be controlled by simple measures, you should seek medical help, because the symptoms may indicate a more serious condition such as esophagitis (inflammation of the esophagus).

Treatment During an attack of heartburn, sit up. If it's a bad attack at night you may find it more comfortable to sleep in a chair. Antacids are usually effective, and drinking milk can be helpful. Hot compresses placed over the stomach can improve the blood supply to the area and relax the muscles. Conventional over-the-counter medicines, including antacids to neutralize the stomach

---

WHY HEARTBURN BURNS

The cardiac sphincter muscle connects the esophagus with the stomach. If this muscle fails to close properly, stomach acids can flow back into the esophagus. Here, the acids cause the burning pain typically associated with heartburn, since the lining of the esophagus is not as well protected as the stomach lining.

THE STOMACH'S VALVE
The cardiac sphincter muscle stops the contents of the stomach from flowing back into the esophagus.

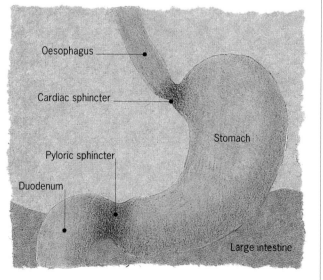

Oesophagus

Cardiac sphincter

Pyloric sphincter

Stomach

Duodenum

Large intestine

acids, usually provide effective relief. Herbalists sometimes recommend an infusion of slippery elm tablets or marsh mallow root. Homeopathic remedies are available; acupuncture and acupressure may also help.

▶ *see also massage, energy, natural therapies*

Painful cough

Any cough is a reflex action to clear irritants or blockages in the breathing passages or respiratory tract. A burning cough felt behind the breast bone can be caused by tracheitis, an inflammation of the windpipe, or trachea. Hoarse coughing accompanied by pain in the throat may indicate laryngitis, or inflammation of the larynx. A sharp pain in the ribs when coughing or taking a deep breath often indicates pleurisy—inflammation of the lining of the lung. This requires immediate medical attention.

Treatment Conventionally, a cough may be treated with cough medicine and a painkiller such as acetaminophen. Homeopathic remedies for coughs are also available. To help ease the pain, an essential oil like eucalyptus, myrrh, sandalwood, or frankincense can be massaged onto the chest and back or added to a bowl of hot water and inhaled. Sprinkling a few drops of myrrh on the pillow aids breathing at night.

▶ *see also massage, energy, natural therapies*

Chest infection/Bronchitis

An acute chest infection usually follows a cold or flu and is characterized by a cough with phlegm. The cells lining the respiratory tract produce phlegm to help entrap irritants so they can be coughed out. If you have a chest infection you may also experience shortness of breath and cough that is painful. When coughing, pain is usually felt in the windpipe or in the muscles between the ribs. A chronic cough or one that produces green or yellow phlegm should be reported to a doctor, as this may indicate infection requiring antibiotic treatment.

Treatment The best way to relieve pain from a chest infection is to encourage the removal of phlegm from the body, rather than suppressing it with over-the-counter cough remedies. To keep phlegm loose during a chest infection, drink at least 2 quarts of fluids a day (not milk, however, as this encourages mucus build-up), and get plenty of rest. Avoid cold air, smoke, and fog. If you smoke, try to give up cigarettes. Steam inhalation can be useful for bringing up phlegm. Eating garlic on a regular basis is a proven preventative, which can help reduce the risk of developing a chest infection.

▶ *see also massage, energy, natural therapies*

Angina

Angina is the pain that people experience when the blood supply to the heart is impaired. It is commonly described as a tight constriction, or pressure, across the center of the chest, and can often be felt in the left arm, neck, or jaw. During an attack a sufferer may be short of breath, nauseous, dizzy, and sweaty. Angina can be provoked by a heavy meal, exercise, cold weather, or stress. If you are being treated for angina and experience a new pain, or if pain persists despite prescription medication, or if pain starts without any obvious factors triggering it, consult your doctor at once.

SOOTHING COUGHS

You can make simple cough remedies from natural ingredients in your kitchen.

■ *For a soothing cough mixture, slice an onion into a bowl, cover it with honey, and let it stand overnight. Strain the mixture into a clean bottle or jar and take 1 teaspoon up to 5 times a day.*

■ *For a dry, irritating cough, make a tea from dried marsh mallow leaves, allowing 2 teaspoons per cup.*

■ *If you're suffering from excessive phlegm, try ginger tea or thyme tea, the latter made with 1 to 2 teaspoons of crushed leaves per cup.*

TREATING CHEST INFECTIONS

Although chest infections are rarely contagious, they can cause considerable discomfort. There are several steps you can take at home to relieve the aching pain under the breast bone. However, if the chest infection is accompanied by sinus problems, earache, or pneumonia, medical treatment is necessary.

DRINK MORE LIQUIDS
Drinking extra liquid keeps the phlegm more fluid.

KEEP WARM AND REST
Keeping warm and resting will help the body to recover.

ADD MOISTURE TO THE AIR
Extra humidity will help to bring the phlegm up and out.

EAT GARLIC
Garlic can help to prevent further chest infections.

PREVENTING ANGINA

You can take steps to prevent the onset of angina by watching your diet carefully and learning to listen to your body:

▶ *Stop smoking. You will significantly reduce the risk of dying from heart disease by limiting further hardening of the arteries caused by nicotine and carbon monoxide.*

▶ *Maintain your weight at a level appropriate for your height and age. This will help to keep blood pressure lower and reduce strain on the heart.*

▶ *Reduce animal fats and salt in your diet and incorporate larger amounts of fiber, fish, and garlic. These measures will also reduce the risk of hardening of the arteries.*

▶ *Manage stress with mind therapies (see pages 88 to 90) and gentle exercise.*

HAWTHORN TEA
Try an infusion made with 2 teaspoons of hawthorn berries steeped in a cup of hot water for 20 minutes. It is known to improve heart function and reduce recurring angina attacks.

Treatment Patients suffering from angina are usually prescribed drugs and advised to give up smoking, exercise regularly, and take steps to manage stress more efficiently. A naturopath can offer advice on dietary management and nutritional supplements such as vitamin E. There are many homeopathic remedies that relieve the symptoms and are sometimes used in conjunction with conventional treatments. However, if you observe any changes in the frequency or intensity of your angina pain, consult a doctor as soon as possible.

▶ *see also movement, mind, relaxation therapies*

EXERCISE AND ANGINA
Regular, gentle exercise such as walking can be of enormous benefit to angina sufferers. Exercise strengthens the heart and improves circulation. Start slowly and increase the amount and intensity of exercise gradually.

Heart attack

A heart attack involves the death of heart muscle from an interruption of the blood supply, caused usually by a blockage such as a blood clot, or thrombus, in a coronary artery. It is a life-threatening condition, but with prompt medical attention and sensible changes in lifestyle, many heart attack victims recover to lead long and healthy lives.

Often starting as a mild pain or pressure in the chest, a heart attack is sometimes mistaken for indigestion. As it worsens, the pain is similar to that of angina but more severe and longer lasting. It may be accompanied by sweating, palpitations, breathlessness, vomiting, or collapse. The pain is typically felt in the central chest area and may radiate round to the back, up to the neck and jaw, or down the left arm.

Damage to the heart may lead to heart failure (a reduction in the heart's pumping efficiency). In severe cases, the victim's heart and breathing stop. When this happens, cardiopulmonary resuscitation (CPR) is a first-aid measure. A combination of mouth-to-mouth resuscitation and chest compressions, its purpose is to keep oxygenated blood circulating in the body until medical help is available. It is best performed by those trained in the method.

Treatment An aspirin given immediately to a conscious heart attack victim can improve blood flow and ease the symptoms. Medical staff may use drugs and/or defibrillation (electric shocks applied to the chest) to stabilize an erratic heart rhythm. This is followed by oxygen and strong painkillers such as morphine. In some cases, drugs to dissolve blood clots, and surgery to repair damaged heart muscle and improve blood flow through the heart, may be necessary. On recovery the heart attack patient must follow a rehabilitation program that incorporates sensible diet and exercise (see advice on preventing angina, opposite page).

▶ *see also movement, massage, energy, natural, mind, relaxation therapies*

Pulled muscle

Pain from a pulled chest muscle usually follows injury caused by a sudden strain, for example when lifting a heavy weight. The pain is felt along the line of the muscle as a dull ache or cramp-like sensation. The affected muscle is often tender.

Treatment Application of cold compresses to the damaged muscle is a simple but effective treatment. An icepack, wrapped in a towel (see page 155), can be used in cases of severe inflammation. Manipulative treatments such as physiotherapy (see page 73) and rolfing (see page 72) can also be beneficial. Homeopaths recommend arnica for sprains and muscle aches: to make a tincture, mix 10 ml of arnica with 1 cup of water and apply it to the affected area. A poultice of ginger can also bring relief. Over-the-counter painkillers, such as aspirin, liniment ointments, and sprays are available at drug stores.

▶ *see also manipulative, massage therapies*

Shingles

Shingles occurs in people who have been previously exposed to the virus that causes chicken pox. The virus lies dormant in the nerve root and becomes active again when the body's immunity is low. People over the age of 50 are mainly affected by the disease because the efficiency of the immune system generally declines with age. Stress also affects the immune system and many people suffer from the disease after experiencing a period of emotional turmoil or pressure.

Shingles usually starts as a sharp burning pain that follows the route of the nerves around the chest, parallel to the ribs. The disorder causes a painful rash of small blisters on the skin. Pain from an attack can persist long after the blisters have healed. This chronic pain condition is called postherpetic neuralgia and is caused by damaged nerves producing strong pain impulses.

Treatment Conventional treatment for shingles includes antiviral drugs and painkillers. The early use of antiviral drugs can help minimize nerve damage, but if treatment is delayed, postherpetic pain may be a major problem. Dabbing the sores gently with mixture of 2 drops each of essential oils of lemon and geranium in 1 cup of water can relieve the pain. Eating a well-balanced diet and increasing your intake of vitamins A, C, and E to boost your immune system can help to prevent the symptoms from recurring. The treatment of postherpetic neuralgia may require help from a pain clinic or acupuncturist.

▶ *see also massage, natural, relaxation therapies*

Broken rib

A broken rib is usually caused by a fall or a blow. In rare cases, however, it may result from excess stress on the rib cage brought on by coughing or even laughing. Pain is felt as a sharp, stabbing sensation over the affected area. It is particularly severe when a person takes a deep breath or coughs.

Treatment The pain of a broken rib is usually treated with over-the-counter drugs such as aspirin or acetaminophen. If necessary, stronger drugs may be prescribed by a doctor. The rib must not be strapped, as this increases the risk of developing a chest infection. After the broken rib has healed sufficiently, treatment from a chiropractor or osteopath (see page 70) can help to rebuild muscle and ligament mobility.

▶ *see also manipulative, massage therapies*

ASPIRIN PASTE

An aspirin paste is a gentle way to relieve pain caused by shingles:

■ *In a bowl, crush two aspirin tablets into a powder.*

■ *Mix the crushed tablets with a skin cream or lotion until the tablets are dissolved.*

■ *Apply the mixture to the affected area.*

SELF HELP AND SHINGLES

There are a number of safe treatments you can try at home to relieve the pain of shingles.

▶ *Apply aloe vera gel, fresh leek juice, or compresses soaked in goldenseal or peppermint tea to shingles blisters.*

▶ *Mix carrot and celery juice with 1 tablespoon of parsley juice and drink.*

▶ *Soak in a tepid bath containing a cup of colloidal oat meal or baking soda to relieve the discomfort of blisters.*

▶ *Try TENS, or transcutaneous electrical nerve stimulation (see page 83), for chronic nerve pain.*

▶ *Relieve pain with reflexology directed at the diaphragm, glands, and spine.*

ABDOMINAL PAIN

The abdominal area is very sensitive to stress, and many recurrent abdominal pains respond well to relaxation therapies. Some kinds of pain, however, may indicate a serious problem.

Abdominal pain may arise from the wall of the abdomen (skin, muscles, and abdominal lining), the contents of the abdomen, or the nervous system. On occasion, abdominal pain may be referred from the organs of the chest or pelvis.

In many cases abdominal pain is short-term and can be safely treated at home. However, if the pain occurs together with vomiting or a high fever, you should consult a doctor immediately, because these symptoms may indicate a serious condition such as appendicitis, stomach ulcer, or kidney infection. A precise description of the type and site of your pain will help your doctor to diagnose the underlying cause and suggest appropriate treatment. In broad terms there are five types of pain associated with the abdomen: generalized abdominal pain, pain of the upper middle abdomen, pain of the center abdomen, pain of the lower abdomen, and pain of the rectal area.

GENERALIZED ABDOMINAL PAIN

Generalized abdominal pain is a term used to describe acute pain that affects the whole area of the abdomen. A serious cause of this wide-ranging pain is peritonitis (inflammation of the membrane called the peritoneum that lines the abdomen). The pain is acute and severe and requires urgent medical attention. Peritonitis is usually caused by infection, which can occur when there is a leakage from the bowel due to perforation of an ulcer, a burst appendix, or rupture of an infected gall bladder. One of the most tell-tale signs of peritonitis is a board-like rigidity of the abdominal wall.

PAINS IN THE UPPER MIDDLE ABDOMEN

Pains in the upper middle abdomen are mainly the result of problems in the lower esophagus, stomach, liver, gall bladder, duodenum, pancreas, heart or lungs.

Indigestion

The term indigestion covers a variety of symptoms—from burping and a feeling of fullness to more painful sensations—that may occur after eating a meal. Pain is felt as a mild to moderate aching or burning sensation in the upper middle abdomen and occasionally radiates to the back. While overeating is the most common cause of indigestion, stress, smoking, and heavy drinking may all aggravate the condition.

INSIDE THE ABDOMEN

The abdominal cavity is located between the lower ribs and the pubic area. It is lined by a membrane called the peritoneum and contains the digestive organs, the bladder, and the rectum.

ABDOMINAL PAIN
Pain in the abdomen often starts as a vague ache affecting the general abdominal area, but then it gradually can be pinpointed to a particular organ.

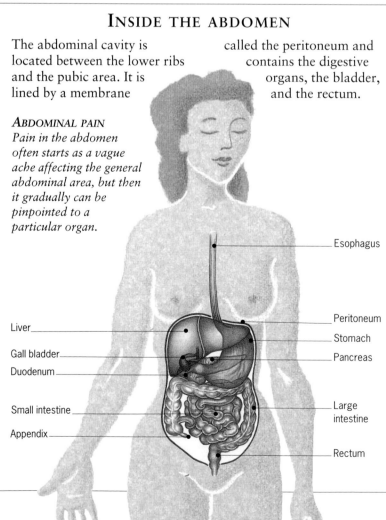

Esophagus

Peritoneum

Stomach

Pancreas

Large intestine

Rectum

Liver

Gall bladder

Duodenum

Small intestine

Appendix

Treatment Over-the-counter antacid drugs can usually relieve symptoms quickly, but they should not be used for a long period of time, since they may hide symptoms of serious disease. Aspirin should be avoided, because it can irritate the stomach and in some cases cause gastric bleeding. Drinking milk or an herbal tea, such as peppermint, fennel, and chamomile after eating can help to ease discomfort. If you suffer frequently from indigestion and also have other symptoms like vomiting, weight loss, or a change in bowel movements, you should consult a doctor.

▶ *see also movement, massage, natural therapies*

Peptic ulcer

A peptic ulcer is a break in the lining of the duodenum, stomach, or esophagus. It is caused by excess acid or a reduction in the mucus layer protecting the lining of the digestive tract, as a result of which the cells in the lining become eroded and an ulcer forms. The pain symptoms of a peptic ulcer are similar to those of indigestion but often more severe. The discomfort is commonly described as gnawing or burning.

Most ulcers are caused by a bacterial infection. Chemicals secreted from the bacteria damage the lining of the intestine, resulting in the formation of ulcers (see below). In these cases, special treatment that includes the use of antibiotics is necessary.

Treatment If you have a peptic ulcer you should be under the care of a medical specialist. Conventional medical treatment for ulcers includes antacids, which work by neutralizing stomach acids. Herbalists may recommend drinking a brew made with slippery elm bark powder, one hour before meals and at bedtime. Homeopathic medicines may also be effective. If abdominal pain continues for several days or becomes more severe, medical advice is necessary.

There are also a wide number of self-help measures for relieving the pain, the most important of which is to stop smoking. Alcohol, caffeine, and aspirin and other non-steroidal anti-inflammatory drugs all irritate the lining of the stomach. If possible, they should be avoided. Eating large meals may aggravate the condition. You may find that eating several small meals at regular intervals is beneficial. Finally, stress, although unlikely to be the direct cause of an ulcer, can aggravate an existing one, so relaxation and meditation therapies should be considered. Maintaining these

HERBS AND INDIGESTION

Various herbal treatments can relieve indigestion symptoms. Taking 1 to 2 oz (25 to 50 g) of aloe vera juice in a glass of water 3 times a day will soothe the digestive tract. Peppermint, ginger, anise, fennel, and chamomile teas can stabilize recurring digestive problems, especially nausea. and gas.

Meadowsweet tea relieves nausea, reduces acidity, and soothes the stomach's mucous membranes. Pour 1 cup of boiling water over 2 teaspoons of dried herb, let steep for 15 minutes, and drink 3 times a day. (Pregnant and nursing women and people allergic to aspirin should avoid this herb.)

HOW A PEPTIC ULCER FORMS

Peptic ulcers develop when acid from the stomach wall erodes the lining of the duodenum, esophagus, or stomach. They can cause a burning, aching pain in the abdomen and are usually accompanied by nausea and vomiting.

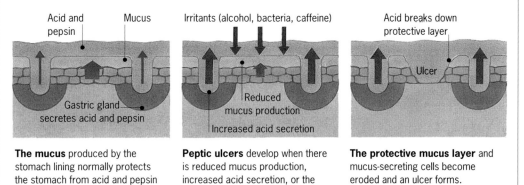

The mucus produced by the stomach lining normally protects the stomach from acid and pepsin secreted by the gastric glands.

Peptic ulcers develop when there is reduced mucus production, increased acid secretion, or the stomach lining is irritated.

The protective mucus layer and mucus-secreting cells become eroded and an ulcer forms.

**DIARRHEA: A
SIMPLE SOLUTION**

Diarrhea attacks while on vacation can be triggered by a change of diet or by consuming contaminated food or water. To ensure that the disorder does not lead to severe dehydration, a potentially serious medical problem, take with you some rehydration salts (available from a druggist). Alternatively you can make your own mixture as follows:

■ *Dissolve 1 tablespoon of salt and 8 tablespoons of sugar in 3 quarts of boiled water and sip this mixture every day while symptoms last. You should keep to these proportions to ensure that the remedy works effectively.*

self-help measures after your ulcer has cleared up should help to prevent a recurrence of the condition.

▶ *see also herbal, massage, movement therapies*

Pancreatitis

Pancreatitis, an inflammation of the pancreas, may be acute or chronic. The disorder is characterized by severe pain in the upper middle abdomen, which in many cases radiates through to the middle of the back. Because the pancreas is an organ involved in digestion, other symptoms may include problems with breaking down food, diarrhea, and weight loss.

Acute pancreatitis is often associated with excessive alcohol intake but may also be caused by gallstones, trauma, metabolic disease, or certain drugs. Chronic pancreatitis may lead to diabetes. Because the pancreas produces insulin, lack of which is a factor in diabetes, any damage to the pancreas can cause a drop in insulin production.

Treatment Both acute and chronic pancreatitis require hospitalization for treatment. In some cases, removal of the pancreas may be necessary. This can lead to problems in digesting food, but these can be corrected by taking oral supplements of the digestive enzymes produced by the pancreas.

Gall bladder disease

The gall bladder stores the bile necessary for digesting fats. Most painful disorders of the gall bladder are associated with gallstones,

which form when there is a chemical imbalance in the bile and some of its components solidify. If you have acute pain in the upper part of the abdomen on the right side, it may be due to inflammation of the gall bladder, known as cholecystitis. This happens when gallstones become trapped at the outlet of the gall bladder into the bile duct, and the flow of bile is stopped. Other symptoms of cholecystitis are nausea, indigestion, and jaundice, in which the skin and whites of the eyes acquire a yellowish tint. If you experience gall bladder pain you should consult a doctor as soon as possible.

Treatment Some small gallstones may remain in the gall bladder for years without causing any problems. Others may pass harmlessly out of the body in the feces. You can help to stimulate the flow of bile by incorporating bitter salad greens such as chicory in your meals at least three times a week. Herbalists recommend alfalfa tablets and dandelion capsules to enhance gall bladder function. In addition, reducing your intake of animal fats and dairy products and having no more than one or two alcoholic drinks a day can help prevent gall bladder pain if you already suffer from it.

Stones that cause pain or inflammation of the gall bladder must be removed. If the stones are small enough, they can be dissolved by drugs. Larger ones are usually removed by endoscopy; this involves inserting a flexible viewing tube into the stomach and duodenum. Sometimes removal of the

GALL BLADDER

The gall bladder is a small muscular sac located under the liver. Bile from the liver is stored in the gall bladder until it enters the duodenum after a meal, where it aids in digestion of fats. If a gallstone becomes trapped in the outlet between the gall bladder and the bile duct, it can cause extreme pain and block the flow of bile to the duodenum. To reduce the likelihood of developing gallstones, avoid becoming overweight and limit your intake of sugar and fat.

GALL BLADDER PAIN
Gall bladder pain often radiates to the shoulder blades and is aggravated by deep breaths and pressure on the right abdomen.

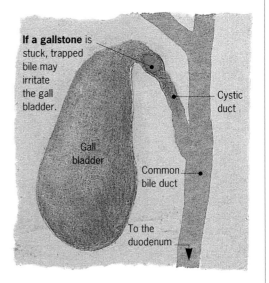

If a gallstone is stuck, trapped bile may irritate the gall bladder.

Cystic duct

Gall bladder

Common bile duct

To the duodenum

gall bladder is recommended. This presents few problems, because the digestive system can function normally without a gall bladder, although dietary changes to reduce the intake of fats may be recommended.

▶ *see also movement, massage, natural therapies*

PAIN IN THE CENTER ABDOMEN

Pain in the center abdomen usually indicates an illness that is causing inflammation of the stomach or small intestine.

Gastroenteritis

The most common cause of pain in the center abdomen is gastroenteritis, or inflammation of the stomach and intestines. It is often caused by consuming food or water that has been contaminated with food poisoning microorganisms. The pain is acute but generally vague and the sufferer may also have a distended abdomen, nausea, and vomiting or diarrhea. Usually the symptoms last for only a few days, but in more severe cases, dehydration, shock, and even collapse may occur. If severe pain persists for more than a few days and is accompanied by vomiting, you should consult a doctor. The symptoms may indicate a more serious disease, such as cholera or typhoid, which are common in developing countries.

Treatment It is vital to drink plenty of water, taken frequently in small amounts, to replace fluids lost through diarrhea and vomiting and prevent dehydration. Flat ginger ale or cola may be taken; or a rehydration mixture (see opposite page) can also be effective. Antibiotics may be necessary in some cases. After the diarrhea and vomiting have subsided, the BRAT diet (bananas, rice, applesauce, and toast) is recommended. Eating yogurt with live acidophilus cultures may also be beneficial, as it repopulates essential bacteria in the intestines.

PAIN IN THE LOWER ABDOMEN

Pain in the lower abdomen usually indicates a problem of the large intestine (colon) such as inflammation (colitis), which is a feature of Crohn's disease (see page 112). Another cause of pain in this area is appendicitis, acute inflammation of the appendix. The appendix is a small closed tube branching off the colon. Disorders affecting the kidneys, the bladder, and the sex organs may also cause pain in the lower abdomen. These pains are covered in Chapter 7.

Diverticulitis

If there are areas of weakness in the wall of the large intestine, the lining may be forced through the wall forming small sacs known as diverticula. Usually these sacs do not cause any problems. Sometimes, however, they can become inflamed, resulting in a condition called diverticulitis. Abscesses may form in the tissues and bleeding may occur. The pain is often cramping, causing the affected part of the abdomen to feel rigid. Nausea, vomiting and a change in bowel habits (for instance diarrhea or constipation) are frequently associated with the condition. In rare cases rupture of the sac may cause peritonitis (see page 108).

Treatment Diverticulitis is usually treated successfully with antibiotics. In more severe cases, the affected part of the lower intestine may be removed by surgery. Slippery elm can help to soothe the pain of inflamed diverticula: mix 1 teaspoon of slippery elm powder with a little honey, then slowly add warm water while stirring to a consistency suitable for drinking or eating with a spoon. Take three times daily. Massaging the abdomen in the morning might also be helpful. You may be able to prevent diverticulitis simply by including more fiber in your diet (but avoid foods with seeds, because these tend to collect in the sacs) and by drinking at least 2 quarts of water a day. These measures will deter constipation, which can further inflame the intestine.

▶ *see also movement, massage, natural therapies*

APPENDICITIS OR INDIGESTION?

Knowing how to spot the warning signs of appendicitis is vital, because it requires prompt medical treatment. If an inflamed appendix is not removed it may rupture, causing peritonitis (see page 108). In general, the initial pain of appendicitis is felt around the navel. When the abdominal lining becomes inflamed, the pain is focused on the right, just above the groin, and is severe, continuous, and made worse by movement and coughing. Most sufferers lose their appetite, feel nauseous, and may vomit or have diarrhea. A mild inflammation, known as grumbling appendix, may cause discomfort but is not a cause for concern.

AIDING DIGESTION WITH MASSAGE

Massaging the abdomen can help to relax the abdominal muscles and aid digestion. You can do this in a chair while remaining fully clothed, but for best results try massaging directly on the skin, using an essential oil mixed with a carrier oil. A drop of oil of peppermint or ginger in a teaspoon of almond oil is particularly effective.

MASSAGING THE ABDOMEN
Place one hand over the other and with small circular movements gently knead the stomach in a clockwise direction.

Crohn's disease

Crohn's disease is a chronic inflammation of the large or small intestine. The condition causes severe spasms or continuous, aching discomfort. It can also produce a lot of pain in the anus and rectum. The causes of the disease are not fully understood. Some authorities believe a diet high in processed foods may be a factor, while other theories suggest that the disease is an autoimmune response in which the immune system attacks body tissues.

Treatment With Crohn's disease, intravenous feedings are sometimes necessary, especially for children who cannot otherwise eat enough for proper growth and development. Adults need a special diet planned by a dietitian, and during a flare-up should eat bland, low-fiber foods. Because stress can aggravate the condition, regular relaxation techniques and aromatherapy can be helpful. Hot and cold compresses applied to the abdomen can improve the function of the intestine and relieve colic.

▶ *see also movement, massage, energy, natural, mind, relaxation therapies*

Irritable bowel syndrome

Irritable bowel syndrome is a painful condition of the lower intestine that causes irregular bouts of diarrhea or constipation or alternating bouts of both. Sufferers develop cramp-like abdominal pains and may have a feeling of distension in the abdomen. As in Crohn's disease, the symptoms are aggravated by emotional stress. Little is known about the causes of the condition although it is thought that abnormal functioning of the muscles in the large intestine may contribute. Food intolerance, specifically an intolerance to lactose (a sugar found in milk), may be a factor in the development of the illness.

Treatment Although irritable bowel syndrome has no cure, you can take steps to alleviate the painful symptoms. Eating a well-balanced diet that includes fiber-rich foods (a daily intake of 20g to 35g of fiber is recommended) can help to prevent attacks. Good sources include fresh and dried fruits, vegetables, beans, and whole-grain cereals. Eating yogurt with live acidophilus cultures helps keep the balance of

YOGA FOR REGULAR BOWEL MOVEMENTS

Starting each day with this simple yoga exercise can be helpful in establishing regular bowel movements. If you are reasonably supple, you could extend the two-step exercise below into the shoulder stand (right).

If you have a back disorder or suffer from some other serious condition, consult your doctor before attempting these exercises.

1 *Lie on the floor with a foam mat or folded blanket underneath you. If this is the first time you have tried this exercise, or if your shoulders are stiff, place extra cushioning beneath your shoulders to support your neck.*

2 *Pressing your hands against the floor, breathe in deeply, bend your knees, and lift your legs over your waist. Keep your shoulders down. Take 10 breaths, moving your abdomen in and out rhythmically with each breath.*

Bring your legs forward so your weight is spread over arms, elbows, and shoulders.

SHOULDER STAND
Keeping your elbows close together, lift your pelvis off the floor and raise your legs straight up, placing your hands under your hips to support your weight. Hold this position for 3 minutes, breathing normally. Slowly lower your legs to the floor.

bacteria in the gut healthy, which should also improve the condition. It is better to avoid coffee and chocolate, because they contain a chemical that causes contraction of the bowel and can lead to abdominal pain. Herbalists suggest drinking peppermint, ginger, chamomile, or fennel tea, since these herbs have a soothing effect on the stomach and intestines. Aromatherapy can be effective for reducing stress and soothing muscle spasms; therapists recommend soaking three or four times a week in a bath with rose oil added to it. Hypnotherapy can also be beneficial, not only for lessening stress but also for dealing with the symptoms of irritable bowl syndrome.

▶ *see also movement, massage, energy, natural, mind, relaxation therapies*

Constipation and flatulence

A sedentary lifestyle and poor dietary habits can lead to irregular bowel movements. When the feces are hard, it becomes more difficult to excrete them from the bowel, resulting in constipation, flatulence, and considerable lower abdominal discomfort. If you experience a sudden, unaccountable change in your normal pattern of bowel movements, it may indicate a condition requiring further investigation.

Treatment Eating plenty of fiber-rich foods like bran, whole-grain breads, brown rice, and fresh fruit, and drinking plenty of liquid is vital for keeping feces soft. Regular exercise, for example, walking, cycling, or swimming, plus yoga exercises (see opposite page) every morning will help stimulate bowel movement. The discomfort of constipation can be relieved by taking 2 teaspoons of psyllium or ground linseed in your cereal or coffee. If the constipation attack is an isolated one, dried prunes, figs, and apricots are excellent natural laxatives.

Although some amount of flatulence is normal, it can become a problem if large quantitiesof undigested food pass into the intestine. The bacteria that settle on this food produce excess gas. Some products, such as bran, beans, broccoli, cauliflower, Brussels sprouts, cabbage, dark beer, and fizzy drinks, are more gassy than others. If you suffer from chronic flatulence it may help to try eliminating some of these foods to pinpoint the cause. As beans and peas are also a rich source of fiber and protein, it's best not to leave them out of your diet

FOODS TO FIGHT CONSTIPATION

Every diet should contain sufficient dietary fiber and liquids, to keep stools bulky yet soft enough to pass painlessly through the colon. Nutritionists recommend consuming between 20g and 35g per day from a variety of high fiber foods rather than laxatives.

FIBER AND FLUIDS
Fiber—from vegetables, fruits, whole grains, and beans—prevents constipation. Lots of fluids help, too.

completely. One way of making them less gaseous is to cook them according to the following method. Place the beans in bowl water to cover and soak overnight. Drain the soaked beans, cover with fresh water, and cook for 30 minutes. Drain and replace the water again and cook for another 30 minutes. Finally, drain once more, cover with fresh water, and cook until tender.

▶ *see also movement, massage, natural therapies*

Stitch

The term "stitch" is used to describe pain that is felt in the side during exercise. The condition often follows a heavy meal and is caused by insufficient blood supply to the muscles, because blood has been diverted to the intestines to aid digestion or the exercise is too intense. If the pain of a stitch persists, the muscle may have developed a spasm or possibly a tear.

Treatment If you have a stitch during exercise, stop your activity and gently stretch the affected area. Breathe deeply for a few minutes, and the pain should subside. You can help to prevent a stitch by avoiding heavy meals prior to exercise. Always allow at least one hour to digest your food before engaging in physical activity. Eating foods like pasta that are high in complex carbohydrates at least an hour before you work out may also help prevent the onset of a stitch. Don't exercise for too long at any one time and make sure that the exercises are within your fitness level.

▶ *see also movement, massage, natural therapies*

IMPROVISED SITZ BATH
You can have sitz-bath therapy at home. First fill the tub with about 4 in (10 cm) of warm water. Sit in the bath, keeping your knees up, and splash water onto your abdomen. Stay in for 15 minutes, then refill the bath with cold water and rinse. You can also add herbs or oils to the hot bath (see below).

RECTAL PAINS

The rectum, the lowest part of the large intestine, connects the intestine to the anus. A variety of painful disorders, including inflammation, polyps (growths), and cancer may affect the rectum and anal canal.

Hemorrhoids

Hemorrhoids, commonly known as piles, are swollen blood vessels in the lining of the anus. They may occur inside the anus or close to the anal opening. They can lead to intense itching and pain and sometimes bleed when feces are passed. These swellings are caused by increased pressure on the blood vessels in the anus, for example, when straining to pass hard stools, when lifting heavy items, or during pregnancy.

Treatment Applying witch hazel to the sensitive area may give some relief from the pain of piles, or you can make your own ointment: simmer 1 oz 30 g (30 g) of pilewort with 6½ oz (200 g) of vaseline for 10 minutes. Naturopaths sometime recom-

mend a sitz bath to relieve the pain of piles or tears in the anus caused by straining to pass hard stools. A sitzbath has two sections, one containing hot water and another containing cold. The patient sits in the hot water with feet in the cold water for two or three minutes and then reverses the procedure for one minute. You can also improvise your own sitz bath (see left). In some cases, an injection is given to make hemorrhoids shrink. Surgery is necessary only if hemorrhoids are very large or troublesome.

Constipation is one of the main causes of piles. Altering your diet to produce softer stools can alleviate the pain considerably (see page 113). Also, try to avoid foods that cause irritation; coffee and spices are examples. Consuming sufficient liquids to soften the feces is important. Aim to drink at least eight glasses of water a day. Natural laxatives such as prunes, figs, and bran can help prevent the pain caused by straining.

▶ *see also massage, natural, relaxation therapies*

SOOTHING HEMORRHOIDS WITH HERBS

Chamomile has long been recognized for its ability to soothe sore, inflamed, or itchy skin. Adding it to a bath will help heal skin damaged by hemorrhoids.

Hemorrhoids can also be soothed by adding to a bath 4 drops of peppermint and cypress essential oils, along with 2 tablespoons of bicarbonate of soda.

Hold the pan carefully with both hands, using a pot holder to ensure you do not scald your fingers.

1 *Mix ¾ oz (20g) chamomile flowers and 3 quarts cold water in a large pan. Bring to a boil, cover, and simmer for 10 minutes.*

2 *Strain the liquid carefully into a bowl. Add the liquid to warm bath water, mix well, and climb in.*

CHAPTER 7

MALE AND FEMALE COMPLAINTS

Disorders relating to the female and male reproductive and urinary systems can threaten fertility and health as well as causing pain. In most cases, the first course of action must be to seek medical help. But there are natural remedies, both old and new, which you can use along with your doctor's advice, not only to ease pain but also to prevent conditions from recurring.

WOMEN'S COMPLAINTS

By taking good care of your body and using natural therapies, you can often avoid or relieve many painful disorders that affect the breasts and the reproductive and urinary systems.

Many of the more serious disorders affecting women—such as breast and cervical cancer and chlamydia, an infection that is a common cause of female infertility—can be treated successfully and leave no lasting damage if caught in the early stages. When you are able to recognize the warning signs of illness, you can seek early treatment and so improve the chances of a complete cure. Better yet, if you understand the possible causes of female disorders, you can take positive steps to avoid such problems.

PAIN AND THE FEMALE BODY

The first step in the early detection of disorders is to get to know your body: how it normally looks, feels, and reacts. Examine your body regularly for any abnormal changes such as menstrual irregularities or the sudden appearance of lumps, swellings, or skin blemishes, or any other warning signals your body may reveal.

▶ *Headaches may be frequent prior to menstruation, due to hormonal changes.*

▶ *The breasts are susceptible to swelling and tenderness before menstruation.*

▶ *The lower abdomen contains the female reproductive organs, which may be affected by growths, infection, abnormal bleeding, and inflammation.*

▶ *The vaginal area is prone to infection and inflammation.*

A HEALTHY BODY
Regular exercise can do much to prevent and relieve many painful disorders.

BREAST PAIN

Most women suffer from breast pain at some time. The most common discomforts are premenstrual breast pain, a chronic condition, and mastitis, an acute disorder.

Premenstrual breast pain

Before menstruation the breasts may feel tender and lumpy, and in some women the pain may be severe. The condition is linked to hormonal changes: raised levels of estrogen in the blood cause water retention in the breasts, making them feel full and tender. This kind of pain usually disappears once menstruation begins, but if it continues, a doctor should be consulted.

Treatment Premenstrual pain can often be treated effectively with over-the-counter painkillers. Evening primrose oil, taken in capsule form, is also effective at reducing pain. Massaging the breasts with geranium oil or adding a few drops to a bath can be soothing. To help counteract water retention you can try natural diuretics such as freshly chopped parsley. In some cases, hormone therapy may be required to alleviate the condition.

▶ *See also massage, energy, natural therapies*

Mastitis

Mastitis, inflammation of the breast tissue, is usually associated with breastfeeding and is most often caused by bacterial infection entering via small cracks in the nipples. The breast becomes red, painful, and swollen. In some cases, an abscess may form in the breast and fever may develop.

Treatment The affected breast should be fully emptied, either by breastfeeding or expressing the milk. Antibiotic pills are usually prescribed, but if an abscess forms surgery is required to drain it. Vitamin E cream can help soothe cracked nipples.

▶ *See also massage, energy, natural therapies*

ABDOMINAL PAIN

Any persistent pain, especially if it is accompanied by other symptoms—bleeding between periods, increased menstrual bleeding, pain during sexual intercourse, or abnormal vaginal discharge—could be an indication of a more serious condition, and the opinion of a gynecologist should be sought as soon as possible. (For information on abdominal pains other than those caused by gynecological problems, see page 108.)

Premenstrual syndrome (PMS)

The physical and psychological changes experienced by women in the days before menstruation are known as premenstrual syndrome (PMS). The physical symptoms include breast tenderness, swelling of the abdomen, abdominal pains, headaches, appetite changes, and cramps. Psychological symptoms include depression, tearfulness, anxiety, irritability, and lack of sexual interest. Symptoms may start up to 14 days prior to a period and disappear at the onset of bleeding. Distressing and sometimes severe enough to disrupt work and family life, PMS is complex and there is still no agreement over its definition and treatment.

Treatment Evening primrose oil capsules have been shown to alleviate symptoms. The recommended dosage is two 250mg tablets after breakfast and dinner, beginning three days before the expected onset of symptoms and continuing until menstruation starts. Herbalists also recommend preparations of diuretic herbs such as juniper. Naturopaths suggest supplements of vitamins B$_6$ and E and calcium or magnesium to calm the nerves, and reducing salt in the diet to discourage bloating. Raspberry leaf or valerian tea can be soothing. Light exercise like swimming or yoga may also be of value.

▶ *See also massage, movement, energy therapies*

Painful periods

Dysmenorrhea, or painful menstruation, is most often caused by changes in hormone levels and an abnormal increase in prostaglandins. Pain is usually worse during the first two days, with cramp-like abdominal pains and an aching back. Painful periods sometimes indicate a gynecological disorder like pelvic inflammatory disease or endometriosis (see page 118). An intrauterine contraceptive device (IUD, or coil) may also cause painful periods.

Treatment Progesterone may be prescribed to correct the hormonal imbalance. The estrogen-progesterone oral contraceptive pill is effective, because it causes shorter periods with lighter bleeding. A hot-water bottle or heating pad placed on the abdomen and lower back can help to relieve pain. Massaging the abdomen with aromatic oil of juniper or taking a hot bath to which a few drops of lavender or juniper oil have been added can be soothing.

Painkillers, such as aspirin and ibuprofen, that inhibit the release of prostaglandins are usually effective. Magnesium supplements

LOOKING AFTER YOUR BREASTS

By maintaining a healthy lifestyle you can help to avoid breast disorders:

■ *Cut down on salty foods, to reduce water retention.*

■ *Eat foods rich in vitamin A to soothe pain and vitamin B$_6$ to reduce water retention.*

■ *Drink alcohol only in moderation, avoid cigarettes, and decrease intake of fats to reduce the risk of cancer.*

■ *Invest in well-fitting support bras to prevent sore chest muscles.*

■ *Examine your breasts regularly for lumps and other abnormalities.*

DIETARY CHANGES

Dietary changes about 10 days before menstruation can help to alleviate some of the painful symptoms associated with PMS. For example, cutting back on the amount of sugar and salt in your diet may lessen breast pain, and decreasing your caffeine intake can help to reduce anxiety and irritability.

Increase your intake of fiber by eating whole grains, fruits, and vegetables, to avoid constipation.

Eat regular meals rich in vitamins and minerals, to maintain blood sugar levels and promote health.

Reduce your intake of caffeine, which can make you feel tense, anxious, nervous, and irritable.

Cut down on salt and junk foods high in fat and sugar, to reduce sluggishness and bloated feelings.

EXERCISES TO REDUCE MENSTRUAL PAIN

Cramp-like pain or discomfort prior to or during menstruation, a condition known as dysmenorrhea, is common and may be severe enough to affect work or leisure. If you frequently suffer from menstrual cramps, exercise may help to relieve the pain.

1 *Lie face down on the floor with your hands flat on the floor at breast level.*

2 *Gently raise your head and chest. Gradually slide your arms forward and push forward, stretching your back.*

help reduce cramping. Herbalists suggest teas of ginger, valerian, or chamomile.
▶ *See also massage, movement, energy therapies*

Pelvic inflammatory disease
Pelvic inflammatory disease (PID) is an infection of the female reproductive organs that causes pain in the lower abdomen, fever, irregular periods, and abnormal discharge. If untreated, PID may lead to chronic pain, heavy periods, and infertility.
Treatment PID sufferers are usually treated with antibiotics. Severe cases may require hospital admission and sometimes surgery. Naturopaths recommend hydrotherapy to improve the circulation, plus vitamin supplements to strengthen the immune system.
▶ *See also massage, movement, energy therapies*

Endometriosis
In this condition, pieces of endometrium (the lining of the uterus) become attached to organs outside the uterus, the Fallopian tubes, for example. The tissue continues to react to hormonal changes, causing painful cysts and excessive menstrual bleeding. In some cases, it may lead to infertility.
Treatment Mild pain can be relieved by anti-inflammatory painkillers like ibuprofen. Drugs may be given to prevent menstruation, and surgery may be necessary to remove cysts. In severe cases, removal of the uterus and ovaries may be considered, particularly for older women. The condition sometimes clears up with pregnancy.
▶ *See also massage, energy, natural therapies*

Uterine fibroids
Uterine fibroids are benign tumors of the uterus that may occur without symptoms. Large fibroids can give rise to colicky pain, heavy periods, pelvic pain, painful intercourse, and complications in pregnancy.

THE FEMALE REPRODUCTIVE SYSTEM

The organs in the female pelvic cavity enable a woman to have sexual intercourse, produce eggs, develop a fetus, and give birth. Painful disorders affecting this area may be caused by a variety of problems, ranging from hormonal imbalances and structural abnormalities to infections and growths.

WARNING SIGNS
Painful symptoms of the lower abdomen may indicate an infection or other disorder and should never be ignored.

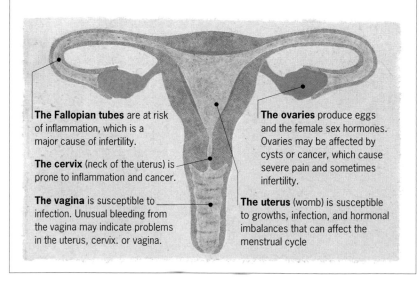

The Fallopian tubes are at risk of inflammation, which is a major cause of infertility.

The cervix (neck of the uterus) is prone to inflammation and cancer.

The vagina is susceptible to infection. Unusual bleeding from the vagina may indicate problems in the uterus, cervix. or vagina.

The ovaries produce eggs and the female sex hormones. Ovaries may be affected by cysts or cancer, which cause severe pain and sometimes infertility.

The uterus (womb) is susceptible to growths, infection, and hormonal imbalances that can affect the menstrual cycle

SEX THERAPIST

Sex therapy is a form of treatment, mainly involving counseling, that helps couples to overcome sexual problems primarily psychological in origin. The therapy is based on the assumption that sexual problems arise from a range of causes, past and present, but the problems are maintained by the situation that the couple currently finds itself in. A therapist aims to modify the situation by clarifying the nature of the problems and exploring the factors contributing to the dysfunctional relationship. A couple will usually visit a sex therapist together, although individual consultations are possible. After the two have been assessed, it is hoped that they will have a better understanding of their problems and how to approach them. For example, the sex therapist might help a woman to identify emotional problems causing painful sex, or a man to discover the underlying cause of impotence or premature ejaculation. A simple explanation of sexual anatomy may help a couple to understand the physical causes of a sexual problem. The therapist can then discuss a program of treatment.

Treatment In severe cases, surgery may be necessary. Fibroids sometimes respond to homeopathic remedies.
▶ *See also massage, natural, relaxation therapies*

Ovarian cysts
An ovarian cyst is a fluid-filled sac that forms in an ovary. It may cause abdominal pain, especially if the cyst places pressure on the bladder or ruptures or twists, and heavy and painful periods. Most are benign, but about five per cent are malignant.
Treatment Surgery is often necessary to remove a cyst. Naturopaths believe cysts are part of the body's attempt to detoxify itself and suggest drinking at least two quarts of water a day and also avoiding highly processed foods, alcohol, and caffeine.
▶ *See also massage, energy, relaxation therapies*

Bartholinitis
Bartholin's glands (two of them) are located at the opening of the vagina and help to lubricate the vulva during intercourse. They can become infected, a condition called bartholinitis.
Treatment Antibiotic drugs are prescribed to fight the infection and painkillers to ease the pain. If an abscess has formed, surgery may be necessary to drain it. In severe cases, the gland may have to be removed. This does not affect the lubrication of the vagina, as other glands also secrete lubricants.
▶ *See also massage, energy, natural therapies*

PAIN DURING SEXUAL INTERCOURSE
Pain during sexual intercourse may affect the vagina or be felt deep in the pelvic area. Possible causes are vaginal damage, a pelvic disorder, or psychological problems.

Vaginismus
Some women experience involuntary contractions of the muscles around the vagina, making sex impossible or painful. This may be due to fear of penetration or follow vaginal damage caused in childbirth.
Treatment If the problem is psychological, sex therapy (see above) may be necessary. Relaxation methods such as yoga, aromatherapy, and massage can help. Damage due to childbirth should start to heal within 10 days but may stay painful for several weeks.
▶ *See also massage, movement, mind therapies*

Vaginal atrophy
Vaginal atrophy, or thinning of the vaginal tissue following menopause, causes vaginal dryness and may lead to painful intercourse.
Treatment Hormone cream may help, as well as over-the-counter vaginal lubricants, vegetable oil, or vitamin E cream.
▶ *See also natural, mind, relaxation therapies*

INFLAMED BARTHOLIN'S GLANDS

Ducts leading to the glands can become blocked, causing pain and swelling. In some cases, a painful abscess forms. Other glands in the vagina can become infected, a condition known as vestibulitis, making intercourse painful—sometimes impossible.

PAIN RELIEF
Some women suffer repeated bouts of inflamed Bartholin's glands. A warm bath followed by aloe vera gel applied to the inflamed area often provides relief.

Labels: Clitoris, Opening of urethra, Labia, Vagina, Bartholin's glands, Anus

PAIN RELIEF AND CHILDBIRTH

Pain management during childbirth is a very personal issue. The use of painkilling drugs is widespread and for many women is essential for pain control. Becoming informed about the drugs available is vital to making the right choices during the birth. However, many women prefer the concept of a natural birth, with minimal medical intervention and the avoidance of drugs. The use of relaxation techniques and being well informed about the birth process are both key features of natural pain control.

NATURAL TECHNIQUES

Thorough preparation for childbirth helps to reduce the need for pain relief. Attending prenatal classes, exercising to strengthen back and pelvic muscles, practicing relaxation and breathing techniques, and seeking emotional support can all help reduce the fear of labor so that pain is not experienced so acutely, and to improve the ability to cope with it.

During contractions, many women find that walking around helps to distract the mind and that kneeling, squatting, or sitting can all be more comfortable than lying down. Massaging the back and buttocks with

COMFORTABLE LABOR
Ask your partner to massage your back during labor to soothe the pain and help you relax.

EXERCISING THE PELVIC MUSCLES
Strengthening the pelvic muscles through exercise can help to improve your stamina during labor.

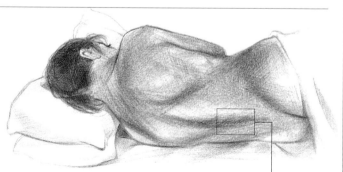

Lie flat, with arms at your sides and knees bent. While pressing your back against the floor, tighten and then relax the muscles used to control urine flow. Repeat 10 times.

talcum powder can also be effective. Between contractions, the woman's partner should use slow, firm strokes, working from the center of the back to the sides. During contractions, light circular strokes on the base of the spine are the most effective.

Massaging the acupressure point between the inner anklebone and the Achilles tendon may provide some pain relief. Use your thumb and massage the point for 60 seconds, first on one foot, then the other.

Acupuncture (see page 80) may also make labor easier, and some birthing centers now offer jacuzzi baths to help mothers relax. Another approach is TENS (see page 83). This provides mild pain relief in early labor but may be less effective in later stages.

ORTHODOX TECHNIQUES

Narcotic drugs such as demerol are commonly prescribed. They provide some degree of pain relief for a few hours but are not effective for all women. Side effects include nausea, vomiting, and drowsiness in the mother. Also, the baby may have problems breathing after delivery, but this is remedied with medication. Many hospitals now give analgesics in combination with other sedative agents and antinausea drugs.

An epidural, an injection of anesthetic into the spinal area, is a reliable form of orthodox pain relief during labor. Side effects are rare, although some women suffer headaches or backache afterwards; there is minimal effect on the baby. A woman may feel less in control of her labor, however, and forceps deliveries are more common with this method because the mother doesn't feel the same urge to push.

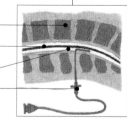

HOW AN EPIDURAL IS ADMINISTERED
The anesthetic is injected into the epidural space by means of a flexible tube called a catheter.

Vertebra
Spinal cord
Epidural space
Catheter

MEN'S COMPLAINTS

Disorders of the male reproductive system—the testicles, penis and prostate—can cause pain and embarrassment. If left untreated, they may put a man's health and fertility at risk.

Disorders affecting the male genitals often go untreated for too long because, through fear or embarrassment, many men are reluctant to discuss sexual health matters with their doctor. A knowledge of the causes and consequences of such disorders, and of the orthodox and complementary methods used in their treatment, can help men to prevent or alleviate many complaints that might otherwise cause psychological as well as physical pain.

PENIS PROBLEMS

The male sex organ, the penis, can be the source of considerable pain if the nerves, blood vessels, or skin become damaged through infection or, more rarely, injury.

Paraphimosis

An overtight foreskin (phimosis) that does not retract easily can cause painful erections and discomfort during sexual intercourse. In paraphimosis the foreskin is so tight that it becomes caught behind the head of the penis, or glans, causing swelling and pain.
Treatment Swelling may be reduced by applying an ice pack. The foreskin can then be returned to its normal position by squeezing the glans. In some cases, minor surgery may be needed to cut the foreskin.
▶ *See also massage, energy, natural therapies*

Priapism

Very rarely, an erection may occur without sexual stimulation and not subside with time. Known as priapism, this painful condition is due to disease or damage to the blood vessels supplying the penis.
Treatment If an erection fails to subside, medical treatment should be sought immediately to avoid permanent damage to the penis. Treatment usually involves taking blood from the penis to reduce the erection.
▶ *See also massage, energy, natural therapies*

Balanitis

An uncircumcised penis may become infected under the foreskin, making the area red, moist, and itchy. Known as balanitis, the condition can be caused by irritation from clothes or an allergic reaction of the skin to a chemical in soaps or condoms.
Treatment Balanitis is usually treated with ointment or antibiotics. Applying aloe vera gel to the affected area after washing and drying the penis may also be effective.
▶ *See also massage, energy, natural therapies*

PAIN AND THE MALE BODY

The male reproductive organs and urinary tract together form a complex system that can be prone to a variety of painful disorders. The older male, in particular, may suffer from pain associated with prostate disorders.

▶ *The bladder is susceptible to infection, which may cause pain on passing urine.*

▶ *The prostate gland, which lies below the bladder, gradually enlarges with age. It may start to press on the bladder, causing pain and obstructing the flow of urine.*

▶ *The penis, which carries urine and semen outside the body, may be affected by infection or inflammation.*

▶ *The testicles, which are so sensitive that even the slightest injury can cause severe pain, may become swollen or inflamed.*

STRESS AND HEALTH
Many men neglect their emotional health. Relaxation and stress reduction play an essential role in the relief of illnesses.

121

LOOKING AFTER YOUR PENIS

Healthy diet, exercise, and good hygiene can help a man to avoid some of the disorders that affect male sex organs:

■ *Always wash the penis carefully when taking a bath or shower. If you are uncircumcised, pull back the foreskin to clean the head of the penis and avoid a build-up of oily secretions called smegma.*

■ *At least once a week, massage the penis with essential oil of tea tree, an antibacterial agent, mixed with a carrier such as almond oil.*

■ *Exercise regularly to improve sex drive and general performance.*

■ *Keep the genital muscles (which control urine flow) well toned by regularly squeezing the muscles for 3 seconds and then releasing.*

ANATOMY OF THE PENIS

The penis, the male sex organ, is susceptible to inflammation and infection through unprotected sexual intercourse and poor hygiene practices. Infection is most likely to develop underneath the foreskin in uncircumcised men, and in the urethra, the tube that conducts semen and urine along the penis. Using condoms and regular washing can help to prevent many of the disorders that may affect the penis.

CROSS-SECTION OF THE PENIS
The penis is the male organ through which semen and urine pass out of the body. It consists of three groups of spongy tissue. When a man becomes sexually aroused, these tissues fill with blood under pressure, expand, and lengthen to produce an erection.

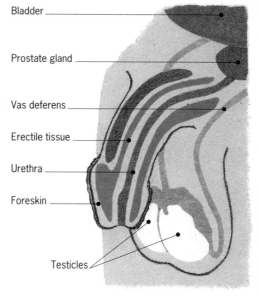

Bladder
Prostate gland
Vas deferens
Erectile tissue
Urethra
Foreskin
Testicles

Peyronie's disease

With Peyronie's disease, part of the sheath of fibrous connective tissue in the penis becomes thicker, causing an abnormal bend during erection. In some cases the penis becomes so distorted that intercourse is painful or even impossible. Little is known about the causes of this disease, which usually affects men over the age of 40. Even if the condition persists, pain on erection normally eases within 12 to 18 months.
Treatment Corticosteroids are usually prescribed to alleviate the pain. If the condition persists, surgery may be necessary.
▶ *See also energy, natural therapies*

TESTICLE PAIN

Hanging behind and below the penis in a pouch of skin called the scrotum are the testicles, or testes, which produce sperm and the male sex hormone testosterone. They are vulnerable to injury and pain, especially during sports activities. A heavy blow to the testicles may tear the testicle wall, causing severe pain and bleeding into the scrotum, and will require surgery to repair.

There are a range of disorders that can affect the testicles (see below), but not all of them cause pain. Cancer of the testicle, for example, is usually painless. You should see a doctor if you experience inflammation or abnormal pain in the testicles or notice any abnormal swelling when doing a regular testicular examination (see page 124).

Hydrocele

Occasionally, fluid accumulates in the scrotum around the testicles, due to inflammation, infection, or injury. This may cause a painless swelling.
Treatment The fluid may be drained off under a local anesthetic. If the problem persists, surgery may be necessary.
▶ *See also energy, natural therapies*

Varicocele

Aching in the scrotum may be due to a varicocele, a usually painless condition almost exclusively affecting the left testicle. The condition is caused by a valve in the testicular vein failing to close properly, so that blood drains back and collects in the vein.
Treatment Any pain associated with varicocele can usually be relieved with simple painkillers such as acetaminophen. Surgery may be necessary to tie off the swollen vein. Supporting the scrotum with tighter underpants or an athletic support can be helpful.
▶ *See also energy, natural therapies*

Torsion of the testicle

The spermatic cord, which connects the testicle to the bladder, can suddenly twist and obstruct the blood supply. The pain is acute and often very severe.
Treatment You should consult a doctor immediately, as surgery may be necessary to restore the blood supply to the testes.
▶ *See also energy, natural therapies*

Man with Painful Urination

Once young people get caught up in the social whirl of student life, it is easy for them to fall into the trap of excessive drinking and smoking, poor diet, casual sexual affairs, and insufficient sleep. The body may react to this unhealthy lifestyle by becoming prone to infections and developing chronic painful disorders that can be difficult to treat and tend to recur.

Alan is a single, outgoing, 22-year-old student who enjoys socializing with friends most evenings and who lives on a diet of junk food. Recently, he experienced an aching pain in his groin, genitals, and lower back and he constantly had the urge to pass urine. The pain gradually became more severe and he noticed his urine was cloudy and contained some blood. His doctor prescribed antibiotics but Alan's pain continued, so he was referred to a urology specialist who diagnosed inflammation of the prostate (prostatitis). In spite of a further course of antibiotics the symptoms have persisted. Because of the constant pain, Alan finds it difficult to concentrate and his social life and studying are suffering.

WHAT SHOULD ALAN DO?

Alan should consult a specialist at a pain management center. There he will have access to a multi-disciplinary health team offering treatments such as acupuncture, TENS, and hypnotherapy. Alan should also look at his diet and general lifestyle, which are probably adding to his problems. He is not in a steady relationship but has had several casual affairs, which may have put him at risk of a sexually transmitted infection. Psychologists at the center can offer advice on cutting down on drinking and smoking. Alan should begin to exercise regularly, walking every day as much as his pain allows. A course of antidepressants may help relieve the pain.

Action Plan

DIET
Avoid alcohol, which irritates the bladder. Increase water intake to eight glasses per day to dilute the urine and wash out bacteria.

LIFESTYLE
Make time for relaxation exercises to reduce stress levels, and restore balance to a hectic lifestyle by sticking to a regular schedule that ensures adequate sleep.

SEX LIFE
Follow safer sex practices, such as always using a condom if he has multiple sexual partners or his partner's sexual history is unknown to him.

DIET
Spicy foods, caffeine, alcohol, tobacco, and foods high in fat and sugar can irritate the prostate and negate the effects of essential nutrients such as zinc and vitamin C.

SEX LIFE
Inflamed prostate is often caused by an infection such as chlamydia, which can be passed on during sexual intercourse.

LIFESTYLE
Lack of sleep and broken rest patterns, together with excessive smoking, drinking, and irregular meal times, can have a detrimental effect on the immune system, leading to chronic or recurring infections.

HOW THINGS TURNED OUT FOR ALAN

The antidepressants made Alan feel drowsy and he found it harder to pass urine. TENS proved to be helpful, but Alan did not feel that it provided a long-term solution. However, acupuncture and relaxation have been effective and counseling has increased his self-esteem. He is now in a steady relationship, so with an improved diet, regular exercise, and a supportive girlfriend, his life has become more stable and his health has greatly improved.

Testicular examination

An abnormal swelling of the testes may indicate a serious problem, such as testicular cancer, and should be reported to a doctor as soon as possible. You should regularly examine both testicles—cancers are usually firm to the touch and neither tender nor painful when pressed.

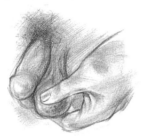

EXAMINING THE TESTICLES
Hold the scrotum gently and feel the entire surface of the testicle for any abnormal lump.

Epididymitis

The epididymis, the coiled tube that carries sperm to the penis, can become infected, causing a dull, aching pain and, in severe cases, inflammation of the scrotum. The pain may be worse during ejaculation and the semen may contain blood or pus.

Treatment The condition usually responds to antibiotics and simple painkillers. If the condition becomes chronic, patients need the specialist care of a urologist and possibly a pain management clinic.
▶ *See also energy, natural therapies*

Orchitis

A virus, such as mumps, can cause inflammation of the testes, known as orchitis. Pain is severe and often accompanied by fever.

Treatment Inflammation and pain can be eased with painkillers and by applying icepacks to the testes. Alternating warm and cold sitz baths may also be beneficial. If the pain persists in spite of treatment, medical advice must be sought to exclude the possibility of torsion of the testicle (see page 122).
▶ *See also energy, natural therapies*

PROSTATE PROBLEMS

Pain in the lower abdomen in men may be due to disorders of the prostate. Situated under the bladder and in front of the rectum, the gland produces some of the secretions in seminal fluid, and it may become inflamed, enlarged, or cancerous.

Inflamed prostate

If the prostate becomes inflamed, the need to urinate becomes more frequent and often there is pain or difficulty in passing urine . This condition is called prostatitis and is usually caused by a bacterial infection that has spread from the urethra. The urine may be cloudy and ejaculation painful.

Treatment Prostatitis is usually treated with antibiotics. The condition has been linked to a zinc deficiency, so eating zinc-rich foods, such as seafood, meat, and whole-grain cereals, or taking zinc supplements may be helpful. Occasionally the condition does not clear up, despite no visible evidence of infection. Treatment of chronic prostatitis can be difficult, requiring the expertise of a urologist and possibly a pain management specialist.
▶ *See also massage, energy, natural therapies*

Enlarged prostate

The prostate gland often enlarges from middle age onwards. In most men this does not cause any symptoms, but in some an enlarged prostate constricts the urethra, blocking the flow of urine. Symptoms include difficulty urinating or incontinence. The bladder may also become distended, causing pain in the abdomen. Cancer of the prostate may also cause similar symptoms, so it is important to consult a doctor as soon as possible if you experience any of them.

Treatment Mild symptoms usually do not require treatment, although increasing your intake of zinc may be useful (see above). some naturopaths advocate special massage via the rectum to improve the drainage of the gland and reduce congestion. In severe cases, surgery may be necessary.
▶ *See also massage, movement, natural therapies*

SOOTHING THE PROSTATE WITH YOGA

Yoga can help to improve blood circulation to the prostate and thus stimulate proper functioning of the organ. It also aids relaxation and reduces stress, which might otherwise inhibit the immune system and delay recovery. Try to make yoga a daily activity; it can be very useful in preventing stress from building up.

2 Put the soles of your feet together and lower the knees. Relax your groin. Hold the position for 5 minutes.

1 Lie on your back, using a blanket for support, if necessary. Bend your knees, placing your feet close to your buttocks.

MEN'S AND WOMEN'S COMPLAINTS

Some painful, debilitating disorders of the urinary system affect both men and women. They can often be avoided by careful attention to diet and hygiene and by using safer sex practices.

The urinary system includes the kidneys and bladder, the tubes (ureters) connecting the kidneys to the bladder, and the tube (urethra) connecting the bladder to the outside. Some urinary tract infections are caused by sexually transmitted diseases (STDs). If an STD is left untreated, it can not only cause bladder and kidney infections but also spread to other reproductive organs and lead to infertility. If you think you may have an STD, both you and your sexual partner should seek medical attention at once. You can reduce the risk of STDs by following safe sex practices.

URINARY SYSTEM DISORDERS

The urinary system is susceptible to a wide variety of disorders. Although these are generally not life threatening, they can cause extreme discomfort and distress.

A burning pain when passing urine is usually due to inflammation of the bladder (cystitis) or urethra (urethritis). Infection of the bladder is more common in females—the urethra is much shorter so infection can spread more easily. Painful urination may be a symptom of vaginal thrush (candidiasis), a sexually transmitted disease, or an allergy to perfumed soaps or deodorants.

Kidney and ureter problems

The kidneys play an essential role in filtering the blood and removing waste products and excess water from the body. They can easily become swollen by an infection, tumor, or cyst in the ureter or in the kidney itself. This swelling, or distension, can cause extreme pain but is not generally life endangering. Kidney pain is usually felt in the lower back, and there may be blood in the urine. A common problem affecting the

ureter is kidney stones, which cause extreme pain as they move down the tube.

Treatment By caring for your kidneys you can help to prevent many painful conditions associated with the urinary system. Drinking more than 2 quarts (about 2 liters) of water a day helps keep the urine diluted and thus decreases the risk of kidney stones

URINARY TRACT

The urinary tract is a complex system for ridding the body of waste products. Infections of the system may affect both men and women, although urethral infections are more common in men, while bladder infections are more common in women because of their shorter urethra.

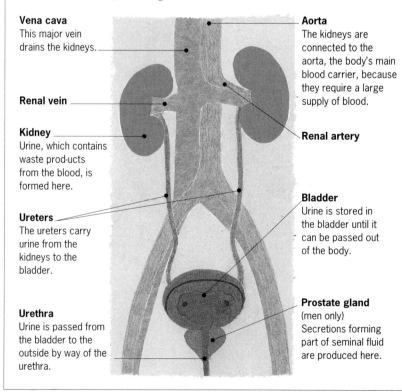

Vena cava
This major vein drains the kidneys.

Renal vein

Kidney
Urine, which contains waste prod-ucts from the blood, is formed here.

Ureters
The ureters carry urine from the kidneys to the bladder.

Urethra
Urine is passed from the bladder to the outside by way of the urethra.

Aorta
The kidneys are connected to the aorta, the body's main blood carrier, because they require a large supply of blood.

Renal artery

Bladder
Urine is stored in the bladder until it can be passed out of the body.

Prostate gland
(men only)
Secretions forming part of seminal fluid are produced here.

CYSTITIS RELIEF

Neutralizing your urine can counteract the burning pain of cystitis. You can do this by eating watermelon regularly, or by mixing a teaspoon of baking soda with a glass of water and drinking it twice a day.

FIGHTING CYSTITIS

Cystitis can be brought on by a variety of factors, including stress, bruising during sexual intercourse, diet, oral contraceptives, and bacteria spreading from the rectum. You can help to prevent cystitis by simple measures.

▶ *Never delay the desire to urinate.*

▶ *Always apply a lubricating jelly before intercourse.*

▶ *Try different positions, if sexual intercourse brings on attacks.*

▶ *Shower and pass urine after intercourse to help flush out infection.*

▶ *Wipe from front to back after going to the toilet, to avoid spreading bacteria to the urethra.*

▶ *Avoid perfumed soaps, deodorants, or douches that may cause irritation.*

---

and infection. Emptying your bladder as soon as you feel the need is also important for preventing stones from forming and bacteria from breeding. Drinking one or two glasses of wine a day can also reduce the risk of kidney stones developing.

▶ *See also massage, movement, natural therapies*

Cystitis

Cystitis is an inflammation of the lining of the bladder, which causes a continuous burning ache deep in the pelvis. Pain may radiate to the back, lower abdomen, urethra, and external genitals. Sufferers often experience painful or urgent urination, blood in the urine, and low-grade fever. Most urinary infections are caused by *E. coli* bacteria. In men acute cystitis may be due to inflammation of the prostate.

Treatment Acute cystitis is best managed by taking antibiotics and drinking plenty of fluids to flush out the infection. Eating yogurt with live acidophilus cultures restores beneficial bacteria killed by the antibiotics. Drinking cranberry or blueberry juice regularly is effective for treating and preventing urinary tract infections, because it makes the bladder less hospitable to bacteria. It should be pure juice or the concentrate, not a juice cocktail. If you like, mix it with apple juice to offset the tartness. Aromatherapy may help to relieve the pain. Add 20 drops of essential oil of juniper, eucalyptus, or sandalwood to a warm bath. Recommended herbal remedies include uva ursi (bearberry) capsules or tea, which must be taken with milk or a teaspoon (5 ml) of baking soda to be effective, and buchu tea (1 teaspoon of dried leaves per cup).

▶ *See also massage, movement, energy therapies*

Urethritis

Urethritis is an inflammation of the urethra, usually due to infection. The condition can cause pain when passing urine, fever, and a frequent urge to urinate. Urethritis may result from a sexually transmitted disease (see page 125), a bacterial infection, or, in men, an enlarged prostate.

Treatment The prevention and treatment of urethritis are the same as for cystitis.

▶ *See also massage, energy, natural therapies*

Candidiasis (Thrush)

This is a fungal infection that mainly affects the vagina, although it can be passed to and from a male partner during sexual intercourse and cause a rash on the penis. It produces soreness and intense itching of the vulva and vagina, a thick, creamy discharge, and sometimes painful urination and intercourse. The *Candida albicans* microorganism that causes the condition occurs naturally in the vagina but is usually held in check by bacteria that also exist there. Anything that affects this natural balance, for example, taking antibiotics, wearing tight clothing, or using highly perfumed soaps or deodorants, can lead to infection.

Treatment Candidiasis is usually treated with antifungal pessaries and creams. The condition is often relieved by applying plain yogurt to a tampon and inserting it into the vagina. Herbal, homeopathic, and naturopathic remedies can also be effective.

▶ *See also massage, energy, natural therapies*

Genital herpes

Genital herpes is a sexually transmitted disease caused by the herpes simplex virus. Common symptoms include a burning rash and multiple painful genital blisters, swollen lymph nodes, headache, fever, and painful urination. Medical attention should be sought as soon as possible.

Treatment This condition cannot be cured but antiviral drugs may help to prevent outbreaks of blisters or make attacks less severe. Both the severity and frequency of attacks should subside as your body builds up its own resistance. Pain may also be relieved by over-the-counter pain relievers and warm salt baths.

▶ *See also massage, energy, natural therapies*

Chlamydia

Chlamydia is a sexually transmitted disease. In men, urination is painful, the testicles are swollen, and often there is a discharge from the penis. Women may experience abnormal vaginal discharge and pain during urination and sexual intercourse, but often there are no symptoms. If the condition is left untreated it can lead to pelvic inflammatory disease (see page 118). It is a major cause of infertility and miscarriage in women.

Treatment Chlamydia is usually treated with antibiotics. You can help prevent chlamydia from recurring by eating yogurt with live acidophilus and by building up your immune system with a healthy diet.

▶ *See also massage, energy, natural therapies*

CHAPTER 8

BACK AND LIMB PAIN

Probably all of us will suffer from back or limb pain to some degree at some point in our lives, yet it is poorly understood. Although in most cases medical attention is not necessary, there are some instances when these musculoskeletal pains require investigation and specific treatment. This chapter looks into a variety of types and causes of back and limb pain, and their possible treatments.

BACK AND NECK PAIN

Back and neck pain may be caused by injury, inflammation, or stress. They may also be referred from another site, due to a problem in that area.

Back and neck problems can cause severe, debilitating pain. Yet in many cases examination and X-rays fail to show a cause, and conventional medical techniques often provide inadequate or no relief. Alternative therapies like acupuncture and reflexology can help ease the pain and enable sufferers to lead more normal lives. Strengthening back and abdominal muscles is a major key to recovery.

DEFINING BACKACHE

Backache can affect anybody at any time, regardless of age, occupation, or level of health or fitness. The pain is felt somewhere along the spine between the coccyx and neck. This area can be divided into three sections, each of which is prone to particular kinds of pain: the lower back (lumbar, or sacral, spine); upper back (thoracic spine); and the neck (cervical spine)

THE LOWER BACK

The lumbar spine, five jointed vertebrae that make up part of the lower back, are under a lot of pressure during the act of lifting. For this reason lower back pain, or lumbago, often affects people whose jobs involve heavy lifting or carrying. But anyone who has weak back and abdominal muscles or is overweight can injure this area with a simple twisting or bending movement, by lifting a heavy load incorrectly, or sitting too long in one position.

Back strain

Many people experience low back pain after a heavy session in the garden or after working on a car engine over the weekend. The cause of these attacks is almost invariably back strain—an overstretched ligament, muscle, or joint. For reasons that are poorly understood, back strain is sometimes accompanied by leg pain that is similar to that of sciatica (see opposite page). Unlike

THE SPINE

The spine is the curved column of bones and cartilage that extends from the base of the skull to the pelvis. Resembling a child's building blocks, the bones are supported by various ligaments, additional joints at the back, and a range of muscles both around and in front of the spine itself. In a canal behind the vertebrae is the spinal cord, an extension of the brain and a vital part of the central nervous system.

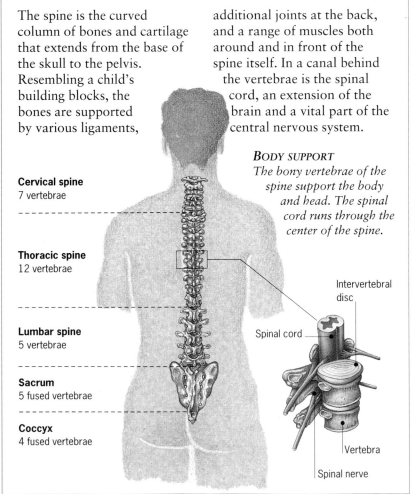

BODY SUPPORT
The bony vertebrae of the spine support the body and head. The spinal cord runs through the center of the spine.

Cervical spine
7 vertebrae

Thoracic spine
12 vertebrae

Lumbar spine
5 vertebrae

Sacrum
5 fused vertebrae

Coccyx
4 fused vertebrae

Intervertebral disc

Spinal cord

Vertebra

Spinal nerve

DID YOU KNOW?
At least 80 percent of North Americans suffer an occasional backache, and for 15 percent the problem is chronic. Fortunately, most backaches go away by themselves or with simple home remedies.

that condition, however, back strain is not due to pressure on a nerve.

Treatment You can usually ease the pain of back strain with rest or by taking mild painkillers. A word of caution, however: too much rest can cause stiffness of the lower back, which in itself creates pain because the muscles tighten and become resistant to exercise. It is important to strike a happy balance between rest and activity.

If the strain recurs or becomes chronic, take a close look at activities that may be causing it. For instance, if your work involves heavy lifting or long periods of standing or sitting, specialized machinery or a revision in routines or techniques may help to overcome potential difficulties. Inadequate abdominal tone and poor posture are often major culprits. Abdominal exercises and conscious improvement of posture (see page 63) can rectify this problem. Women should also look at how they carry their handbags and how much weight is contained in them. Habitually carrying a heavy object on one shoulder is the cause of many back problems.

If symptoms persist, seek the help of a physiotherapist or other practitioner of manipulative therapies (see page 73). Ultrasound and infrared treatments can be very effective. More important, however, is to begin an exercise program to minimize stiffness and help to prevent recurring prob-

lems. A pain clinic, physiatrist, physiotherapist, or family doctor can usually advise you on a regimen best suited to your needs. And relaxation techniques can help prevent or offset depression about the condition, which would compound the original pain.

▶ *See also manipulative, movement, massage, energy, natural, mind, relaxation therapies*

Disc disorders and sciatica

The spongy discs between the vertebrae consist of a soft, jelly-like core surrounded by a hard outer ring (annulus fibrosus). This outer layer is fairly elastic and is under constant pressure. If it tears, the inner jelly-like material leaks into the spinal cord and puts pressure on a nerve root.

This very painful condition, known as a slipped or prolapsed disc, usually produces severe pain in the lower back, because the nerve root is very sensitive. It is often accompanied by shooting pains and needles and pins down the leg as far as the foot. This latter condition is called sciatica, because the pain follows the path of the sciatic nerve.

Treatment In most cases a slipped disc is relieved within six weeks with the aid of rest, mild painkillers, and physiotherapy. However, if the pain persists over a longer period, surgery may be necessary. Placing a wrapped ice pack and a hot-water bottle alternately on the site of the pain for about 10 minutes twice a day can help reduce the

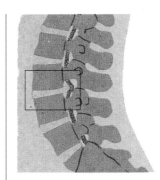

PROLAPSED DISC
If a spinal disc ruptures and its soft spongy core (shown in blue) leaks out, it may put pressure on a nerve (shown in purple), causing severe pain and disability.

RELIEVING PAIN FROM A SLIPPED DISC

A slipped disc can respond well to simple bed rest. To ease pressure on the spine, lie flat on your back with your shoulders, hips, and ankles aligned. Elevating 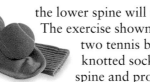 the lower spine will also ease pressure. The exercise shown below requires two tennis balls placed in a knotted sock; they raise the spine and provide relief.

ELEVATING THE SPINE
Lie on the floor and place the balls under your lower back, one on either side of the spine. Hold the position for 5 minutes. Remove the balls and relax for 2 minutes, then place the balls under your buttocks and repeat the exercise.

Keep knees bent
and your feet placed flat on the floor

129

Man with Slipped Disc

A healthy back is remarkably resilient, able to cope with a wide range of pressures during work and leisure activities. Sudden excessive strain, however, especially if coupled with overweight and reduced flexibility due to lack of exercise, can lead to painful back injuries. In this situation, changes in diet, lifestyle, and work practices may be necessary to correct the problem.

Eric is a 32-year-old construction worker presently working on a demolition site. Though he keeps active with football on the weekends, a taste for fast foods, especially french fries, have left him a few pounds overweight. One day at work, Eric was wheeling a heavy wheelbarrow of bricks across the site, when he suddenly felt the most excruciating pain in his back; he was unable to work for the rest of the day. A dull, intermittent pain radiated into his leg. His doctor diagnosed a prolapsed intervertebral disc and referred him to a chiropractor. Eric finds the pain unendurable and a threat to his livelihood, as he is afraid to try any activity that might aggravate it.

WHAT SHOULD ERIC DO?

Eric should see a chiropractor for treatment. Manipulation of his spine will help ease pressure on the disc by relaxing the surrounding muscles, relieving inflamed ligaments, and separating the vertebral spaces. He could also try a course of acupuncture, which can relieve some of the acute pain and muscle spasm. Eric has been advised to get plenty of bed rest and he finds it takes the pressure off his back. To prevent future back strain, Eric must lose weight and begin to strengthen his back and abdominal muscles with regular exercise. If he joins the YMCA or a health club, a trainer can help him plan a fitness regimen that is suited to his particular needs.

DIET

Fast food is usually poor in nutritional value and high in fat and cholesterol.

LIFESTYLE

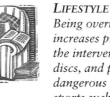

Being overweight increases pressure on the intervertebral discs, and potentially dangerous contact sports such as football put further strain on the body.

WORK

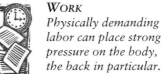

Physically demanding labor can place strong pressure on the body, the back in particular.

Action Plan

DIET
Replace fatty foods with more vegetables, fruits, lean meats, and whole-grain cereals to lose weight without a reduction in energy.

LIFESTYLE
Cut out football for now. Regularly stretch and do low-impact aerobic exercise to help strengthen the back muscles. Allow time for warm-up exercises before physical activities.

WORK
Employ safe lifting and carrying techniques so that the back is not strained. Try to economize on effort used to perform each task.

HOW THINGS TURNED OUT FOR ERIC

Eric found that several sessions of acupuncture and a course of chiropractic treatment relieved his back pain effectively. The stretches and exercises that a back specialist taught him are also proving beneficial. He swims twice a week and eats healthier meals. He is losing weight at a steady rate and now feels much better, which encourages him to continue his diet. He is also getting useful advice from a friend who dealt with the same problems.

pain of sciatica.

▶ See also manipulative, movement, massage, energy, natural, relaxation therapies

Arthritis of the spine

Discs dry out and become narrower with age, and this process can cause chronic back pain. If the disc exerts pressure on a nerve, the back pain may be accompanied by acute attacks of sciatica. As the disc becomes narrower, the facet joints behind the spine change shape and alignment and they too become worn. If this process continues, arthritis can develop, causing chronic pain and stiffness. In some people the condition may lead to narrowing of the spinal canal (spinal stenosis), which causes leg pain when walking and limits activity significantly.

Treatment People with arthritic spines usually have to restrict their activities, because exercise, bending, stretching, and lifting cause flare-ups. This may mean changing jobs. Back supports have been prescribed in the past, but if worn for more than a day or so during an acute attack, they can compound the problem by weakening and stiffening the back. A balanced approach with rest, anti-inflammatory drugs, and an exercise program is the best form of treatment under these circumstances, and a pain clinic (see page 69) or your doctor can advise you.

A natural alternative to orthodox anti-inflammatory drugs is a tincture consisting of equal parts of meadowsweet, willow bark, black cohosh, prickly ash, celery seed, and nettle taken three times a day in half teaspoon amounts. To prevent stiffness, try drinking aloe vera juice or applying aloe vera gel to the affected areas. Rolfing (see page 72) helps many arthritis sufferers. The founder of this technique, Ida Rolf, discovered that exercising the body's connective tissues helped to cure her own arthritis.

▶ See also manipulative, movement, massage, energy, natural, relaxation therapies

Ankylosing spondylitis

In ankylosing spondylitis, a chronic, progressive joint disease, the spine becomes inflamed and vertebrae fuse together, causing pain and stiffness in the lower back. Symptoms tend to be worse early in the morning and in some cases the stiffness may affect daily activities. The condition predominantly affects males, and the first symptoms typically show up between the ages of 15 and 30. Early indications are severe pain and stiffness, usually in the lower back, and these may be accompanied by fatigue, loss of appetite, and sometimes a low-grade fever. A form of the disorder has been linked to colitis, an inflammation of the colon (lower bowel).

Treatment Pain and stiffness caused by ankylosing spondylitis may be minimized by heat therapy, massage, deep-breathing exercises, posture training (see Alexander Technique, page 76), stringent exercise programs—especially daily swimming and T'ai chi (see page 75). Stretching exercises can help to prevent curvature of the spine. For controlling pain, nonsteroidal anti-inflammatory drugs in the ibuprofen category. seem to be the most effective. Acupuncture

EXERCISES FOR BACKACHE

Backache is one of the most common forms of chronic pain. Regular light exercise helps to keep the muscles working efficiently and the joints supple. Have a trainer help you develop a daily exercise regimen to meet your needs. Even if your mobility is severely limited, the exercise below can promote flexibility and relieve pain.

1 *Sit with your right leg straight out. Bend your left knee and place your left foot on the outside of your right knee.*

2 *Bend your right elbow and put it on the outside of your left thigh just above the knee. Breathe in deeply and try to straighten your back.*

3 *With your left hand behind you, slowly twist your upper body and head to look over your left shoulder. Hold for 20 seconds and repeat for the other side.*

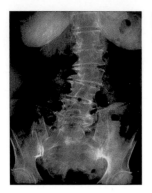

AGE AND THE SPINE
The X-ray above of an elderly woman shows the characteristics of an advanced form of osteoarthritis: curvature of the spine and reduction of space between vertebrae. Increasing your intake of calcium can do much to prevent the onset of the disease. Good sources of calcium include low fat milk and yogurt, canned sardines with bones, green leafy vegetables, and soybeans.

may also be helpful. To relieve aching and stiffness try a few drops of arnica tincture in your bath. Because of the connection with colitis in some people (see page 111), making changes to your diet may help prevent the onset of the condition. A low-fat, low-starch, and low-sugar diet is recommended to help starve and limit the growth of undesirable bacteria.

▶ *See also movement, energy, natural therapies*

Osteoporosis

As the body ages, the bones naturally become thinner. In the condition known as osteoporosis the density of the bones decreases, making them brittle and less capable of withstanding stress. Women are particularly vulnerable to this condition after menopause, when the ovaries cease producing the hormone estrogen, which helps to maintain bone density. Osteoporosis can cause minute fractures in the vertebrae, which leads in turn to ligament and muscle strains as the overall posture of the spine is changed. Eventually, the vertebrae may collapse completely, producing severe localized pain and tenderness.

Treatment It is difficult to replace bone tissue once it has been lost. However, it is possible to reduce the risk of osteoporosis by exercising regularly and by maintaining a balanced diet that includes plenty of foods containing vitamin D and calcium. Supplements may also be necessary.

Calcium citrate and calcium carbonate are the most easily absorbed A patient who lies in bed loses muscle and bone mass. Walking, running, aerobics, and other weight-bearing exercise are all good for helping to minimize the loss of bone. Hydrotherapy exercises in a pool heated to body temperature 98.6°F (37°C) may also be effective. Calcitonin, a thyroid hormone that regulates calcium metabolism and inhibits calcium loss from bones, shows promise as a drug to halt osteoporosis. The following herbs used alone or in combination may be effective for treating estrogen deficiencies: liquorice, black cohosh, ginseng, and red raspberry leaf.

▶ *See also manipulative, movement, massage, energy, natural, relaxation therapies*

Back pain in pregnancy

In the last months of pregnancy the increased weight of the fetus places greater strain on the muscles and ligaments of the lower back, causing pain. The pain may also be due to hormone imbalance or gynecological complications such as a retroverted uterus. However, the pain almost always subsides after the birth.

Treatment Careful prenatal screening and advice on posture and suitable activities can help to minimize back pain in pregnancy. Swimming is an ideal exercise right up until the later stages. The body is supported by the water, which eases the strain on weight-bearing joints. Massage is very beneficial for relieving back and neck pain.

THE UPPER BACK

Back pain in the thoracic spine is often the result of a strain in the latissimus dorsi muscle, caused by lifting. In the elderly, upper back pain may be due to osteoporosis. Pain may also be referred from another site; for instance, duodenal ulcers or gallstones can cause aching in the upper back.

THE NECK

The neck, a delicate structure, is vulnerable to several painful disorders. A person may suffer greatly from any swelling or inflammation of muscles or joints in the neck, because they are so tightly packed together.

Acute neck strain

If you sit over a book or work at a keyboard for a lengthy period of time without a

MASSAGE IN PREGNANCY

Back, shoulder, and neck pain are extremely common during pregnancy. Massage can help to relieve some of these pains. However, it's important to avoid manipulating the spine; instead concentrate on the muscles that surround it.

SOOTHING AN ACHING BACK
Sit so that you are leaning over the back of a chair. Your partner should use long sweeping strokes, starting from the base of the spine and gradually moving upward and outward.

break, acute neck strain may result. A change in position or work habits can help to prevent or alleviate this problem.

Treatment Simple stretches are useful for preventing neck strain. Clasp your hands and cup them over the back of your head. Drop your head forward and feel your neck stretching. Using one hand, push your head to one side and then do the same in the opposite direction. Anti-inflammatory painkillers or infusions of valerian may help to ease pain. Compresses of an anti-inflammatory herb such as willow bark can help relax stiff muscles. You could also try pressing on acupressure points at the top of the shoulders, a few inches out from the base of the neck, to ease pain and stiffness.

▶ *See also manipulative, movement, massage, energy, natural, relaxation therapies*

Whiplash injury

In a rear or head-on collision in a car, the head is thrown backward and forward by the impact. This may cause whiplash, which is felt as an acute neck strain a few hours or even a few days after the accident. Head restraints on car seats can prevent damage to the cervical spine in collisions, but must be at the appropriate level. Severe injuries, including fractures and dislocations, tend to occur only in the most violent collisions.

Treatment Immediately after a whiplash injury, an ice pack should be held against the painful area for 10 minutes, then a hot-water bottle wrapped in a towel applied for another 10 minutes. This routine should be repeated every morning and evening. After the initial shock has subsided, the pain usually diminishes, but if it does not, treatment should be sought from a specialist such as a neurologist. A chiropractor, osteopath, or physiotherapist (see pages 70, 71, and 73) can help with pain relief. Acupuncture can also be effective.

The muscles around the spinal column are very strong and support the head on the neck for all activities. For this reason, after a whiplash injury surgical collars should be worn only if there is a risk of instability, as they weaken the muscles and cause further pain and stiffness. However, soft foam collars can be worn at night, because this is the time when the muscles of the head and neck are relaxed. The essential oils of rosemary and sweet marjoram can relieve pain: add 2 drops of each to your bath or put them in 2 teaspoons of carrier oil and rub it in night and morning. Simple painkillers may also be effective. Symptoms usually ease within two to three weeks—sticking to your rehabilitation schedule is essential to prevent development of chronic symptoms.

▶ *See also manipulative, movement therapies*

Cervical spondylosis

Cervical spondylosis, or arthritis of the neck, affects the joints between the vertebrae in the neck. The discs gradually lose fluid after early middle age and become narrower. This causes pain and stiffness in the neck and numbness and tingling in the arms and hands, if the disc is putting pressure on the nerves. The condition occurs in the vast majority of people, but most never suffer from neck pain. Certain individuals, however, may be prone to the problem—manual workers, football and rugby players, and people with other joint disorders such as rheumatoid arthritis, for example. It may also be brought on by whiplash neck injury after a car accident.

Treatment Usually pain can be controlled with over-the-counter painkillers, a collar for night wear, and occasional physiotherapy, particularly if the discs are pressing on a nerve. If the condition persists, surgery may be necessary to relieve pressure on the nerve by fusing the two problem vertebrae with a bone graft.

▶ *See also manipulative, massage therapies*

RELAXING THE NECK

If your neck feels tense and uncomfortable, try swathing it in a silk scarf. The warmth that this brings can help improve blood circulation and relieve muscle pain and tension.

REFLEXOLOGY FOR NECK PAIN

If your neck is too sensitive to touch, let alone massage, it may help to massage the feet instead. According to reflexologists, areas on the feet called reflex zones correspond to other parts of the body. If one of these zones is massaged it can relieve pain in a corresponding area of the body. You can give yourself a simple massage to relieve neck pain, but for a longer course of treatment it is advisable to contact a qualified practitioner.

MASSAGE FOR NECK PAIN
Massaging the ball of the foot and the area where the big toe joins the bottom of the foot can help bring relief from neck pain.

GENERAL JOINT PAIN

Pain in the limbs may be due to conditions arising in the joints of the arms or legs, it could be a referred pain from the back or neck. It might also signal a more general disorder.

JOINT RELIEF

Once the swelling of painful joints has subsided, applying a hot compress or the following mixture can help soothe aches. Expect the first few applications to cause a mild burning sensation.

▶ *Mix a few dashes of ground red (cayenne) pepper with 1 table-spoon (15 ml)of olive oil. Apply with gauze several times a day.*

▶ *Brew a strong infusion of chamomile, using 2 tablespoons dried flowers in 1/2 cup (120 ml) hot water. Strain it, then soak a clean cloth in the liquid and apply.*

There are many disorders that can cause severe pain in the limbs. In some cases, the condition may affect a single joint such as the knee, while in others, several joints such as the hips, wrists, and toes may be affected.

Osteoarthritis

Osteoarthritis is a common disease of the joints characterized by pain, inflammation, and stiffness. It is thought to be a disorder of the cartilage that covers the ends of the bones at the joint. Under normal circumstances this tough and well-lubricated material enables smooth movement of the joint. However, with age, excessive wear and tear, and injury, the cartilage begins to break down into flakes, some of which can form loose bodies in the joint. This causes the lining of the joint (synovium) to become inflamed and the joint to swell with excess fluid. The underlying bone gradually becomes exposed, causing spasm, then stiffness, as the sufferer tries to protect the diseased joint. New cartilage may form but this is usually of poorer quality and can cause osteophytes, overgrowths of the bone. These can hinder movement even further.

The condition can occur for no particular reason or it may be hereditary. Osteoarthritis of the hip is fairly common among the elderly and postmenopausal women who have a close relative, like a mother or sister, suffering from the condition. It can also be brought on by an injury to or a deformity of a joint, or an infection such as Lyme disease. **Treatment** In the early stages, nonsteroidal anti-inflammatory drugs such as aspirin; heat, for example, a warm bath or heating pad; and weight loss are effective for easing pain. If there is a large build-up of fluid in the joint, ice packs may help to reduce inflammation. Should the swelling persist, a doctor may decide to draw off the fluid

with a needle and syringe. It is important to maintain a balance between rest—to avoid aggravating the condition—and activity—to keep joints as mobile as possible. Resting too much can cause more stiffness. Putting all arthritic joints through a daily range-of-motion routine minimizes stiffness and retains joint function. A physical therapist or rehabilitative specialist can recommend the best exercises.

Chiropractic and acupuncture can be effective at relieving joint pain. You can also try massaging the muscles around the inflamed joints, moving with smooth and gentle strokes. Rubbing in an ointment that contains capsaicin (red pepper) is a proven pain reliever. You can also make your own preparation (see far left).

A number of herbal decoctions are recommended for arthritis. One is nettle (2 teaspoons dried leaves to 1 cup boiling water; steep for 5 minutes; strain. Another is dandelion (3 tablespoons finely chopped dandelion root and leaves to 2 cups cold water; boil for 3 minutes; steep for 10 minutes; strain) Both can be taken three times a day. Two other effective remedies are the anti-inflammatory devil's claw, available in tablets, and evening primrose, available both in capsules and as an extract.

▶ *See also manipulative, movement, massage, energy, natural therapies*

Rheumatoid arthritis

Rheumatoid arthritis is a painful disorder, characterized by inflammation and sometimes severe deformity of joints, particularly the fingers, wrists, knees, and hips. Although the cause is unknown, it is considered an autoimmune disorder, in which the immune system attacks the body's own tissues for no apparent reason. In this case, the synovial tissue lining the joints is attacked and becomes inflamed. The disease can also affect the blood vessels. The most common early symptoms are stiffness in the joints of fingers, hands, or feet, especially in the morning. In some people the condition affects only one or two joints, but in others it may spread to almost all joints in the body. Rheumatoid arthritis can afflict anyone, including babies, young children, and the elderly, although it most often occurs in middle-aged women.

Treatment Keeping joints mobile tends to help in the early stages. However, in time, activity becomes progressively more painful. Treatment is similar to that for osteoarthritis and includes anti-inflammatory painkillers, chiropractic, hydrotherapy, and acupuncture. Physiotherapy can help considerably. Also, occupational therapists can advise patients on how to cope with disability and introduce devices such as special bottle openers and cutlery designed for patients with finger joint disorders.

When arthritis is severe and does not respond to treatment, surgery may be considered. It is now possible to repair or replace joints—and thus restore mobility—in severely disabled patients.

▶ *See also manipulative, movement, massage, energy, natural therapies*

Gout

Gout is a joint disease that predominantly afflicts men. The big toe joint is usually affected but other joints such as the ankles, wrists, and knees can be involved. The disorder is caused by a build-up of the waste product uric acid in the blood. Crystals of uric acid form within the joint, causing acute inflammation, which usually lasts from 7 to 10 days. The affected joint becomes swollen, very tender, and hot, and the patient may develop a light fever.

Treatment Elevating the affected joint and rest are essential. Applying an ice pack for 3 to 5 minutes at regular intervals may help to ease the inflammation caused by an acute attack. If a large joint is affected, a doctor may decide to remove excess fluid with a needle and syringe. In some cases, tablets that help to reduce the level of uric acid in the blood will be prescribed.

As uric acid levels can be raised by high levels of a substance known as purine, avoiding foods that are high in purine, such as liver, poultry, and beans (see below), may help to reduce the risk of suffering future attacks.

According to some naturopaths eating celery seeds helps to eliminate excess uric acid in the blood. You can make an infusion by pouring boiling water over 2 teaspoons of crushed seeds. Allow the mixture to steep for 15 minutes and drink a cupful three times a day. Cutting down on alcohol and losing weight may also help to prevent the frequency of acute gout attacks.

▶ *See also manipulative, movement, massage, energy, natural therapies*

Cure from the sea
A simple marine creature called the sea cucumber may offer hope for osteoarthritis sufferers. According to a 1993 study by the University of Queensland in Australia, eating sea cucumbers can help alleviate the pain of osteoarthritis, because they contain chemical agents that attack the disease. After successful trials at the university, the Australian Department of Health authorized the use of the active ingredients isolated from sea cucumbers as an arthritis treatment.

FIGHTING GOUT

Naturopaths believe that a change of diet can help to reduce the risk of recurring attacks of gout. They suggest eating more foods that tend to lower the amount of uric acid in the blood and avoiding those foods that tend to raise it.

FOODS TO FIGHT GOUT
Eat cherries and other berries, apples, citrus fruits such as oranges and lemons, and vegetables such as leeks, broccoli, and celery.

GOUT-CAUSING FOODS TO AVOID
Stay away from peas and beans, mushrooms, cauliflower, and asparagus. Also cut down on organ meats, fish, seafood, and poultry.

Nightshade
An arthritis specialist in the United States, Dr. Robert Bingham, found that a third of his rheumatoid arthritis patients were sensitive to plants of the nightshade family, such as potatoes, tomatoes, peppers, and eggplant. To test whether they are contributing to your arthritic pain you can try eliminating these foods from your diet.

Problems Affecting Specific Joints

Joints may be affected by inflammation of surrounding tissues such as tendons. Rest and manipulative treatments can help to ease the pain, but occasionally, surgery may be necessary.

Two of the most common conditions affecting joints are inflammation of the tendons (tendinitis) and inflammation of the bursa (bursitis). Bursas are fluid-filled pads that act as shock absorbers and permit smooth movement of the joints.

THE SHOULDER

The shoulder is an extremely complicated joint. Pain can arise for a variety of reasons, but is often associated with rheumatoid arthritis or a previous injury. Athletes, in particular football and soccer players, are especially prone to shoulder injuries. People in certain occupations are also susceptible.

Tendinitis and bursitis

Many painful shoulder disorders are caused by problems in the subacromial space, just above the shoulder joint and below the collarbone, or clavicle. This space houses a tendon and a bursa. The tendon may be injured or the bursa inflamed. Both problems cause pain when the arm is raised.

Treatment Applying an ice pack to the area for 20 minutes at a time, three to four times a day, for the first 48 hours will diminish swelling and inflamation and ease the pain. After two days, apply moist heat with a poultice, hot pack, or hot shower for 20 minutes at a time, several times a day if possible. To restore movement, swing the arm gently and loosely. As soon as you can, begin to raise both arms over your head several times a day, reaching higher each day. It may help to visualize the pain as a sword in the joint. Imagine that ice is applied to the site and the sword is gradually drawn out; feel the pain gradually decreasing. If symptoms persist, a doctor may suggest corticosteroid injections.
▶ *See also manipulative, movement therapies*

Arthritis of the shoulder joint

Where the collarbone meets the shoulder blade there is a flat joint, the acromioclavicular joint, which moves very little. It can become arthritic, particularly in athletes and workers, such as hod carriers, who carry loads on their shoulders.

Treatment Injections of cortisone directly into the shoulder can help, but surgery may be necessary. Problems in the joint can cause it to press down on the subacromial space, leading to symptoms similar to those of tendinitis.
▶ *See also manipulative, movement therapies*

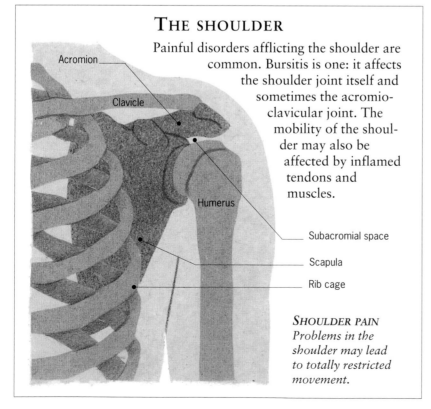

THE SHOULDER

Painful disorders afflicting the shoulder are common. Bursitis is one: it affects the shoulder joint itself and sometimes the acromioclavicular joint. The mobility of the shoulder may also be affected by inflamed tendons and muscles.

Acromion

Clavicle

Humerus

Subacromial space

Scapula

Rib cage

SHOULDER PAIN Problems in the shoulder may lead to totally restricted movement.

Frozen shoulder

When a painful injury or inflammation prompts a person not to move his shoulder, the inactivity allows adhesions, constricting bands of tissue, to form. Adhesions make it even more painful to move, and eventually the capsule lining the shoulder joint shrinks because of scar tissue from the adhesions. The condition particularly affects diabetics and people recovering from a stroke.

Treatment Frequent application of ice packs and a course of gentle but gradually progressing exercises are necessary to keep the shoulder mobile (see opposite page). Hydrotherapy can be effective, and massaging the muscles of the shoulder and those extending into the chest, back, and neck will help relieve tension and encourage movement. Osteopathic or chiropractic treatment can ease pain and restore mobility. Acupuncture and rolfing may also be beneficial.

▶ *See also manipulative, massage therapies*

THE ELBOW

Painful disorders affecting the elbow include arthritis and injuries to the joint and the surrounding muscles, ligaments, and tendons.

Tennis elbow

Overuse of the extensor muscles on the thumb side of the elbow causes strain on the tendon that attaches the elbow to the bone of the upper arm. The tendon can become inflamed, causing a painful condition called tennis elbow. The disorder is usually brought on by injury or a repetitive activity such as painting, keyboard work, or racket sports. If you're a tennis player, have a professional appraise your grip and check to see if your racket is correct for you.

Treatment To reduce inflammation, rest the arm and apply ice packs for the first 24 hours. Then bathe the elbow alternately in hot and cold water or apply ice packs, followed by a warm rub and brisk towel dry. This stimulates circulation and aids healing. Compresses or poultices of comfrey or arnica are also said to speed up healing. Acupuncture and frequent massage of the affected area with essential oils of lavender or rosemary helps stimulate blood flow. A steroid such as hydrocortisone injected into the area may be effective, but if symptoms persist, surgery to repair or reattach the tendon may be necessary.

▶ *See also manipulative, massage therapies*

Golfer's elbow

Overuse of the flexor muscles, which bend the wrist and fingers, causes inflammation and tenderness or pain on the inner side of the elbow. The condition, commonly known as golfer's elbow, is particularly prevalent in people who exercise frequently and in workers engaged in digging.

Treatment Follow the same procedures as for tennis elbow.

▶ *See also manipulative, movement therapies*

THE WRIST

Wrist pain may be caused by a variety of conditions, including degenerative joint diseases such as arthritis and inflammation of the tendon, tenosynovitis, for example.

Carpal tunnel syndrome

The median nerve, which passes into the hand via a passageway called the carpal tunnel, may become compressed and cause numbness, burning, and tingling in the hands. Symptoms tend to be worse at night. People whose jobs call for repeating the same motions over and over are vulnerable to the syndrome. Pregnant and overweight women, anyone with an underactive thryoid gland, and diabetics are also at increased risk.

Treatment Chiropractic, acupuncture, TENS, and ultrasound can help relieve pain. Wearing a cast (removed only when showering) may improve the condition. In severe cases, surgery to relieve the pressure on the nerve may be necessary.

▶ *See also manipulative, movement, massage, energy, natural therapies*

Acupressure points for carpal tunnel syndrome

An acupressure point that can be used to relieve wrist pain is found in the middle of the inner forearm two and a half finger lengths above the wrist crease. Firmly press this point on the affected arm for 2 minutes and repeat three times daily for a month. Alternatively, try a point the same distance above the wrist crease on the outside of the forearm between the two bones.

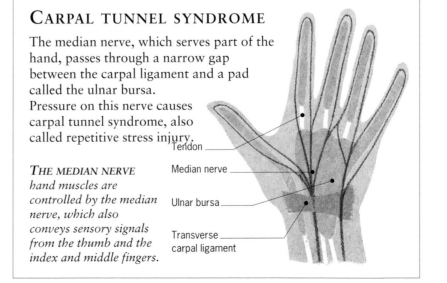

CARPAL TUNNEL SYNDROME

The median nerve, which serves part of the hand, passes through a narrow gap between the carpal ligament and a pad called the ulnar bursa.
Pressure on this nerve causes carpal tunnel syndrome, also called repetitive stress injury.

THE MEDIAN NERVE hand muscles are controlled by the median nerve, which also conveys sensory signals from the thumb and the index and middle fingers.

Tendon

Median nerve

Ulnar bursa

Transverse carpal ligament

Tenosynovitis

If the inner lining of the sheath surrounding a tendon becomes inflamed, generally from overuse, it can become swollen, tender, and even severely painful. This condition, known as tenosynovitis, usually affects the wrist and hand and is most often seen in people whose jobs involve repetitive actions—factory workers and keyboard operators, for instance.

Treatment Wearing a splint, resting the wrist, and taking anti-inflammatory drugs usually help to alleviate the pain. However, if pain persists, corticosteroid drugs may be injected into the wrist. Surgery might be necessary if fibrous bands develop between the tendon and its sheath.

THE KNEE

Knees are complicated joints that are prone to injury. They are subject to inflammation of the joints, tendons, and bursas, bleeding into the joint, and arthritis.

Sports injuries

The menisci, or crescent-shaped cartilages, in the knee that aid in joint stability, can tear and cause severe pain. Tendon strains and ruptures, muscle tears, and tendinitis are also common injuries among people active in sports.

Treatment Ice packs, rest, and physiotherapy help to relieve acute pain. More severe injuries may require surgery.

▶ See also manipulative, movement, massage, energy, relaxation therapies

Occupational knee problems

Miners and other people who work in the same position for long periods are prone to tears in the cartilage. Kneeling on all fours for a long time, for example while fitting a carpet, can cause prepatella bursitis, or housemaid's knee, when the bursa in front of the kneecap (patella) becomes swollen and inflamed. Kneeling in an upright position for a long period places great stress on the patella, tendons, and shin area. This causes symptoms similar to those of housemaid's knee and is known as parson's knee.

Treatment These injuries require the same treatment as athletic injuries. If the joint is severely inflamed, apply an ice pack three times a day (see page 155). Leave it for 5 minutes, remove for 5 minutes, and then replace for another 10 minutes. Once the swelling has gone down, apply a hot compress to the knee to aid healing. Corticosteroid injections in the bursa can help to reduce inflammation, and surgery is rarely necessary. Protective kneepads can prevent the problem from occurring.

▶ See also manipulative, movement therapies

THE FOOT

There are a number of causes of painful feet. In some people the balls of the feet are prominent, which can be a cause of pain. In such a case the problem can be managed by placing appropriate insoles in the shoes.

Foot disorders

These include swellings in the nerve at the front of the foot, which can be intensely painful. This condition is known as Morton's neuroma. Occasionally a bunion, a swelling of the bursa around a big toe joint, can cause pain. Arthritis may arise in the big toe joint, which can become stiff and require wider shoes or even surgery.

Treatment An ice pack on the painful area for 10 minutes while sitting with the leg raised can reduce swelling and relieve pain. Repeat every 10 minutes. To prevent chronic pain from bunions, which result from wearing narrow, high-heeled shoes, switch to roomy, flat shoes and insert arch supports and special pads to relieve pressure. Exercise your toes whenever possible. While seated, lift one bare foot six inches off the floor. Make six small circles in both directions, then stretch toes out and upward as far as possible. Repeat with the other foot.

FOOTBALL INJURIES
Soccer players are frequently afflicted with knee injuries. Sports physiotherapists are specially trained to relieve the pain caused by common strains and tears.

CHAPTER 9

LIVING WITH CHRONIC PAIN

Sufferers of chronic painful disorders can all too easily fall into a negative cycle of depression, tension, and irritability. This not only worsens the original pain but can also have serious consequences for the person's job, family, and social life. Learning to live with chronic pain means breaking out of this cycle by first accepting and then mastering the pain.

COPING WITH PAIN

Finding a positive way to live with chronic pain is a two-step process: the first step is to come to terms with the pain, and the second is to master it.

POSITIVE IMAGERY
Try digging deep down into your memory to remember and relive some of the positive experiences in your life, such as pleasant family holidays, the first days of your relationship with your partner, the day you were promoted. Once you can learn to push the pain to the back of your mind and stop thinking about it, your condition and general mental health should start to improve.

Unlike acute pain, which serves as a distress signal to warn of injury or illness, chronic pain often appears to have no purpose. It is sometimes regarded as useless because it may persist long after an injury has healed, or it may be caused by a chronic disease or disorder, such as cancer or arthritis, long after the onset of the disease has made any warning sign redundant. In some cases there may even be no apparent physical cause.

The persistance of chronic can seriously interfere with daily activities. In fact, for some people the situation may seem hopeless, but an understanding of chronic pain and the way it is linked with emotions and lifestyle can help a sufferer to rise above the condition and the problems it causes.

SURVIVING CHRONIC PAIN

Chronic pain poses emotional and psychological problems that can be at least as damaging as the physical consequences. Anyone who is in chronic pain suffers from a complex web of negative feelings, which in turn can affect not only the sufferer's well-being but also that of family, close friends, and colleagues at work.

The unpredictability of pain

Because persistent pain is unpredictable and often without apparent cause, a major worry for sufferers is feeling that they are not believed. One day the pain may stay at a manageable level and the next day flare up and force the person to take a day off from work, miss a family outing, or cancel a vacation The erratic nature of chronic pain makes it hard for colleagues, family, and friends to understand the problem and sympathize. Even doctors can be confused by some cases of chronic pain, as X-rays and other tests may show no signs of a disorder.

Coping strategies Chronic pain sufferers have to realize that there may be no simple explanation for their problems. Many patients go to a doctor with their hopes raised, expecting their illness to be named and an antidote prescribed. When this fails to happen they become depressed. Instead of leaving it all up to a doctor, it's better to take responsibility for one's own health. If you have a pain problem, try to find out all you can about your condition and the underlying cause of the pain. For example, learning that healing has taken place even though the pain continues, may help ease your anxieties about it.

You can also prepare yourself for a visit to a doctor by keeping a pain diary and marking a pain scale daily (see pages 42 to 45). The information gathered in this way can help allay your fears and improve communication with your doctor. Deep breathing exercises (see page 142) can promote release of tension and focus your mind before a consultation, and positive imagery (see far left) can aid in controlling the pain and also foster an optimistic outlook.

Avoiding irritability and depression

When pain dominates your life, it can become very wearing both for you and those around you. Constant discomfort can deplete energy levels and interfere with regular sleep. It can also be humiliating if you need assistance to do things that previously you had taken for granted. The most ordinary of tasks such as getting up in the morn-

---

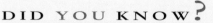

DID YOU KNOW?
The term chronic comes from the Greek word *khronos,* which means "time" and refers to consistent pain experienced over a long period. The Greek philosopher Aristotle believed that pain, like pleasure, was one of the passions of the soul and that it could be conquered with reason.

ing, dressing, or climbing stairs can become an ordeal. Inevitably, feelings of frustration and uselessness, mood swings, irritability, and bad temper may result.

Being so beleaguered can lead to negative thinking: many chronic pain sufferers start to believe that their pain is a punishment, and they become burdened with guilt and bitterness. These thoughts only serve to increase the downward spiral of depression, tension, and dependence on pain relievers, which worsens the sufferer's condition as well as quality of life.

Coping strategies To keep intrusive levels of pain from dominating your life, you need to distract your mind. Relaxation therapies (see pages 91 and 92) can help provide some relief, not just from pain itself but also from constant concern about it. Of particular value is biofeedback training (page 92), because it teaches how to override bodily responses that may be fostering pain. Visualization exercises (see below) are also useful. Positive thoughts can affect more than the mind: they can actually bring about physiological changes, because blood flow is stimulated, more endorphins are released, and the body functions more efficiently.

Maintaining relationships

Family relationships are put under stress by chronic pain. The sufferer's emotional state may change on an hourly basis in response to fluctuating pain levels, which makes them unpredictable and irritable. Tension and resentment can result, especially if family members do not understand what the sufferer is feeling.

Coping strategies Communication is the key to overcoming tension between you and your family and friends. Try to explain your experience of pain as clearly as possible, describing its pattern (or its unpredictability) and intensity. In this way those who care about you can come to a better understanding of the nature of your pain and find it easier to accept that it exists when you say it does. You may find that family counseling is helpful during this difficult period.

Pain clinics and self-help organizations can introduce you to counselors who can advise you and your family individually or together on these issues. Family members, in particular, need to know how to strike a balance between giving adequate support and allowing the chronic pain sufferer to become increasingly dependent.

GOING BACK TO WORK

Losing your job through illness can have a huge impact on your self-esteem, causing depression and feelings of uselessness. If you're absent from work for a long period, it may be difficult to summon up the enthusiasm and confidence to return to your job. Take the following steps to readjust to working life:

▶ *Accept that your condition may require a reappraisal of current employment. You may be able to work only part-time, for example, or you may have to consider retraining for another position.*

▶ *In the weeks preceding your return to work, try to increase your level of mobility. Set daily targets for exercise, such as walking a little farther every day.*

▶ *Accept the new limitations: compare your efforts with your performance when you were at your lowest ebb rather than your abilities before you fell ill.*

▶ *Once back at work, don't overdo it, but build up gradually until you approach your former levels of activity.*

TAKING CHARGE OF YOUR BRAIN

Visualization exercises can help ease stress and tension and in turn lessen the degree of pain you experience. A particularly effective visualization could be imagining yourself walking through your own mind, taking charge of emotions, memories, and the pain sensation itself. Picture yourself as the engineer in charge of your brain, prioritizing positive thoughts and memories and consigning negative thoughts to the waste bin.

MIND POWER
Recent research has shown that positive thoughts actually bring about physiological changes such as increased blood flow.

141

*BREATHING EXERCISE
Building up a relaxation
program will help you to
push pain to the back of
your mind. Eventually
you will find you feel
calmer for increasingly
longer periods of the day.
Breathe deeply from
your diaphragm and each
time you breathe out, tell
yourself that you are
releasing all of your
anger and sadness.*

Readjusting at work

Chronic pain can make a demanding job seem much more difficult. The physical symptoms sometimes pose very real problems in the work place; for example, back and neck pain can be exacerbated not just by physically taxing activity but also by immobility, such as sitting at a desk for long periods. Psychological factors are equally important. Chronic pain may diminish your sense of autonomy in your job and your self-esteem and confidence in turn may be lessened.

Coping strategies It is important for psychological health to try to keep working in some capacity, in order to maintain a sense of independence and purpose, to keep up social contacts, and to refocus your mind away from the pain. Many employers are now more sympathetic to chronic pain. Discuss the implications of your condition with your manager and talk about options for part-time or less demanding duties.

Lifestyle changes

The impact of chronic pain on your lifestyle depends on its nature and severity. Many sufferers find that their favorite leisure activities, such as participating in sports, and even their basic mobility are seriously affected by pain. Boredom and frustration can be very real problems if you're unable to keep active. Your sense of independence and self-worth can be adversely affected if you find yourself dependent on others for things previously taken for granted.

Coping strategies Housework, further education, hobbies, shopping, and socializing do not have to be abandoned altogether, they simply need to be approached at a more relaxed pace and with adequate rest periods. The most important factor is to remain active. Even if you're unable to work, there's no reason why you should have to give up hobbies and other interests.

Doing something creative, such as painting or growing special house plants, can help distract you from pain and raise your self-esteem. You can also learn a great deal from others who are in similar circumstances. Some clinics offer the opportunity for pain sufferers to share problems and collaborate to find lifestyle solutions.

Being in control of your pain

Perhaps most important of all is to acquire the ability to accept chronic pain and to be realistic about your capabilities. While positive thoughts are helpful in relieving depression and the perception of pain, having expectations that are too high can lead to disappointment. Become well informed about the nature of your pain, its mechanisms, and the exercises and therapies that you can undertake. The key is to find as many ways as possible to be in control.

THE REP PROGRAM

There are three key principles to managing your own pain effectively: relaxation, exercise, and pacing—the REP program. Balancing these three elements on a daily basis can pay real dividends. Practice relaxation methods such as deep breathing and autogenics (see page 88) to help overcome depression and negative mind-sets. Relaxation can also be valuable after exercise to soothe any pain problems. Use exercise to combat muscle tension and relieve stress; and pace yourself, both to avoid overstraining and to measure progress. For example, use a pain journal to plot exercise goals and achievements on a daily or weekly basis.

Relaxation therapies can establish a positive mind-set, both for undertaking the next stage of the REP program, exercising, and dealing with existing pain flare-ups and stress.

Exercise will relieve muscle tension and improve mobility. Increased independence of movement will also lift your mood and stimulate the body's own painkillers, endorphins.

Pacing will ensure that you never overstrain yourself, but that you do gain a real sense of progress as physical and psychological goals are reached. Even setting the smallest of goals, such as extending a walk by an extra 3 minutes a day, provides long-term results.

Chronic Pain Sufferer

Chronic pain not only affects the sufferer but can also put a strain on relatives and close friends, who may need to show great patience and tolerance. To manage chronic pain effectively requires a new approach to the problem, including measures such as counselin, relaxation therapies, and enlisting the active support of the whole family.

Jane is 41 years old, is married to John, and has two children ages 12 and 6. A former nurse, she injured her back at work two years ago and was diagnosed as having a prolapsed disc. She now has persistent pain, which prevents her from sitting for long periods, and she cannot walk far. Although her doctor prescribes painkillers, she finds that these make her feel lethargic and irritable, and she tries to avoid taking them as much as possible. She can perform few tasks around the house, spends most of the day in bed, sleeps badly, and feels angry that she can no longer look after her family. Her family, which now takes on all domestic responsibilities, feels distressed about her pain but is unsure how to help.

WHAT SHOULD JANE DO?

Jane should ask for a referral to a local pain clinic. Initially she will attend weekly sessions with a pain management psychologist and a physiotherapist. The pain specialists will also review her medication. They can provide details of helpful booklets and tapes and put her in touch with a self-help group where she can learn relaxation techniques to assist her in coping with the stress of chronic pain. The consultants will suggest a weekly family conference to discuss existing problems and help members to understand Jane's new self-help approach. An occupational therapist will visit the home in order to assess the possible introduction of useful equipment and to advise on necessary adaptations.

Action Plan

THE FAMILY
Take charge of pain management rather than depending on others. Encourage the family to be patient and to allow her to cope as best she can on her own.

STRESS
Practice relaxation strategies daily to cope with stress, and work through problems one by one.

EMOTIONAL HEALTH
Seek counseling to confront the wider implications of pain and its long-term effects on the family. A weekly conference will let the family discuss practical and emotional issues.

STRESS
Jane's pain causes health, money, marital, and family tensions that add extra strains.

THE FAMILY
Jane's family is overprotective and does everything for her. It also lets her indulge in too much pain talk and behavior.

EMOTIONAL HEALTH
Jane is depressed and bitter about her losses, her career, and her lack of mobility. She feels that she is letting down her family by no longer being able to care for them adequately.

HOW THINGS TURNED OUT FOR JANE

Jane learned more about chronic pain and began to appreciate the possibilities for self-help. Listening to her family at the weekly conferences made Jane realize how much they too were suffering, and motivated her to work at her self-help pain management. She practices relaxation exercises regularly and finds that these help her to deal more effectively with pain. She has become more active around the house.

CARING FOR PEOPLE IN CHRONIC PAIN

Caring for someone who suffers from chronic pain means trying to find a balance between providing support and love on the one hand, and allowing independence and self-help on the other.

Every sufferer of chronic pain has unique care requirements, and the nature of the care they need is determined by a range of factors. In each case there is a different pattern of pain, and sufferers lie at different points along a spectrum of disability. At one end are those who are effectively crippled by pain. At the other are people who need moral support and practical help when they suffer an occasional flare-up, but are otherwise physically fit, mobile, and functioning well in all areas of their lives. Nonetheless, common principles apply in all cases.

LEARNING TO PROVIDE CARE

Being a caregiver poses many problems. People who are close to someone with chronic pain can feel helpless and even guilty for being healthy. On the other hand, they may grow to resent the attention that the patient demands—and then feel guilty about their reaction.

In fact the most useful role for a caregiver may be to relieve a sufferer's major frustration, which is having to continually explain an illness. People in chronic pain frequently report that trying to educate others about the quirks caused by their disability, without relinquishing their independence or causing a fuss, can be a major difficulty. By acting as an intermediary and taking on the burden of explanation, a caregiver can relieve this pressure and in so doing help to remove the pain from center stage.

The care giver should try to become familiar with the particular pattern of pain that their friend or loved one is experiencing. Are there any triggers that set off the pain or things that help to soothe it? Does it follow a daily pattern? How much can the sufferer manage at any one time? By knowing these facts the caregiver can plan to help when severe bouts occur, affecting the sufferer's concentration or mobility, and aid in protecting the sufferer against triggers without having to be overprotective generally.

Giving round-the-clock care

While emotional and social support may be all that some sufferers require, others will need help with difficult or personal tasks. Some may even need round-the-clock care and intensive nursing. These people are at particular risk of becoming invalids. Until recently, for example, it was common practice for bed rest to be prescribed for anyone with severe chronic back pain—for months and even years. This is now known to be a cause of muscle wasting—as much as 3 per cent of muscles can be wasted per day—and general weakness. Experts in the field now acknowledge that, except for a small minority who are seriously disabled, enforced immobility and inactivity causes more pain in the long run.

In most chronic pain cases, current practice now favors active, gentle mobilization and early rehabilitation through physical therapy. People in chronic pain are encouraged to do as much as they can for themselves, within both sensible and humane parameters. Caregivers are persuaded to stand quietly back and allow sufferers to care for themselves as much as possible and in their own time.

When it is necessary to provide 24-hour care, it is important that client and care giver ask for a case conference with their doctor, nurse, psychologist, physiotherapist, and any other essential healthcare agents.

This will help them to establish a well thought out rehabilitation plan and learn about any local and national support organizations. Caregivers should also make sure to ask about the financial and personnel support they are entitled to.

Taking care of yourself

Both caring and being cared for can exhaust anyone's good nature or worse. Failed surgery, unsuccessful treatments, poor sleep, and even pain medications can cause extremes of mood. Counseling support should be accessible for the care giver as well as the patient. If this help is not forthcoming, the support person may develop symptoms similar to those of post-traumatic stress syndrome, and family relationships may suffer as well. If managed properly, however, caring for someone and being cared for can be an enriching and enlightening experience.

CARING FOR ELDERLY PEOPLE

Older people may feel lonely and isolated if they have outlived many of their friends and relatives, so often the best care is simply companionship and a sympathetic ear. Research shows that an elderly person's experience of pain can be influenced more by environment than the pain itself.

Staying active

Keeping an elderly person mentally, socially, and physically active is important. Passive interests such as watching television and reading do not provide as much distraction from pain as more active pursuits like knitting, sewing, and domestic chores. Teaching self-help pain management techniques or providing contact with self-help, social, and recreational groups can all increase activity levels.

Another finding of research is that for many elderly people peace of mind, and thus the ability to deal with chronic pain, depends largely on how they view their past. Memories are of particular importance in old age, and good ones can be a tremendous boon to sufferers. People with regrets and bad memories, on the other hand, are more likely to feel lonely and depressed. Caregivers can help by encouraging their charges to discuss their memories and how they feel about them, talking them through to try to see bad memories in a more positive light.

Getting sufferers to plan their memoirs, for instance, can be an excellent starting point.

Other factors also affect how an elderly person copes with pain. Among them are the loss of friends and family, financial difficulties, and domestic problems. In these cases the caregiver should provide practical help when necessary and social support during periods of adjustment.

CARING FOR THE TERMINALLY ILL

Terminally ill people suffering from chronic pain may falsely believe that their pain and other symptoms are inevitable. This is rarely the case. Pain, nausea, fatigue, constipation, loss of appetite, and incontinence can all be relieved with the right help from a doctor, nurse, or well-informed caregiver.

When the condition of a loved one or friend deteriorates and he or she becomes terminal, it is time for the patient and those providing care to reassess things together. This may be a good time to call another conference and make a detailed care plan. It is also the time for a caregiver to try to prepare for the inevitable by finding out what will happen in the last stages.

Putting the sufferer in control

If the sufferer is to stay on top of pain and deal with it successfully, he or she needs to retain control over the treatment plan. More specifically, putting patients in con-

COMMUNICATING PAIN
To help children express pain issues, foster a positive creative atmosphere in which the problem can be discussed by all the family.

HELPING A CHILD IN PAIN

Children feel pain just as intensely as adults. A parent's reaction to a child's pain can have a huge influence on the way he or she deals with it Here are some ways in which parents can help their children to cope:

▶ *Become fully informed on the latest treatment and care options.*

▶ *Ease anxiety and distress by explaining procedures and the hospital environment.*

▶ *Formulate an action plan to minimize pain levels and distress, and teach skills for coping with flare-ups to reduce fear of pain.*

▶ *Incorporate visualization, stretching and exercises, and relaxation techniques into daily activities.*

▶ *Make sure that other siblings don't feel left out, by involving them in the care of the patient.*

trol of their painkilling medications has been shown to be the most effective way of avoiding overdependence, and reducing the attendant side effects.

Keeping patients well informed about their conditions and involved in monitoring and assessing their own progress also helps reduce their anxiety and pain. Involving them in simple procedures like measuring blood pressure and temperature can help.

CARE OPTIONS

Caregivers need to be aware of the options that are available for their charges. The terminally ill often need a very demanding level of 24-hour care, and there may be technical difficulties associated with giving medications, feeding, and bowel problems that make professional help a necessity. It would be useful to attend a case conference comprising the health professionals that are treating the patient, and check out all relevant sources of information to find out what help is available.

For a terminal cancer patient, a local hospice team may supervise care for the patient and the close family. For terminal patients with noncancererous conditions, care systems vary considerably. A nurse may oversee the care under the direction of a general practitioner and specialists.

When home nursing care is needed for a patient, agencies exist for the purpose of screening such attendants, but the caregiver usually has to interview them and make the selection. This can be a difficult process. If possible, obtain references from former patients. Also, enlist the help of family members and friends for back-up support.

Hospices

If home and hospital care options have been exhausted for terminally ill patients, the best choice may be to admit them to a hospice. Because of their high staff-to-patient ratio, such institutions almost always offer the best standard of care that is available. Not only are they experienced in dealing with the difficult aspects of chronic physical pain, but also they can cope with the emotional and spiritual pain that the terminally ill may be facing. Staff at hospices are also well able to handle other symptoms that can afflict the very ill, such as bed sores, dehydration, and constipation.

A hospice provides a positive spirit and a supportive atmosphere, enabling the terminally ill to come to terms with approaching death. The aim is for patients to live out their final days with a feeling of peace, calm, and dignity, in an environment that is free from needless pain, fear,and stress.

Origins

Dame Cicely Saunders was responsible for a major breakthrough in the management of pain when she established Saint Christopher's Hospice in south London in 1967. The hospice was not only dedicated to the care of patients, but also to research and teaching on all aspects of pain. Among her theories of pain management was that fear and anxiety directly enhanced pain by increasing tension, and that patients needed to be informed about the details of their condition in order to understand their pain and reduce their fear. She also recognized that hospices needed to provide advice to care givers looking after patients at home. Saint Christopher's has since become a model for similar centers throughout the world. Her motto, adopted by the whole hospice movement, is to keep patients "dignified, alert and pain free."

DAME CICELY SAUNDERS
Dame Cicely was medical director of the first modern hospice in the UK from its establishment in 1967 until her recent retirement.

CHAPTER 10

PAIN CAUSED BY INJURIES

The pain of minor injuries can be quickly relieved using appropriate first-aid measures and simple natural remedies that can be found in any well-stocked kitchen. In cases of more serious injuries that require expert medical attention, prompt first aid can still ease the casualty's pain and distress and may even save a life.

RELIEVING THE PAIN OF MINOR INJURIES

Accidental injuries are an ever-present possibility. Knowledge of first aid and a well-planned medicine cabinet that contains natural remedies can ensure pain relief and speedy recovery.

ARNICA
Arnica montana, or wolfsbane, is a toxic plant with medicinal uses. The flowers contain compounds that reduce inflammation and aid circulation. It is effective as a tincture or salve for bruises, sprains and muscle pain. As the herb is toxic, it should not be applied to cuts or broken skin or taken internally except as a homeopathic remedy (in which the ingredient is present in minute amounts).

Head, chest, and abdominal wounds, severe burns, deep cuts that produce heavy loss of blood, and bone fractures, require immediate medical attention. When you are in any doubt as to the nature or seriousness of an injury, always seek medical help immediately.

The best way to prepare for dealing with injuries is to take a course in first aid. The Red Cross and many community hospitals offer courses that usually take no more than one day. First-aid treatment, carried out as early and swiftly as possible, can reduce the risk of shock—and may save a life. It can also assist the body in beginning the repair process sooner, and thus minimize pain.

Keep a first-aid cabinet in your home and a kit for your car fully equipped at all times. At the minimum, supplies should include adhesive bandages; antiseptic; cotton tip applicators; cotton balls; sterile gauze pads; tweezers; scissors; an elastic bandage, instant ice compress, and oral thermometer; ipecac syrup; and a flashlight and batteries. In addition to conventional equipment, it's a good idea to keep a variety of household and natural remedies on hand to provide relief for a range of injuries.

NATURE'S FIRST-AID REMEDIES

Many natural remedies that can ease the pain of superficial skin wounds are found in a well-stocked kitchen or garden. Simple remedies can often hasten healing and prevent infection with few, if any, side effects. Olive oil, for instance, is effective at reducing the inflammation caused by bruising and can be used straight from the bottle.

Other remedies may have to be prepared in advance so they are ready for use when needed. For example, the mashed heads of young marigolds (calendula) preserved in alcohol (vodka is best) makes an excellent tincture for relieving insect stings. The following common ingredients can form the basis of a natural first-aid chest: butter, salt, sugar, honey, cucumber, apple, onion, potato, cabbage, fresh parsley, garlic, yogurt with live acidophilus cultures, red wine vinegar, cider vinegar, tea bags, skim milk, cornmeal, oatmeal, cayenne pepper, castor oil, safflower oil, olive oil, lemon juice, glycerine, alcohol, baking soda, papain (found in meat tenderizer), and ammonia.

With a little planning, your garden can also be a rich source of natural remedies. Skullcap (mad dog weed), valerian root, St. John's wort (hypericum), juniper, lavender, burdock, comfrey, marigold, geranium, basil, aloe vera, and chickweed can all be beneficial for alleviating pain resulting from superficial injuries such as grazes and burns.

It is also useful to keep a selection of essential oils on hand for easing pain, encouraging tissue renewal, and helping to guard against infection. Basic essential oils include tea tree oil, myrrh, calendula, lavender, vitamin E oil, hyssop, juniper, geranium and eucalyptus (see page 79).

Certain homeopathic remedies such as cantharis, aconite, ledum, and arnica can also be kept in your natural remedy first-aid chest. These medicines have various properties that are useful in accident situations. some alleviate bruising and inflammation others are good for relieving pain and stress. They will not interfere with the body's normal healing processes or affect any orthodox treatments that may be necessary.

The following pages explain how to use these items for the first-aid treatment of a range of common injuries.

NATURE'S FIRST-AID CHEST

Keep a stock of natural remedies close at hand so you have ready access to a range of effective treatments for minor household injuries and ailments.

Many items, such as honey, olive oil, cornstarch, and vinegar, are not only as effective as comparable manufactured products, but also sometimes more economical too. If you make a list of the items you might need for first-aid purposes and note where they are being stored, you will be able to find them quickly when the need arises.

Check all items regularly, to ensure that you have an adequate supply for an emergency, and replace anything that has passed its "use-before" date or is showing signs of degenerating.

Top row (left to right): cornstarch, oatmeal, baking soda, glycerine, vitamin E tablets, essential oils, castor oil, slippery elm, massage oil

Middle row (left to right): cloves, cayenne pepper, salt, cinnamon, honey, olive oil, sunflower oil, brandy, red wine vinegar

Bottom row (left to right): lemon, milk, sugar, yogurt, cider vinegar, apples, cucumber, garlic, potato, cabbage, butter, parsley, aloe vera

SAFE STORAGE
Make sure that natural products for use in first aid are as fresh as possible. Keep highly perishable items, such as dairy products, in the refrigerator and store other items in a cool, dark cupboard where they will be safe from insects and other pests.

Injuries to Skin

The skin is well supplied with nerve endings that alert the brain immediately to any injury. Pain from a wound indicates that there may be loss of blood and a risk of infection, so urgent attention to the injury is required.

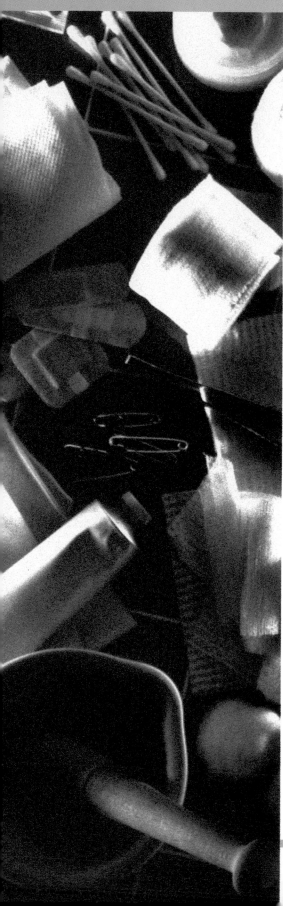

The skin is a versatile protective cover for the body. It is waterproof, supple, and sensitive, and capable of stretching to accommodate the movement of the body. The skin plays a vital role in retaining bodily fluids and keeping infection out.

To function efficiently the skin must be kept supple and healthy. Excessive washing of the face and hands, especially during cold weather, can make the skin rough and sore. As the natural oils that keep the skin supple are washed away, the skin dries out and may crack. This common condition, called chapping, can be avoided by using a barrier cream and making sure your hands and face are thoroughly dry after washing them. Regular use of a lanolin-based hand or face cream, moisturizer, or bath oil will minimize further chafing and the pain associated with chapping.

If a skin condition is no better after two weeks of self-treatment, it may indicate a problem such as eczema or psoriasis. In such a case you should see your family doctor, who may refer you to a specialist. If the skin becomes damaged it must be protected with a dressing such as a clean gauze or an adhesive strip bandage, depending on the wound.

TREATMENT FOR SHOCK

After an injury blood pressure may drop, leading to potentially fatal shock. Look for warning signs such as pale, cold, clammy skin; rapid, shallow breathing; weak pulse; dizziness; weakness.

FIRST AID FOR SHOCK
Lay the injured person down on his side and check that he can breathe easily. Loosen any tight clothing around the waist, chest, and neck and keep him warm with a coat or blanket. Seek medical help immediately.

MINOR CUTS AND GRAZES

Children in particular are prone to minor cuts and grazes, or scratches. Grazes are less serious than cuts because damage is superficial and there is little loss of blood. However, they are often more painful because layers of skin have been removed over a wider area, exposing more sensitive nerve endings. Minor cuts involve damage only to the small blood vessels near the surface of the skin known as capillaries, and although they may bleed profusely at first, the bleeding soon stops. Cuts and grazes can both become very painful if infected, and thorough cleaning and disinfecting of the wound is extremely important.

Natural treatment for cuts

There are a variety of natural remedies that help to heal minor cuts and grazes. Tea tree oil is a natural antiseptic—add a few drops to the water you use to wash the wound. Aloe vera can be applied directly to the wound as a gel or a concentrated liquid. It is a natural antibiotic and also relieves the pain. You should then cover the wound with a sterile dressing. To promote healing, add calendula cream or comfrey oil to the bandage. You can also mix a few drops with the water you use for washing the wound.

Plain granulated sugar or honey accelerates healing, soothes pain, and helps prevent scarring. It can be packed onto a cleaned cut or wound and then covered with gauze, but make sure the wound has stopped bleeding, because sugar can make the bleeding worse.

When dressing a cut, you can add any of the following to the bandage or gauze to promote healing:

▸ *A tincture of myrrh, consisting of one part myrrh to six parts water, acts as a natural antiseptic.*

▸ *A tincture of calendula.*

▸ *Comfrey oil or an infusion of the herb.*

▸ *Gel squeezed from the leaf of an aloe vera plant (see right).*

✚ For minor skin wounds

■ Rinse the injured area under cold running water to wash the wound and slow or stop the bleeding.

■ Gently remove any debris, such as gravel or glass splinters, using cotton swabs, gauze, or tweezers.

■ Clean with antiseptic wipes, or use gauze or cotton swabs dipped in a mild antiseptic. Once it is clean, dab the injured area dry and then cover it with a plaster or a dressing held in place with a bandage.

USING ALOE VERA

Grow your own aloe vera plant for a ready source of fresh gel to apply to cuts and bruises.

1 *With a pair of scissors, snip off a large leaf; using a sharp blade, cut a slit along its length.*

2 *Open out the leaf and squeeze the contents onto a moistened, absorbent cloth. Place over the cut.*

BRUISES

Any blow to the body that damages the capillaries under the skin will cause bruising as blood leaks into the tissues. Most bruises are not serious but can still be painful. Heavy bruising to the face, head, chest, back, or abdomen could indicate internal injuries and should be examined by a doctor.

Natural treatment for bruises

There are several natural remedies that can reduce the pain and swelling of bruises, such as bathing the injury with herbal witch hazel skin toner or applying arnica or comfrey ointment (if the skin is not broken). A cold compress soaked in a lavender infusion is also effective. Honey and vegetable, olive, or safflower, mixed together or used individually, are

✚ For bruises

■ You can ease the pain of bruising with a cold compress: soak a cloth in cold water, then wring it out and apply to the bruised area for 10 minutes. This restricts the internal bleeding and reduces swelling. Or you can make an ice pack by wrapping a packet of frozen peas in a towel: do not leave an ice pack in contact with the bruise for longer than 10 minutes.

natural remedies that can ease the pain of a bruise. Spread over the bruised area several times a day or take 3 ml by mouth twice daily. Similarly, cornmeal mixed with water or vegetable oil applied externally will relieve pain, as will a tea of St. John's wort.

SUNBURN

Some cases of sunburn are severe enough to cause blisters, in which case they should be treated like any other minor burn (see below). If you also experience chills, nausea, fever, and intense itchiness, or feel faint, you may be suffering from sunstroke and should seek medical attention as soon as possible.

Natural treatment for sunburn

Place a cold compress on the burn to reduce inflammation and then apply calamine lotion to soothe the pain. Your kitchen can also provide some natural remedies to bring relief from the inflammation and pain of sunburn. For example, slices of apple, cucumber, or raw potato, also plain yogurt, cider vinegar, moist tea bags, even compresses of skim milk applied to the face and body are safe, natural, and inexpensive treatments.

These can be combined with skin moisturizers. Aloe vera, calendula, and witch hazel are soothing, too. Adding 5 drops of lavender essential oil to a base such as almond oil and massaging it in brings rapid relief. Hypercal cream or lotion (a mixture of hypericum and calendula) can also encourage rapid healing.

+ For sunburn

For milder cases of sunburn, taking aspirin or acetaminophen can offer quick relief from the pain, itchiness, and swelling, and there are many after-sun skin creams and lotions that can be effective. Ointments containing hydrocortisone, benzocaine, and lidocaine can also be applied to the skin to ease the pain of sunburn.

SOOTHING BATH
Five drops each of lavender and calendula essential oils added to a warm bath can soothe the sting of mild sunburn.

MINOR BURNS

Burns to the skin can result from fire, hot metal, hot liquid, steam, intense cold, electricity, chemicals, or the sun. The seriousness of a burn depends upon the area of the body that is affected and the depth to which the skin has been damaged.

In superficial, or first degree burns, only the outer layers of skin are damaged, causing soreness, redness, and slight swelling. Such burns are most often caused by steam, a hot drink, the sun, or by touching a hot object like a saucepan. Pain can be reduced by keeping the burn under cold running water for a few minutes. (For chemical burns, flush with cool water for 15 to 30 minutes.)

Seek emergency medical help if the burn affects an extensive area, if the skin is broken, severely blistered or charred, or if the victim is suffering severe pain. A doctor should always be consulted for burns to the eyes, feet, and pelvic and pubic areas; any

burn where you are not sure of the depth or extent of the injury; and any wound that shows signs of infection or has not healed properly within 10 days.

Natural treatment for minor burns

After immersing a burn in cold running water, add a few drops of calendula tincture to cold water and apply this to the burned area as a cold compress. After 24 hours, you can apply vitamin E oil or lavender oil (4 drops per $\frac{1}{4}$ cup (60 ml) of water to promote healing. Calendula ointment, witch hazel, and aloe vera gel (see page 151) can also soothe the pain of a burn. The homeopathic remedy cantharis 3c, taken every hour, can provide pain relief. One dose daily of aconite 12c also has a soothing effect. A diet high in protein and supplemented with vitamin C will help speed healing.

+ For burns

- Cool the burn as quickly as possible by first immersing it under cold running water; then apply a compress of cold water or any available safe liquid such as milk and elevate the burned area.

- Do not apply ointment or cream to a burn for the first 24 hours. If blisters form do not burst them, as this increases the risk of infectiion.

- Remove any watch, belt, or jewelery that may constrict the burned area, before it starts to swell. Don't remove any clothing that is stuck to the wound.

- Cover the burn with a clean non-fluffy material such as a sterile dressing or clean handkerchief. You don't need to cover a burn to the face.

- Seek immediate medical attention for any serious burn, especially around the face or pubic areas.

BLISTERS

A blister is a pocket of fluid that forms under the skin. In addition to burns, a common cause of blisters is friction, for example, from wearing new or badly fitting shoes. If a blister has become inflamed, swollen, and painful, or is exuding a cloudy or unpleasant smelling fluid it may have become infected, in which case you should see a doctor.

Natural treatment for blisters
Natural pain-relieving remedies include a cornmeal poultice and vegetable oil lightly applied to the blister before bandaging. Aloe vera gel or the liquid from a capsule of vitamin E applied to the blister can help soothe the pain and hasten healing. Application of lavender essential oil can also be effective.

✚ For blisters
■Avoid bursting a blister, if possible, because this increases the risk of infection. If the blister is likely to burst, however, wash the area with soap and a mild disinfectant, and then carefully puncture it with a sterilized needle or blade and cover it with a sterile dressing. Avoid getting the dressing wet.

STINGS AND BITES

Insect stings are rarely dangerous, unless the victim has multiple stings, is allergic to bee venom, or the stings are around the mouth or throat, which can cause swelling that may obstruct breathing. Stings from certain types of jellyfish, sting rays, and a Portuguese man-of-war can not only be painful but also poisonous. If weakness, dizziness, nausea, muscle spasms, or sweating are evident, seek medical help immediately.

Natural treatment for stings and bites
Once the stinger has been removed and the area cleaned, the alkaline sting of an ant or wasp can be eased with lemon juice or vinegar.

Bee stings are acidic, so use baking soda, ammonia, or meat tenderizer. Cider vinegar and garlic are natural antiseptics, while raw onion alleviates swelling and pain.

For insect bites, a pulped fresh marigold flower can be applied to the wound and bandaged in place to aid healing. A warm moist compress of burdock also works. A poultice of cornstarch and lemon juice soothes itching. Butter and salt (moistened with water) are natural antiseptics.

For jellyfish stings pour rubbing alcohol, ammonia, or sea water over the injured area and remove any remaining stingers with tweezers. Apply a paste of meat tenderizer or baking soda and water.

STINGER OR BITER?

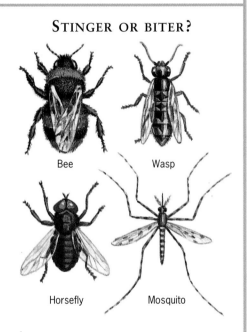

Bee   Wasp

Horsefly   Mosquito

AIRBORNE ATTACK
Stinging insects such as bees and wasps inject poison under the skin. Biting insects such as mosquitoes and horseflies break through the skin to draw up blood.

✚ For stings
■If a stinger has been left in the flesh, remove it using your nail or a pair of tweezers or scraping it out with a credit card.

■Try to avoid squeezing the poison sac that constitutes the stinger, as this may release more poison into the bloodstream.

■Apply hydrocortisone cream or a cold compress to reduce swelling. If the injury is in or around the mouth or throat, give the patient ice to suck and seek medical help.

■If the patient feels dizzy, has swelling, a rash, severe itching, or difficulty breathing, he may be suffering anaphylactic shock, a life-threatening allergic reaction to the sting. He needs an immediate injection of adrenaline, or epinephrine. He may be carrying his own source. If not, get him to a hospital immediately.

STING AND BITE PREVENTION

There are many ways to prevent insect bites and stings. Food supplements of zinc and garlic are released through the skin in tiny amounts and repel insects. Other natural repellents include 5 drops of eucalyptus or citronella oils added to a cup of water and applied to exposed skin areas.

Cider vinegar is also effective. Dark clothes attract insects, so wear light clothing, especially in the evening, and keep wrists, arms, and legs covered. Place insect screens over windows and, in tropical countries, sleep under a mosquito net that has been sprayed with insecticide.

Strains and Sprains

It is helpful to know how to differentiate the different types of musculoskeletal injuries—strains, sprains, and fractures. Many injuries can be treated at home using simple first aid measures, while others may need expert medical attention.

Sports injuries can result in damage to muscles and other soft tissues, particularly around a joint. Ligaments, tendons, and muscles may be twisted or torn. Joint strains and sprains usually cause pain and swelling and restricted movement in the limb. Sometimes it is difficult to tell the difference between them (see below). In many cases, these injuries can be treated safely at home with a combination of conventional and natural therapies.

Telling the difference between muscle or tendon damage and a broken bone (fracture) can also be difficult. Serious fractures can sometimes be identified by sight, for example if a limb is badly swollen or hanging at an unusual angle, or (in the case of compound fractures) if the bone protrudes through the skin. Movement is difficult or impossible and pain can be throbbing, shooting, stabbing, aching, or unbearably sharp. Often, the only way to identify a fracture for certain is to have an X-ray taken. To avoid further damage of a broken bone, movement should be restricted. If in any doubt about an injury, treat it as a suspected fracture, provide support for the injured limb, and arrange transportation to a hospital.

STRAIN OR SPRAIN?

A sprain is damage to a ligament at or near a joint, whereas a strain is damage to a muscle. One way to identify the injury is to note which movements cause the most pain. Ask someone to bend the limb for you without your making any effort. If it still hurts or is restricted, the problem is a joint injury (sprain). If it no longer hurts or is restricted when someone tries to straighten it, it is a muscle injury (strain).

KNEE INJURY
The pain of a knee injury may stem from the joint itself or from soft tissues around it.

CRAMPS

A cramp is a painful muscle spasm caused by a sudden excessive contraction of the muscle fibers. It is usually involuntary, strikes unexpectedly, and can be quite crippling temporarily. Often cramps occur at night and affect the calf muscle, particularly after a day of unaccustomed exercise, which produces a build up of lactic acid in the muscles. They can also be caused by repetitive actions, poor circulation, sitting in an awkward position, or swimming in cold water.

Muscle cramps are common during or after exercise, due to excessive loss of salt and body fluids from sweating. Replenishing these fluids with water or electrolytic sports drinks during exercise can help to prevent the problem. Cramps sometimes occur if muscles are cold when starting exercise. You can avoid this problem by doing a warm-up routine before working out.

Strenuous physical activity carried out too soon after eating a big meal can also lead to cramps, because the blood supply is diverted to the digestive system and there is insufficient blood reaching the muscles. Always wait at least one hour after eating before exercising.

Natural treatment to prevent muscle cramps

Ensure that your diet contains an adequate supply of vitamin D and calcium (see page 58) to reduce the risk of muscle spasms. Vitamin E supplements have also been shown to prevent night cramps.

Hot and cold compresses can improve circulation to affected muscles, and a mustard foot bath may help to relieve leg cramps.

Basil, marjoram, and lemon grass essential oils added to a warm bath or mixed with a base oil and massaged into the muscles can help to alleviate the problem of recurring cramps.

✚ For muscle cramps

- A good way of forcing a muscle with a cramp to relax is to stretch the muscle out again.

- If you have calf cramps, you can stimulate blood circulation to the muscle by massaging the leg in upward movements toward the heart. This helps to flush out lactic acid and prevent muscles from becoming stiff again later.

- A hot shower will help improve circulation and bring further relief.

FIGHTING MUSCLE CRAMPS
This exercise can help you avoid cramps in the calf muscles: stand about 3 ft (1 m) away from a wall, with your feet flat on the floor and legs straight. Lean toward the wall and press against it with your palms. Stretch and hold for 10 seconds. Repeat several times.

Bend your arms slowly as you lean your body toward the wall. Hold the position as soon as you feel your calves tighten.

Keep the legs straight to stretch the fibers in the calf muscles and counteract the effect of cramps.

MAKING A COMPRESS

For minor strains and sprains, a cold compress is a good way to reduce inflammation, swelling, and bleeding under the skin and soothe pain. An ice pack is effective for reducing swelling in serious joint injuries. To make an ice pack, fill a plastic bag with crushed or cubed ice (or use a bag of frozen peas). Wrap the pack in a towel and apply to the injury. Repeat as necessary. (Never apply ice directly to the skin as it can cause ice burns.) After swelling diminishes, a hot compress is helpful for improving circulation and promoting healing.

1 *Take a piece of soft, non-fluffy cloth and soak it in cold water. The cloth should be sterile, even if the skin is unbroken, as is usually the case with a bruise or sprain.*

2 *Squeeze or wring out the cloth so that it is damp but not dripping and place it firmly on the injured area.*

3 *Replace the compress with a fresh one regularly, so that the cooling effect is maintained. If necessary, hold the compress in place with an open-weave bandage.*

STRAINS AND SPRAINS

All joints are vulnerable to strains and sprains, especially from accidental falls and injuries sustained in contact sports such as football.

The knee is particularly prone to damage because it is made up of a complex arrangement of cartilage, ligaments, muscles, tendons, and bones that must allow movement and support the weight of the body (see below). If any of these structures are damaged, the effect can be painful and the knee may stiffen or be unable to support the weight of the individual. The pain of a strained or sprained knee is described as sharp, intense, stabbing, or tender.

A sprained ankle is a painful injury involving any one of a number of ligaments and tendons at different sites on the joint. The ligament at the top of the foot is the most vulnerable to injury. If you trip and put your weight heavily on one foot, this ligament absorbs most of the impact and can be damaged. This type of injury can take a long time to heal, because the ligaments have a poor blood supply. Treatment includes resting the injury to aid healing and lessen pain and swelling.

Natural treatment
Once first aid has been applied (see box, right) a number of natural therapies can help reduce pain.

✚ For sprained joints

- Rest the injured part by supporting the limb in a comfortable position.

- Apply ice every 20 minutes for a few hours to reduce pain, swelling, and bruising. This treatment should be repeated four or five times over the first 24 hours.

- Compress the injured joint by padding with a cotton pad or plastic foam and securing with a roller bandage. You can compress and chill the injured area at the same time by using a roller bandage to hold an ice pack in position.

- Elevate and support the limb to reduce blood flow to the joint and thus reduce swelling and bruising.

Lightly massaging the injury will help to improve circulation and drain any fluid that has built up. Comfrey leaves applied as a poultice can aid the repair of tissue and cartilage. To use, bruise the leaves and wrap in a dressing. Avoid placing the leaves directly on the skin as they may cause irritation.

The homeopathic remedy Arnica mother tincture, added to water, can be applied on a moist compress to reduce swelling. Rhus tox or Ruta graveolens can assist the long-term repair of ligaments and tendons, while Ledum can ease the pain.

FIGURE OF EIGHT BANDAGING

An elastic bandage must be wide enough to cover the injury and extend 1 in (2.5 cm) beyond. It should be wound firmly but not too tight. Check regularly and adjust as necessary.

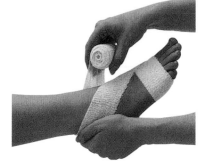

1 *Holding the foot with one hand, wind the bandage once around the top of the foot, working from the inside outward. Make sure that the bandage is not too tight.*

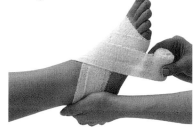

2 *Wind the bandage from the inside of the ankle across the foot to the little toe. Take it under the foot and then up by the big toe. Now take it under the foot again.*

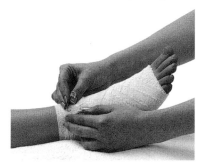

3 *Wind the bandage across the top of the foot and behind the ankle in a figure eight pattern. Continue until the foot is covered. Wind around the ankle and secure.*

THE KNEE JOINT
The knee joint is lined with smooth pads of cartilage (menisci) and cushioned by fluid-filled sacs (bursas). Knee tendons link the tibia, a bone in the lower leg, with the quadriceps muscle, and ligaments add support. The knee is an unusual joint in that a special bone, the knee cap, or patella, is incorporated in the tendons to add protection. The knee is vulnerable to torn or sprained cartilage, tendons, muscles, and ligaments; dislocated patella; and inflamed bursas.

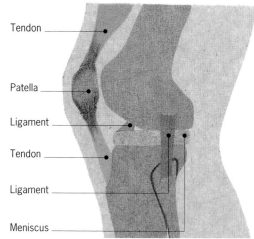

Tendon

Patella

Ligament

Tendon

Ligament

Meniscus

INDEX

ACKNOWLEDGMENTS

Carroll & Brown Limited
would like to thank
Sharon Freed
Madeleine Jennings
Trish Shine

Editorial assistance
Jennifer Mussett

Design assistance
Rachel Goldsmith

Photograph sources
8 Wellcome Institute Library, London
9 (Top) Mary Evans Picture Library; (Bottom) Carroll & Brown Ltd
11 Alvis Upitis/Image Bank
12 Zefa
17 Professor P.M. Motta/ University 'La Sapienza', Rome/ Science Photo Library
19 Matt Meadows/Peter Arnold Inc/Science Photo Library
25 Kobal Collection
26 Boston Medical Library, in The Francis A. Countway Library of Medicine, Boston, Mass, USA
28 Kobal Collection
29 (Top) Angela Hampton/ Family Life Pictures; (Centre) J. Wakelin/Trip; (Bottom) Frank Schneidermeyer/ Oxford Scientific Films

34 Zefa
36 Kobal Collection
38 Eye of Science/Science Photo Library
42 Wellcome Institute Library
47 Deni Bown/Oxford Scientific Films
50 Scott Camazine/Oxford Scientific Films
60 National Back Pain Association
62 S. B. Paul McCullagh/Oxford Scientific Films
66 National Back Pain Association
68 Zefa
71 Science Photo Library
72 David Kirk-Campbell/Rolf Institute of Structural Integration, Boulder, Colorado, USA
73 Simon Fraser, Hexam General Hospital/Science Photo Library
76 The Society of Teachers of the Alexander Technique
106 Marc Romanelli/Image Bank
132 CNRI/Science Photo Library
138 Tony Stone Images
140 (Top) Zefa (Bottom) Gilda Pacitti
146 Photograph courtesy of St Christopher's Hospital
148 Jos Korenromp/Oxford Scientific Films

Illustrators
Joanna Cameron
Karen Cochrane
John Geary
Sandie Hill
Christine Pilsworth
Lesli Sternberg
Sarah Venus
Paul Williams

Photographic assistants
M. A. Hugo
Mark Langridge

Hair and make-up
Kim Menzies

Picture researcher
Sandra Schneider

Research
Stephen Chong

Index
Richard Emerson